Redemptive Change

THEOLOGY FOR THE TWENTY-FIRST CENTURY
CENTER OF THEOLOGICAL INQUIRY

Theology for the Twenty-first Century is a series sponsored by the Center of Theological Inquiry (CTI), an institute, located in Princeton, New Jersey, dedicated to the advanced study of theology. This series is one of its many initiatives and projects.

The goal of the series is to publish inquiries of contemporary scholars into the nature of the Christian faith and its witness and practice in the church, society, and culture. The series will include investigations into the uniqueness of the Christian faith. But it will also offer studies that relate the Christian faith to the major cultural, social, and practical issues of our time.

Monographs and symposia will result from research by scholars in residence at the Center of Theological Inquiry or otherwise associated with it. In some cases, publications will come from group research projects sponsored by CTI. It is our intention that the books selected for this series will constitute a major contribution to renewing theology in its service to church and society.

WALLACE M. ALLSTON, JR., ROBERT JENSON,
AND DON S. BROWNING
SERIES EDITORS

What Dare We Hope?
by Gerhard Sauter

The End of the World and the Ends of God
edited by John Polkinghorne and Michael Welker

God and Globalization, Volume 1:
Religion and the Powers of the Common Life
edited by Max L. Stackhouse with Peter J. Paris

God and Globalization, Volume 2:
The Spirit and the Modern Authorities
edited by Max L. Stackhouse with Don S. Browning

God and Globalization, Volume 3:
Christ and the Dominions of Civilization
edited by Max L. Stackhouse with Diane B. Obenchain

Redemptive Change:
Atonement and the Christian Cure of the Soul
by R. R. Reno

Redemptive Change

Atonement

and the

Christian Cure

of the Soul

R. R. Reno

TRINITY PRESS INTERNATIONAL
Harrisburg, Pennsylvania

For Blanche and Robert Jenson

Trinity Press International, P.O. Box 1321, Harrisburg, PA 17105

Trinity Press International is a division of The Morehouse Group.

Biblical quotations are from the New Revised Standard Version of the Bible, copyright 1989 by the Division of Christian Education of the National Council of the Churches of Christ in the USA. All rights reserved.

Cover design: Corey Kent

A catalog record for this book is available from the Library of Congress.

Printed in the United States of America

02 03 04 05 06 07   10 9 8 7 6 5 4 3 2 1

Men despise religion; they hate it, and fear it is true.
—BLAISE PASCAL, *PENSÉES*

CONTENTS

ACKNOWLEDGMENTS

My work on the logic of redemptive change began with a research project, "Salvation and Personal Identity," funded by the Pew Evangelical Scholars Program. The year-long leave of absence in 1995–96 allowed me to develop the basic notions of consequential and continuous personal identity, without which I could not have made any real progress in my efforts to understand the role of change in the Christian vision of salvation.

As I was just beginning to orient myself, I was asked by Dr. Eglė Laumenskaitė to give a series of lectures on the topic of my research at the Center for Religious Study of Vilnius University in Lithuania. The discipline of working up my diffuse thoughts into a two-week course of lectures was very helpful, and I enjoyed the discussions with the capable and energetic students at Vilnius University. Their comments and probing questions helped me a great deal. In 1997, I exercised this material yet again, this time to the theology majors at Creighton University, in a seminar under the title "Christianity and Modern Humanism." I appreciate their patient endurance of my less than fully articulate efforts to explain why I thought atonement the central issue in the drama of faith in the modern era.

The crucial support that allowed me to turn ideas, notes, and lectures into a book was provided by the Center of Theological Inquiry in Princeton, New Jersey, where I was in residence in 1998–99. The congenial working environment and supportive staff of the Center gave me the freedom to put pen to paper, and the series established by the Center in conjunction with Trinity Press International allowed me to publish the results under expert editorial guidance. I greatly admire the Director of the Center, Wallace Alston. His commitment to top-notch intellectual work for the church is exemplary, and stands against any who would divide churchmanship from scholarship. I am fortunate to

benefit from his vision, as well as Wallace's gentle reminders that I need
to attend to the good fruits of modernity, not just its failures.

During these leaves and travels, my department chairs, Richard
Hauser, and John O'Keefe, as well as my colleagues in the Theology
Department at Creighton University, generously accommodated my
absences. The Dean of the College of Arts and Sciences at Creighton,
Michael Proterra, ensured that the crazy quilt of benefits properly
meshed with various grants and fellowships. In this and so many other
ways, Creighton University encourages scholarly ambition among its
teaching faculty, and for that I am grateful.

Institutions provide support; people create intellectual community.
I have many to thank. In the early stages of this project, Patrick
Murray and Michael Brown urged upon me a more thorough investigation of the problems of identity. At Vilnius University, David
Burgess, a Fullbright student, offered helpful criticisms. One gray
Scottish day, Fergus Kerr patiently listened to me as I tried to talk my
way through the book for the first time. The Resident Members of
the Center of Theological Inquiry, especially David Tracy and George
Lindbeck, tried to persuade me that I need not be so polemical and
could be clearer in argument and exposition. I have tried, with mixed
success, to follow their good advice. I owe many debts to Kendall
Soulen, not the least of which is for taking time from his own project
to read the whole manuscript and provide invaluable suggestions for
rewriting. While in Princeton, I came to know Ivica Novakovic and
Lynn Robinson. Their friendship was a great boon. As they have for
many other projects, David Dawson, Bruce Marshall, Ephraim
Radner, and David Yeago read drafts and indulged me along the way.
Robert MacSwain read and commented with his usual keen sense for
language. I must also thank Stanley Hauerwas, both for putting me
in touch with Rob and for urging me to connect this analysis of personal change to my earlier work, *The Ordinary Transformed*. I wish
I could and had.

At Trinity Press International, I have benefited from the editorial
advice of Henry Carrigan, the editorial director. Ruthann Dwyer copy-
edited the manuscript, saving me from countless errors and inelegan-
cies. The managing editor, Laura Hudson, has smoothed the way
nicely. I am fortunate to have the opportunity to publish with a press
so committed to high standards.

To all these people and many more (are you reading Kathy,
Maureen and Mary Rae?) I offer a hearty "thank you." But to three

people, I owe a greater debt. I read R. C. Moberly's beautiful book, *Atonement and Personality*, nearly one hundred years after it was written, but it was as if I was hearing a living voice. I cannot begin to lay claim to Moberly's subtlety of thought, but what he taught me in his masterpiece of analytical theology is at the foundation of this book. The other two I must thank can never be separated. Blanche and Robert Jenson have been constant sources of encouragement and counsel while I wrote and revised. Many times I went into Jens's office at the Center of Theological Inquiry, where he is Senior Fellow for Research. He listened to me with a smile that suggested bemused enjoyment of a circus act, and then reassured me that what seems strange may, in fact, be true, especially when one begins to think about things in terms of what they might become rather than what they presently are. My wife and I count ourselves lucky to have come to know both Blanche and Jens. To them I dedicate this book.

R. R. RENO
OMAHA, EPIPHANY 2002

ABBREVIATIONS

CJ   *Critique of Judgment* (Kant)
CPR   *Critique of Pure Reason* (Kant)
CPrR   *Critique of Practical Reason* (Kant)
E   *Enquiries Concerning Human Understanding and Concerning the Principles of Morals* (Hume)
MPL   *Essays Moral, Political, and Literary* (Hume)
NHR   *The Natural History of Religion* (Hume)
R   *Religion within the Boundaries of Mere Reason* (Kant)
T   *A Treatise of Human Nature* (Hume)

INTRODUCTION

I blame equally those who choose to praise man, those who choose to blame him, and those who choose to amuse themselves; and I can only approve of those who seek with lamentation.
—PASCAL, *PENSÉES*

Change is everywhere. Acorns fall from oak trees, sprout, and grow. Snow melts in spring, and rivers run to the sea. A clear morning becomes an afternoon gloomy and violent with thundershowers. These cascading currents of change strike some as the very essence of things. For Heraclitus, all is flux; nothing abides. In the river of time, all things are and are not. For the author of Ecclesiastes, the earth is the stage for endless change filled only with weariness. Nothing is sated with completion; nothing is drained to the rest of emptiness. The wind blows without exhaustion, and without end.

In the history of Western philosophy, dissolution and decay have motivated foundational questions. How can anything *be* against the forces of change? Where are permanence and stability in the endless flux of events? What abides and has the ability to endure against the erosive power of time? Answering these questions has produced doctrines of being, teachings about what makes things what they are with sufficient power and purpose to prevent them from being driven by change into what they are not.

The doctrines of being are many. The goddess Justice told Parmenides to follow the way of that which is and cannot not be. The power of necessity abides, and to that we must cling. Plato felt the power of necessity in the speech and character of Socrates, and Plato bequeathed to subsequent generations a testimony to what he saw and heard. The Old Testament has its own answer to the problem of being. The author of Ecclesiastes is as sensible as any ancient thinker

1

on the threatening meaninglessness of change. He advances no doctrine of being, at least not in the Greek sense, but he does point his
readers toward what is and cannot not be. Amidst the whirlwinds of
change, he tells his readers, "Fear God, and keep his commandments"
(Eccl 12:13). The covenant of the Lord endures forever, and God will
bring every deed to judgment.

Horace's ode to springtime turns the problem of change in a personal direction. Horace begins with an evocation of the renewing
power of seasonal cycles. As winter gives way to spring, "the changing year renews the plain," and the "changing year's successive plan"
testifies to the enduring power of the world. The year may wane, but
"her losses soon the Moon supplies" as day turns to week, and week
to month.

> But wretched Man, when once he lies
> Where Priam and his sons are laid,
> Is naught but Ashes and a Shade.

Unlike the moon's cycles, Horace says, we are cut off from that which
abides. We cannot draw on the limitless fund of being. Indeed, that
which we have piled up as bulwarks against the dangers of a changing world—wealth, honor, virtue, friendship—are naught. The
philosophers might rejoice in the abiding power of the elements, the
high and immutable necessity of being, but Horace's conclusion is a
chilling evocation of our vulnerability to change:

> Not you, Torquatus, boast of Rome,
> When Minos once has fix'd your doom,
> Or eloquence, or splendid birth,
> Or Virtue shall replace on earth.
> Hippolytus unjustly slain
> Diana calls to life in vain,
> Nor can the might of Theseus rend
> The chains of hell that hold his friend.[1]

We are really very different from the snow and the river, from the grass
and the moon. Blond hair turned gray is one of the many signals of our

---

1. Horace, *Odes* 4.7. I follow Samuel Johnson's translation, *The Poems of Samuel Johnson* (ed. David Nichol Smith and Edward L. McAdam; Oxford: Clarendon, 1941), 231—32.

journey to death and corruption. We do not sprout young and tender shoots of life after the winter of our lives. Such darkening thoughts do not require the voice of the distant gods; they are nearer than we wish.

The goddess whispered into the ear of Parmenides, and her guidance is as much riddle as revelation, but she is answering a fear that Horace so powerfully evokes. Ancient philosophers and their teachings about being were, finally, motivated by the need for consolation against change. To be sure, they sought higher things and in so doing undertook journeys of speculation. Nonetheless, these speculative adventures served spiritual purposes, and however much I may fail in speculation, I have no difficulty grasping those spiritual purposes. Ancient philosophers cultivated a cure of the soul that reduced our vulnerability to change, and the logic was simple. If we wish to endure, we must cling to that which abides. However much philosophers fought over how to identify that which abides (*logos, nous, hyle*) and over the spiritual techniques, rational arguments, and moral disciplines necessary to escape the tendrils of change, the proposed cure of the soul had a singular form. Change is a threat, and the project of life is to lay up a fund of being that cannot be overdrawn, not even by the necessity and finality of death. This cure of the soul obtains for Plotinus as for Sextus Empiricus. Whether the fund of being is "beyond being," or nothing more than the singular and inexhaustible knowledge that we cannot know more than that we cannot know, *something* sends an electrical charge through our lives, shocking us out of the flux that threatens to absorb us. Whatever makes me who I am, my identity as a person, must be wrenched from the cascades of change and fixed to the immutable power of being.

Our world is very different from the world of ancient Greece and Rome. One remarkable difference has to do with change and its relationship to our hopes and fears. Where the ancients fled from change as one would flee from a tidal wave that one knows will engulf and destroy, modernity seeks and embraces change. The ancients built monuments in the vain hope of damming up the currents of forgetfulness by putting the past ever before themselves; we move to California in the vain hope of putting the past forever behind us. Socrates wanted to speak the truth and honor justice, but he gave no evidence of wanting to change Athens and regarded her laws as more sacred than life itself. In contrast, no city in North America is without agitators for change; no community lacks activists and reformers. Even if established interests ignore and resist, from country club to coffee house, the universal consensus is that agents of change are a blessing, as a whole, even if painful serially. We fear death and its finality, yet we also fear stagnation, complacency, and missed opportunities. The ancients may have wished to cling to that which abides, but we are not so sure. What is most important, what is best and makes life worth living, we think, is around the corner, in the future. As a result, the modern cure of the soul is very different from the ancient project of preparing for death. It is keyed to convictions and habits, prejudices and disciplines, that embrace the redemptive power of change.

Embracing change raises the difficult question that stands as the center of this study. How can you and I, as finite persons with bounded and vulnerable personal identities, participate in change with joy and thanksgiving? As Horace worries, change disrupts, disjoins, and ultimately destroys. To desire change, then, is to entertain the threat of destruction and dissolution. Therefore, we do not simply desire change. To the extent that our world has turned away from that which abides and has embraced the future, we desire morally meaningful change. We desire change in which our identities as persons matter both for and across the difference between what is and what shall be. The central and contested question, then, can be reformulated more precisely: How can you and I matter in the dynamics of change?

Two Constraints

The ancients did not cling to unchanging being out of atavism; the voice of the goddess was wise. They prized *apathia* as the highest good because the alternatives seemed so inauspicious. It is very difficult to explain how you and I matter in the logic of change; it is very hard to show how change is redemptive. Destruction and dissolution are real threats. In order to counter these threats, two severe constraints, both of which involve personal identity, must shape our answer to the question of how we can matter in change. First, our personal identity must be consequential for change. Change is redemptive only if the difference it makes is, somehow, keyed to what makes me who I am. Morally meaningful change must be personal, not impersonal. The change must be for me, not against me. Second, our personal identity must remain continuous across the disjunctions and disruptions of change. Change is redemptive only if I remain myself. I must be able to see myself "at-one"—atoned—across morally meaningful change. Both constraints guide this inquiry.

Consequential Identity

We cannot matter if the dynamism of change simply absorbs or dissolves us. Being who we are must make a difference for a future that is redemptive rather than destructive. Otherwise, whether we *are* or *are not* is of no consequence. Horace evokes the fear of inconsequential existence. We slip into the underworld, beyond the reach of anything or anyone that defined and shaped our lives as persons. Nothing about us finally matters in the world of interchangeable, spectral, and lost shades. We can neither boast of accomplishments nor make claims of justice. Even the bonds of friendship are broken by death. If we are to overcome Horace's altogether reasonable fears and embrace change as a blessing, then we must have some hope that we matter for and in the logic of transformation. Our identities as distinctive and unique persons must have a consequential role. The future must be mine in the sense that its shape and purpose are imputable to me. In some sense, we need to be able to formulate a sentence about the future that takes the form "Because of who I am . . ."

Many sages and prophets have designated aspects of our lives as the fundamental source of "personality" or "individuality." Freedom, reason, intention, character, feeling, and consciousness are popular candidates. I wish to embrace these possible designations under a formal description of personal identity as whatever makes us who we are rather than someone else. Christianity has its own account of what makes us who we are, and it depends upon assumptions about who Jesus Christ is. I will canvass that account in the final chapter and commend it to the reader. Nonetheless, for most of this inquiry, formalism serves a heuristic purpose. We need to understand the function of personal identity in the problem of change, and if we bog down in the undoubtedly important but contested question of what constitutes our identities as persons, then we may lose sight of this functional relation. Therefore, at the outset I plan to set aside the question of what constitutes personal identity and focus on the more minimal claim that personal identity must matter for change. For if personal identity has no consequential role for the future, then surely the ancients are right: change is to be feared rather than sought with hope.

Continuous Identity

Change cannot break us in two; it cannot rupture or destroy our lives across an unbridgeable chasm that separates present from future. Otherwise, however delightful the ideals we seek, not we but some other, standing in our place, shall enjoy the good fortune. As a consequence, we need to grasp the conditions under which we endure across change. Philosophers and theologians have sought to specify the basis for personal continuity—the soul, memory, the brain. Again, my goal is formal. Just as I wish to abstract from rival explanations of that which constitutes personal identity, I also plan to adopt a heuristic formalism about the question of what secures the continuity of identity.

That formalism is tactical. Christianity advances very definite views about how continuity is ensured, and again such views turn on assumptions about who Jesus Christ is. This account of continuity is most clearly expressed in traditional doctrines of atonement, which emphasize our "at-one-ment" with God, but also provide a basis for seeing ourselves "at-one" across change. Doctrines of atonement, then, supply the crucial premises for the Christian affirmation of redemptive change. In the final chapter I will give such views full play. However, I will not plunge directly into an exposition of Christian accounts of continuous personal identity. I wish to analyze the conceptual constraints that follow from embracing change as redemptive, Christian or otherwise. To do so, I begin with the simple specification that personal identity must endure across change in order for change to be good news for you and me. Even though the question of how we ensure continuity is very much a matter of debate, *that* we must remain continuous, however understood, is an indispensable element of redemptive change.

Three Theses

How can I embrace change as redemptive? The conceptual constraints are now defined. In order to affirm redemptive change, I must be able to affirm that I am consequential and continuous in change. The conclusion is foreshadowed. The Christian account of redemptive change depends upon crucial assumptions about personal identity that make possible the articulation of a cogent doctrine of atonement. However, this study is not merely an existential exercise and a conceptual inquiry. It is a polemical endeavor. The prophets of self-wrought transformation have many followers. These prophets constitute the tradition of modern humanism that will preoccupy most of this inquiry. Modern humanism insists that change is redemptive insofar as it stems from and serves our intrinsic dignity as persons. Thus, the pressing question is not whether or not to embrace change. As I have suggested, modernity answers this question with a presumptive yes. Instead, the pressing and controversial question is whether to embrace change under the rubric of Christianity or modern humanism—or to enter into the labyrinths of postmodern attempts to turn the dangers of redemptive change into a harmless play of difference.

In this study, I hope to defend the claim that this question can be answered rationally and in favor of the Christian cure of the soul. The conceptual constraints, consequentiality and continuity of personal identity, allow us to achieve clarity about just what can and cannot be said about redemptive change. That clarity speaks against modern humanism, for its cure of the soul, based upon the intrinsic dignity of our identities as persons, is entangled in persistent contradiction. I will devote a great deal of effort to exposing and analyzing this contradiction in order to advance a material assessment of modern humanism and its claims and then to weigh it against the Christian promise of redemption. This engagement shapes the structure of the inquiry, and it develops as follows.

The Descriptive Thesis

I argue that the role of personal identity in change constitutes the most perspicuous and decisive point of conflict between Christianity and modernity. The standard Enlightenment account of this conflict tells an epistemological story. Open debate and reasoned argument war against ecclesiastical authority and dogmatic faith. This account gives the false impression that the clash between Christianity and modernity is best understood as a conflict of reason with revelation, science with theology, the head with the heart. Such characterizations obscure the deeper moral collision. Modernity is animated by moral prejudices that stem from a humanistic cure of the soul, and these moral prejudices make the collision with Christianity violent. Change is good, indeed necessary, we are told, in order to overcome the authoritarian diminishments and fanatical temptations of Christian faith. For modern humanism, only a commitment to personal identity as the sole and sufficient basis for the highest good can deliver us from anxiety and misgivings about change. Only the affirmation that we matter most allows change to be redemptive. Thus, the critical task of modernity is to clear away the impediments to such a commitment and the realization of its promise in our lives. Such a critical task necessarily rejects the Christian claim that Jesus Christ matters most for our salvation.

In chapter 1, I demonstrate this descriptive thesis by providing an anatomy of modernity's critical project, showing its moral basis and charting its collision with Christianity. I do so by advancing a differentiated epitome of the many modern objections to faith. This epitome is structured around two objections: the first to crushing authoritarianism and the second to vain overreaching. The objection to authoritarianism is based on the fear that the submissive patterns of faith undermine and obscure the supremely consequential role of personal identity. We do not matter, fears the modern humanist, under the systems of dogma and obedience that define traditional Christianity. The objection to vain overreaching imagines our identities stretched and broken by the unbridled ambitions of supernatural belief. Fanatical efforts and extreme moral discipline attempt to transcend the limits of who we are and in so doing undermine the conditions for continuous personal identity.

The isolation and elaboration of these two modern concerns serve a particular purpose. The most profound conflict between Christianity and modernity rests in a disagreement over how change should be sought and effected. To bring precision to this conflict, as well as clarity to the nature and logic of modern objections to Christianity, I use the constraints of consequential and continuous personal identity to construct a conceptual artifact: we-matter-most humanism. This humanism insists that change is redemptive if and only if we are the necessary and sufficient conditions for the highest good. This formulation is my attempt to characterize the logic of modern humanism. It allows me to take a step back from the diverse traditions of modern humanism, some rationalist and some skeptical, some utilitarian and some romantic. My goal is not to harmonize these diverse modern traditions. Instead, I wish to explicate the underlying humanistic view in terms of the formal relationship between personal identity and the changes necessary to achieve the highest good. My thesis is that this formal relationship fuels the modern alienation from faith because it advances a vision of redemptive change at odds with the very logic and structure of the Christian cure of the soul. For Christians, Jesus is necessary and sufficient, not you or I. To the extent that the conceptual artifact that I call we-matter-most humanism captures the distinctively modern presumptions about personal identity in relation to change and makes the conflict with Christianity immediate and pressing, the critical agenda of modernity can be examined. The cogency of its view of personal identity and change can be tested, and we can make informed judgments about the merits of modern humanism in comparison to Christianity.

The Diagnostic Thesis

Modern humanism encourages us to seek and demand change. We must throw off the burdens of crushing authoritarianism. We must repent of overreaching ambitions. But proponents of this critical urgency cannot make sense out of how we matter for the future we are encouraged to seek. The relationship between personal identity and the highest good that is endorsed by modern humanism cannot affirm that we are both consequential for and continuous across change. Thus, the critical project of modernity encourages us to adopt moral prejudices against authoritarianism and overreaching that have no cogent basis. We must conclude, as I will argue, that the vision of redemptive change that animates the critical project of modernity is irrational.

Demonstrating this failure requires me to do more than deploy logical formulations that capture the formal relationship between personal identity and the highest good in modern humanism. I must show how actual proponents of this humanism fail to satisfy the conceptual constraints of consequential and continuous personal identity. To do so, I undertake close readings of three central modern figures—Jean-Jacques Rousseau, David Hume, and most extensively Immanuel Kant. These figures are, I think, both seminal and representative. Each is extraordinarily influential; none is reducible to another. In my analysis, I track the logic of their humanism, showing how their vision of human destiny moves along pathways circumscribed by the presumptive necessity and sufficiency of personal identity for the highest good, each turning on the difficulty of establishing a life "at-one" across the threatening disjunctions of change.

As I work through these three figures, clarity about the logic of we-matter-most humanism reveals that each of these great modern thinkers holds a view of the relationship between personal identity and the highest good that prevents change from being good news. Rousseau and Hume avoid the most painful consequences of this failure by renouncing (Rousseau) or mitigating (Hume) the reality of change. Kant neither renounces nor mitigates. He insists upon redemptive change and acknowledges the conceptual constraints. Personal identity must be consequential in the strong sense of being the sole and sufficient basis for the highest good, as well as continuous in the sense of placing necessary constraints upon the future we seek. However, as I will show in some detail, without a cogent account of atonement, Kant cannot meet these high standards. Such failure produces a distinct suspicion. The modern humanism that Rousseau, Hume, and Kant so effectively represent seems to lack a cogent basis for insisting upon critical and transformative change in which our identities are consequential and continuous. Thus the humanism they embrace either backslides into an ancient anxiety and fear of change or embraces change without rational hope. Neither alternative is happy.

I pursue this diagnostic thesis in chapters 2—5. Throughout, I resist the temptation to develop these close readings into a larger account of the history of modern humanism. I also repress my impulse to show how the leading postmodern theorists do little more than either rearrange the basic options articulated by Rousseau, Hume, and Kant or return to ancient renunciations of morally meaningful change. I wish to know and explain the logical constraints of the humanistic cure of the soul, and I must restrict myself to tracking the fate of personal identity under these constraints. As a consequence, the analysis is limited to the distinctive thought of Rousseau, Hume, and Kant.

But I am interested in more than these particular figures. Precisely because Rousseau, Hume, and Kant are such seminal and representative modern figures, their failures are visible in the modern form of life that their thought both reflects and continues to shape. As I look up from my books, I see these failures in the flesh and blood of modern life. I do not keep what I see a secret from my reader. I will urge the reader to look up as well, to see what I see. The contradictions of we-matter-most humanism are real. The more I have come to understand the logic of the modern cure of the soul, the more I now see how deeply and extensively modern humanism has betrayed its promises. We have been stripped naked before the demands of change. Now, in the twilight of modernity, to be told "The future is now!" has no taste of delight, for it is the warning that management consultants speak to corporate executives; it is the stark truth that parents must confront as their children are absorbed into the shocking crudity and anger of adolescent culture; it is the bitter truth of the real estate developer; it is the harsh epithet of the orthopedic surgeon filing for divorce. "The future is now!" is the rude hand that will break our necks if we refuse to turn our gaze and love and loyalty away from the past. Nothing abides; all is coal for the engine of change. However shining its rhetoric, the logic of modern humanism has failed. We may either love change or hate it, celebrate it or resist it, but we cannot rationally affirm change as redemptive. Illuminated by this analysis, I have come to see that modernity is a propaganda campaign on behalf of a putatively moral change that can neither be explained nor inhabited, and I am convinced that what is called "postmodern" is best understood as the array of spiritual disciplines necessary for enduring the failed redemptive project of modern humanism.

The Prescriptive Thesis

Where modern humanism fails, Christianity succeeds. Christianity identifies Jesus of Nazareth as the sole source of morally meaningful change. In the sixth and final chapter, I show how this identification allows Christian teaching to provide a cogent account of the way in which personal identity matters for the future. Unlike modern humanism, Christianity offers a doctrine of atonement. Our lives are consequential in divine judgment, and we endure as continuous beings because Jesus is "for us" as the power of incorporation. We are "in Christ" under divine judgment and are judged according to his righteousness. We are "in Christ" in a new life, shaped by word and sacrament into the form of his righteousness. By describing atonement in Christ, Christianity offers a cure of the soul in which we can embrace change in hope, rather than flee in fear or resign ourselves to change with the despair born of knowing that we can have no rational confidence that we will matter.

My conclusion, then, is programmatic. First, we should acknowledge the underlying inhumanity of modern humanism. The pious wishes of the great proponents of human dignity, critical freedom, rational responsibility, and social tolerance are not sufficient to overcome the debilitating logic of insisting that we matter most for redemptive change. As a critical project devoted to changing society, morality, and personality so that personal identity is both consequential and continuous, modernity fails. Second, we should recognize that one of the most important contemporary tasks of theology is to transform the animating assumptions of modern humanism. We must be consequential and continuous in order for change to be good news, and in that sense, modern humanism rightly wishes to affirm the central role of personal identity. However, redemptive change is "in Christ." Our identities as persons are consequential in Christ; our identities are continuous in him. Rather than attack the potency and ambition of faith, as does modernity's criticisms of crushing authoritarianism and vain over-reaching, theology must affirm the incorporative power of Christ, a power that intensifies our dependence upon another and sharpens the edge of change. We matter more insofar as we are more dependent upon and changed by Christ. Such an affirmation is the ground and basis of Christian humanism.

Four Objections

My emphasis on the polemical engagement of Christianity with modern humanism may lead the reader astray. Life does not come in neat packages. Our commitments and projects (modern, humanistic, or otherwise) rarely stem from a single source that admits of formal statement and clear definition. The mind and heart are eclectic, and we tend to seek, rather than possess, the clarity of mind and purity of heart that would bring life into focus. Our convictions rarely admit of propositional formulation without substantial loss. As a consequence, as I identify and formulate the logic of we-matter-humanism, track down its contradictions, and juxtapose the Christian view, readers can feel as though this inquiry seeks both too little and too much. The logical formulations can seem abstruse and detached, and as a result inconsequential. The subtle texture of modern critical ambition, its zeal for human freedom and care for human fragility, can seem lost in the argumentative deployment of formal analysis. Yet, the precision itself yields results that seem overly ambitious. The admittedly troubled modern project, no doubt prone to certain excesses and failed promises, is suddenly pinned with a charge of self-contradiction. This charge seems too bold and grandiose. Something so complex and diverse as "modern humanism," to say nothing of modernity, cannot be reduced to contradiction!

These concerns are well founded. Arguments are rarely just the right instruments for intellectual navigation. Nonetheless, they are almost always useful, and therefore, I must ask the indulgence of the reader. I must isolate and define modern humanism in order to undertake close analysis of its account of the relation between personal identity and morally meaningful change. I must fix semantic content and constrain premises in order to gather argumentative momentum. To proceed in this way will inevitably seem too narrow to capture the flesh and blood of the modern project and, at the same time, will yield entailments that seem to go far beyond what any reasonable humanism would wish to say. Yet, inference requires propositions, and entailments follow with logical force. Insofar as I intend to mount an argument against modern humanism and in favor of Christianity, an argument based on what can be affirmed without contradiction, I cannot see any other way to proceed.

However, objections to my approach exist that involve more than the worry that formal arguments are too narrowly constructed and yield conclusions too forceful. Four such objections emerge that I should anticipate. (1) This approach obscures Christian patrimony of modern humanism, giving the impression that humanism is a strange, inexplicable cancerous growth, antithetical and unrelated to Christianity. (2) Surely modernity is not simply to be repudiated. Modern humanism has made us aware of the great importance of personal freedom and the intrinsic dignity of each individual. A proper engagement with modern humanism requires judicious assessment rather than polemical rejection. (3) The argumentative structure of this study creates the impression that Christianity is the dialectical victor, mandated by its ability to answer a question that modern humanism cannot. If this is so, then the approach seems hopelessly modern. Do the powers of rational analysis deliver us from the clutches of error? Is that not a covert form of humanistic hubris? (4) Modernity has been eclipsed by postmodernity. As such, this study of modern humanism is hopelessly outdated, fighting a superannuated enemy rather than addressing the real spiritual challenges of the present age. These four important objections require answer from the outset.

Christian Patrimony

Christianity is the engine of Western culture, and we rightly assume that the intensely critical and transformative passions of modern humanism are only possible in light of the Christian embrace of redemptive change. Charting the connections between Christianity and modern humanism remains an important task. To a certain extent, this study shows one set of conceptual connections. Christianity and modern humanism are both committed to redemptive change; both require cogent accounts of the continuity of personal identity in change; both turn on the problem of atonement. In this sense, even as I construct an argument against modern humanism, I am drawing together two strains of redemptive hope by exposing a shared problem and a common submission to the necessary consequentiality and continuity of personal identity. Modern humanism, like Christianity, hopes to advocate change in which we matter, and this is a very important common ambition. Indeed, were they not so closely connected on this point, I could not formulate the conflict between the two views with any formal clarity. Because Christianity and modern humanism ride on the same rails of consequential and continuous identity, they collide rather than pass each other at a distance.

The reader may object that I should chart the historical and conceptual interconnections between Christianity and modern humanism rather than develop a polemical rivalry, that I should focus on the common ambition rather than bring logical tools to bear upon the collision between the two. However, to ask for a synthetic appreciation of the overlapping preoccupations of Christianity and modern humanism, and their shared dependence upon the possibility of atonement, is to ask for something I cannot provide. My approach to this fundamental problem is analytical, not historical. I lack the serene disposition that allows for the kind of survey and synthesis that would yield a clear and compelling picture of the role of atonement in Western thought and culture. I have interior mental sketches of the central importance of the doctrine of atonement in Western Christian theology, its connection to legal theories and punitive practices, and its contribution to the emergent dynamism of early modern Western culture. But I cannot paint landscapes. Instead of using a brush and palette, I am much more inclined to take up the scalpel and dissect the cadaver in order to see how the organs of thought and commitment function.

Moreover, I know that the dysfunctions of the Christian Church— its venial compromises, its schismatic failures of charity, its worldly lust for domination—offer an important explanation for the rise of the nontheological philosophies, moralities, and political theories that have shaped modernity. I know that the failures of Christianity have contributed a great deal to the moral prejudices that animate modern humanism. Yet, to acknowledge such connections and causes in no way settles the question of antagonism or comity. Christianity may have to carry the burden of responsibility for the incoherence of modern humanism. But the main goal of this study is not to determine causes and assign blame; it wishes to assess character.[2] A child is not necessarily a friend. A child can become prodigal. Modern humanism, though deeply indebted to and conceptually intertwined with Christianity, is a functional enemy of faith. This prodigal enmity is more important than the ambiguities, subtleties, and historical origins of modern humanism, for each of us must make a personal and not merely intellectual decision. To which cure will we submit our souls—modern or Christian?

Judicious Assessment

The second objection resists the force of the juxtaposition of modern humanism and Christianity. The prodigal son is flesh and blood of his father, and surely we should not overstate the collision between modern humanism and Christianity. The argument is too heated. I should recognize the potentially fruitful correctives that modern humanism offers to the excesses of Christianity. What of the fury of the Inquisition, the burning of heretics, witchhunts, and the theocratic ambitions of clerics? Should we not thank modern humanism for curtailing these aspects of Christianity? Furthermore, the objection continues, I should allow that modern humanism is a great ally against the tendency of the scientific and the technological to advance a reductive view of our humanity. Surely the fact that modern humanism defends personal identity, however imperfectly, should be counted a gain. Thus, the objection concludes, I might debate with modern humanism, but I should do so with the spirit of mutual instruction rather than with polemical intent.

I wish to assess the cogency of modern humanism, not to tally the plusses and minuses of its contribution to history. I have no interest in keeping score. Because I find this humanism inconsistent in its fundamental promise of redemptive change, I cannot adopt a sanguine attitude. Insofar as Christian faith seeks truth, the contradictions of

---

2. For a rich and suggestive portrayal of the ecclesiastical sources of modern habits, moral values, and intellectual presuppositions, see Ephraim Radner, *The End of the Church: A Pneumatology of Christian Division in the West* (Grand Rapids: Eerdmans, 1998). I do not have sufficient historical expertise to fully assess Radner's claims, but I find his approach compelling and his strategies of analysis revolutionary.

modern humanism—and the animating assumptions that entail these contradictions—must be rejected. This may strike readers as reactionary. After all, should we not acknowledge that modern humanism has brought important values to the forefront: human freedom, scientific inquiry, democratic ideals, and religious tolerance? Perhaps, but a sunset in Los Angeles is often filled with lovely colors: pinks, purples, and yellows. One would think it nothing but glorious were it not for the realization that such colors are unnaturally vivid and the shades are but a compensatory final moment of a daylong immersion in suffocating smog. One of my goals in this study of atonement and personal identity is to bring into the open the illogic of modern humanism. We may savor the values and achievements of modernity, but at least we should take an honest look at the toxins through which such values and achievements are refracted. If such honesty is reactionary, then so be it.[3]

Modern Form of Argument

The vigor of my reduction of modern humanism to self-contradiction gives the impression of dialectical victory, as if Christianity is somehow more plausible because of the failure of its rival. The argument is, then, typically modern. It assaults the present age in order to give birth to a new, albeit "reactionary," future. It uses critique in order to apply torque to the wheels of a hoped-for change from modern humanism to a restored Christianity. Thus does the objection draw me back into the circle of the very modern patterns of thought and life from which I seek to escape.

I may be modern by God's providence, and thus suffer its temptations, but I do not wish to be modern by intent and conviction.

---

3. I point readers to a sober mind whose formulations are less heated but substantially the same. At the conclusion of *An Essay in Aid of a Grammar of Assent*, John Henry Newman advances various "evidences" on behalf of the truth of Christianity. However, he prefaces his positive remarks with a negative one. After cataloguing an array of beliefs that serve as a profile of modern humanism, Newman writes, "These opinions characterize a civilized age; and if I say that I will not argue about Christianity with men who hold them, I do so, not as claiming any right to be impatient or peremptory with any one, but because it is plainly absurd to attempt to prove a second proposition from those who do not admit the first" ([Notre Dame: University of Notre Dame Press, 1979], 323). Newman is perfectly willing and able to show the illogic and inhumanity of his "civilized age." However, such efforts are not forms of "arguing with," a turn of phrase that Newman intends as collegial and not adversarial. For Newman, a Christian engagement with the present, "civilized age" takes the form of "arguing against."

Specifically, I do not wish to be read as showing the "dialectical necessity" of Christianity. The logical and cultural failures of modern humanism in no way enhance the plausibility of Christianity in our day. No mental trick can turn *Schadenfreude* into rational advantage, as if, somehow, the inconsistencies of one tradition of objections to Christianity rebound as positive reasons to have faith. I cannot construct a disjunctive syllogism in which the reader must choose: Christian consistency or modern humanistic self-contradiction. The ancient flight from change is a real possibility, both intellectually and spiritually. As I hope to show, Hume offers a mitigated humanism that carefully manages and limits change, and his legacy gives cogency to a "conservative progressivism" that follows in the wake of the disjunctive contradictions of a more full-blooded humanism. Furthermore, postmodern thought, when it is not being filtered through the moral pietism of American academic life, renounces redemptive change and advocates a return to the ancient quest for *apathia*. Those postmodern spiritual directors who wish to habituate us to love difference need not find a consequential and enduring role for personal identity. This may not be appealing, but it is also not illogical. The contradictions of modern humanism do not plague the patrons of difference.

More important than the obvious point that the failure of one view of human life does not prove the truth of another, I wish to advance no illusions of mental or intellectual redemption. Contradictory propositions and irrational prejudices debilitate and diminish our lives. They tempt us to squander our inheritance. I hope that I can give the reader some sense of these effects of modern humanism. But in no way do the grim consequences of certain ways of thinking and acting necessitate a turn to cogency and hope. This confidence in critical insight is a modernist fantasy. Human beings have a long history of living amidst swine. Because our captivity to error is, finally, spiritual, we seem able to tolerate any amount of falsehood, even if we can see how it produces contradictions both logical and existential. No analytical, dialectical, or genealogical tour de force will save the day. The remedy to prodigal thought is ascetical, not intellectual. Only incorporation in Christ will allow us to repent of our journey into the inhumane logic of modern humanism in such a way that we can see how dependence upon Christ and the hope for eternal life are enhancements, rather than diminishments, of who we are. That incorporation may be the object of our prayers, but it cannot be the consequence of our thinking.

Postmodernity

Rousseau's zeal for affirmation of his individuality by society continues to define contemporary politics of recognition.[4] Hume's defenses of ordinary rational expectations retain currency in a culture dominated by experimental sciences. Kant's dream of uniting freedom with reason continues to animate liberal ambitions. Yet, the very irrationality of modern humanism that I hope to make plain in this study makes modernity inhospitable. Although we can live with contradictions, we do so only by enduring the illogic of our hopes and the failures of our dreams. In this way, modern humanism continues to define our age but no longer as a new possibility we champion; rather it is a legacy we defend with ever decreasing conviction. For this reason, I have little doubt that modern humanism is a spent force, even as its very failure continues to shape our souls.

Postmodernism designates the many strategies we develop for defending what cannot be defended. Not by coincidence does postmodernism flirt with misology. Not by accident is postmodernism fixated on the uncontrollable force of change. The theoretical flights of deconstruction amount to elaborate demonstrations of the unstable and vulnerable status of semantic identity in a world defined by modernist assumptions. The same holds true for personal identity. Irony is the defense mechanism of a person who realizes that power is always a threat. No change can redeem; it can only dominate and destroy. Thus, if we grasp the failed logic of modern humanism, then we can better understand the spiritual project of postmodernism: to live in a dynamic culture of change without hope for redemption.

I will not pursue an analysis of postmodernity. Its translation of change into difference alleviates the contradiction that afflicts modern humanism, but in so doing, postmodernism establishes an alternative, rather than rival, vision of human destiny. We are back among the ancients, seeking techniques for building bulwarks against the threats and dangers of change. Christian hope has no greater logical advantages over postmodern irony than it did over the ancient quest for *apathia*. The advantage is spiritual; the gain is moral, for Christianity, unlike postmodernism amidst the fragments of a failed modern humanism, can urge a change that is keyed to personal identity. It is this advantage, this gain, that I hope to champion. For I am convinced that the future of humanism depends upon a return to the Christian vision that succeeds where modernity fails.

---

4. See Charles Taylor, *The Ethics of Authenticity* (Cambridge: Harvard University Press, 1992).

–Chapter 1–

TWO POLES OF CRITICISM

To explain how a philosopher's most remote metaphysical asser-
tions have actually been arrived at, it is always well (and wise) to
ask oneself first: what morality does this (does *he*) aim at?
—FRIEDRICH NIETZSCHE, *BEYOND GOOD AND EVIL*

Criticisms of Christianity are sharpened in many different ways.
Sometimes objections concentrate on the intelligibility of Christian
claims. Beliefs about the nature of God are deemed conceptually confused. "Christianity may have poetic value, but it is insufficiently
coherent to be a candidate for truth." At other times, emphasis falls
upon the lack of evidence for Christian beliefs. "We have no good
reason to think that Christianity is true." "Miracles are intrinsically
incredible." "Full of hypocrisy and malfeasance, the history of the
Church fails to offer even the basic evidence of holiness." Or the
emphasis shifts from questions of intelligibility and evidence to concerns about the effect of Christianity upon our moral sensibilities.
Christianity is decried as a debilitating distraction from the real challenges of human life. "Faith encourages the believer to look up and
away from the everyday tasks of making the world more just."
"Faith is a pie-in-the-sky narcotic that encourages quiescent acceptance rather than critical responsibility." Specific features of the
Christian account of God and human destiny strike the critic as ret-
rograde. "The idea of divine lordship sanctifies the worldly tyranny of
the powerful." "Ancient descriptions of God as Father promote violence against women." "The imagery of ritual sacrifice legitimates violence." The list of these particular failures is endless, but the pattern of

19

criticism is common: Christianity encourages a form of life at odds with human flourishing.[1]

We can easily miss the underlying moral valence of criticisms of Christianity because of the epistemological nature of many of the standard objections. At issue, we are tempted to think, are matters of reason and revelation, or science and religion, or faith and evidence, not morality in any fundamental sense. We tend to think that critics of Christianity are concerned about intellectual responsibility, accurate knowledge, justified belief, good evidence, and not particular questions of right and wrong. As a result, many modern defenses of Christianity have been devoted to producing evidence or demonstrating the critical dimension of faith or producing a religious epistemology. Such efforts have been misguided. Either they fail to persuade because they treat the symptom, rather than the cause, of modernity's critical disposition toward Christianity, or they revise away the essential features of classical Christianity, and the defense becomes a garbled form of pleading guilty.[2]

Clarity about the moral basis of modern criticism of Christianity will allow us to avoid these missteps. This has more than apologetic importance; we should properly grasp the friction between modernity and Christianity so that we can understand the world in which we live. A theological engagement with the moral basis of criticisms of Christianity helps expose the logic of the humanism that animates modernity. The atmosphere of criticism is so highly charged because

---

1. Donald MacKinnon recognized the central importance of this moral criticism: "The philosopher of religion easily tends to think that the greatest obstacles today in the way of religious belief are to be found in the unintelligibility and inadmissability of such fundamental concepts as that of a creator God, an immaterial soul, etc. But it may be that as a matter of empirical fact, the most deep-seated unwillingness to take seriously the claims of the Christian religion has its roots in a sharp criticism of Christian ethics, of the Christian image of the good life" (_Borderlands of Theology_ [New York: Lippincott, 1968], 51). My goal is to show how the "philosophical" criticisms MacKinnon thinks secondary are, in fact, forms of the deeper moral criticisms.

2. For an exposition of the case against a theological focus on epistemology and the doctrine of revelation in the Christian engagement with modernity, see Stephen N. Williams, _Revelation and Reconciliation: A Window on Modernity_ (Cambridge: Cambridge University Press, 1995), 1—23. See, also, my argument against an epistemological interpretation of the modern objections to Christianity, "Pro Nobis: Words We Do Not Want to Hear," in _The Rule of Faith: Scripture, Canon, and Creed in a Critical Age_ (ed. Ephraim Radner and George Sumner; Harrisburg: Morehouse, 1998), 63—76. For an account of the absurd intellectual practices that follow from attempting to formulate an epistemological mediation between Christianity and modernity, see Bruce D. Marshall, _Trinity and Truth_ (Cambridge: Cambridge University Press, 2000), 50—179.

modernity is preoccupied with human destiny. When we step back from the involving claims of Christianity in order to assess their cogency and purpose, we step into a landscape just as swept with compelling truths and urgent demands. We step into the soteriological project of modern humanism, which at the end of this chapter I will define as "we-matter-most humanism."[3]

This distinctively modern cure of the soul may be entering into a crisis called "postmodernism," which is full of claims and counterclaims that seem to have left behind the great themes and ideals of modernity: critical freedom, personal dignity, human rights, rational responsibility. Yet, for all the criticisms and doubts of postmodernity, modern humanism remains a potent vision. The humanistic project, diverse in expression, contested and often resisted by many who fall under its influence, continues to exert ideological force over our minds and over our souls. Whatever its source, whatever its logical status, whatever its current forms, I am interested in this power. I want to understand the demands and promises of modern humanism, not only because, as a Christian theologian, I wish to know my rival but also because, as a citizen of this strange post-Christian world, I too feel its power.

To grasp the saving ambition of modernity, we need to recognize that the disjunction between epistemology and morality is an optical illusion created by the transformative urgency of modern thought. Notions of an objective and dispassionate search for truth are given flesh by various ascetical disciplines of inquiry, as well as pneumatologies of subjective attributes and affections that attend genuine experience and true belief. Both yield a redoubled concern for the proper focus of human life. For example, a patron of the experimental method in natural science embarks on a highly moralistic enterprise. Our inclination to believe what we were taught as children and our tendency to generalize from anecdote must be severely repressed as we discipline ourselves to believe only what may be verified by repeated experiment. For this reason, modern science has been formed by a literature of exhortation and asceticism that, however materially divergent, is formally parallel to Thomas

---

3. Jules Michelet, a great propagandist for the redemptive power of liberty, insisted that the difference between Christianity and modern humanism must be understood religiously: "Nothing is more fatal to the Revolution than to be self-ignorant from the point of view of religion—not to know that it bore a religion in itself" (*History of the French Revolution* [ed. Gordon Wright; Chicago: University of Chicago Press, 1969], 415).

à Kempis's *Imitation of Christ*.[4] In a no less rigorous way, modern philosophy attempts to isolate "clear and distinct ideas" or "sense impressions," and this entails training the human psyche. We must refine our inner sensibilities, undertake thought experiments, do inventories of our experience, search for marks of certainty, all in order to reliably identify the marks of truth. John Locke's project parallels the introspective anatomy of experience found in Saint John of the Cross. At every turn, then, we discipline our minds and reconfigure our lives accordingly. To participate in the modern project of seeking truth, we must repent of our tendency to be absorbed into a community of opinion, to be swayed by passing emotion, to be deceived by the ability of inference to outrun experience. We must undertake a lifelong task of self-criticism. We must get our souls in order.[5]

---

4. See Nietzsche's reduction of modern intellectual values to a pale and desiccated imitation of Christian asceticism in *On the Genealogy of Morals* 3.23—27. For Nietzsche, the great lie of modern humanism is its claim to inaugurate a form of life that serves human needs rather than divine purposes. On closer examination, the surgical tools of asceticism still operate in modern life. The human soul continues to be a site of conflict in which the will-to-power seeks to create something beautiful, something true, something "genuinely human," out of the raw material of our lives.

5. Richard Rorty is an effective opponent of the optical illusions of modern thought. Rorty promotes a view of intellectual discipline as "a matter of coping with reality" and not "getting reality right" (*Objectivity, Relativism, and Truth* [vol. 1 of *Philosophical Papers*; Cambridge: Cambridge University Press, 1991], 1). For Rorty, philosophy offers no "skyhook" by which to swing out of particular prejudices, no "view from nowhere" from which to develop an objective account of reality. Rather, philosophy offers a kind of intellectual and moral practice. Here, Rorty thinks the representationalist approach to philosophy, which treats objectivity as a certain class of sentences (e.g., "This stone is heavy" is objectively true), is "fruitless and undesirable." Such an approach is fruitless because no coherent account may be given of the criteria by which one may determine when the word "objective" is properly predicated of sentences. For Rorty, the proper use of the predicate "objective" is determined by the practical judgment of those engaged in the intellectual practices that constitute our scientific and democratic culture. More importantly, representationalism is "undesirable" because it obscures this contingency, and in so doing tempts us to neglect our responsibility for nurturing the very practices that guide our use of "objective."

To use Rorty's formulation: the transcending ambitions of representationalism, the desire to see things as they "really are," tempt us to think that philosophy has priority over politics. This ambition for intellectual vision purified of anything contingently human creates the illusion that a general question about "truth" has priority over the very concrete and immediate question about moral community and character. The danger is that we shall devote ourselves to "truth" while neglecting the need for conversation; we shall worship "justice" while ignoring the suffering of others. Our ambitions shall carry us away from, rather than into, the things that matter. However, "if you give up on the priority of escaping from 'human peculiarities and perspectives,'" Rorty observes, "then the important questions will be about what sort of human being you want to become" (13). The primary question, then, is ascetical, not metaphysical or epistemological. For Rorty, our judgments about the proper cure of our souls should animate our use of philosophical vocabularies. Throughout this chapter I wish to show how Rorty is right on this point.

The disciplinary impulse of modern preoccupations with knowledge and objectivity places it in continuity with Christianity: cure of the soul is at the center. However, common concern does not guarantee work toward a common purpose. Whether in the spirit of fraternal correction or with a more antagonistic attitude, modern thought has found wanting the classical Christian strategies for guiding and directing human beings toward their proper end. For modernity, Christianity is a dangerous and potentially destructive force. It is not a self-evident good that has the power to save, the power to enroll us in what is best. Modern thinkers disagree about the location of this danger. Strident critics argue that defects are essential to the very nature of Christianity; others argue that destructive tendencies have become attached to Christianity during its historical development. Friendly or unfriendly, revisionary or destructive, the critical intuitions shared by those who engage Christianity are instructive, for the distinct moral logic of modernity reveals itself most clearly in the polemical and transformative passion it directs toward its Christian past.

The criticisms of Christianity move between two poles. The first pole of criticism argues that Christianity produces a crushing authoritarianism. Christian salvation requires dependence upon fixed and external forms of thought and action, and such dependence necessarily undermines the distinctive potential and achievements of persons. We cannot genuinely participate in a destiny forced upon us, for dogmatic conformity compresses and compacts, rather than expresses and enlarges, our humanity. Faith acts upon, rather than stems from, who we are. The second pole of criticism argues that Christianity suffers from a vain and dangerous overreaching that rends the delicate fabric of our humanity. The Christian view of salvation promises such a great difference between human reality and redeemed life that disruptions ensue. Quietism and withdrawal undermine human solidarity and weaken the fragile practices of rational inquiry and democratic self-governance. Fanatical efforts to live up to this promise of salvation damage both society ("Fundamentalist extremism!") and psyche ("Puritanical repression!"). Divisions and separations wound both the interior life of the person and the body of society.

To the extent that modern Christian apologists have sought to provide "objective" evidence and arguments for faith, they have both assumed a fruitless epistemological project and have obscured the fact that the real conflict between modern and Christian claims about truth rests in the kinds of intellectual practices and supporting cultures they seek to engender.

These two poles, crushing authoritarianism and vain overreaching, are not at odds with each other. Quite the contrary, as we shall see, they stem from a common commitment to the singular role of the person in the highest good. They are two poles of the same vision of human destiny. They reflect the positive ambition of modern humanism: to ensure that our identities as persons are consequential for and continuous across morally mandated change. Nonetheless, they mark two very different sensibilities and traditions of criticism.[6] The critic of crushing authoritarianism often underlines the limitless potential of human reason and creativity: "If only we could unleash human potential!" The critic of vain overreaching rarely has such confidence in humanity. The mood is more cautious, and emphasis falls on limiting the extremes and excesses of human ambition.

The divergence of the concerns and presuppositions of modern humanism aid, rather than hinder, the purpose of this survey of modern criticisms of Christianity, for the two poles of criticism capture a wide range of distinctively modern concerns. As such, they provide us with an orientation to the scope and ambition of modern humanism.

Crushing Authoritarianism

The charges of authoritarianism have a familiar ring. Consider these standard criticisms, which are disparate in emphasis but similar in form. "The dogmatic form of traditional Christianity violates the autonomy of the thinking person." "The machinery of institutional maintenance produces conformity and routine rather than creativity and free expression." "Unique individuals are pressed into the narrow and archaic patterns of discipleship as believers attempt to reproduce ancient and static social forms in the flux of contemporary life." "Christian missionaries impose Western morality and belief upon indigenous cultures." This small sample ranges widely, from epistemological concerns about the proper context for the responsible formation of belief, to political and sociological concerns about individual and

---

6. Isaiah Berlin's influential essay "Two Concepts of Liberty" (*Four Essays on Liberty* [Oxford: Oxford University Press, 1969], 118—72) offers a helpful discussion of the different sensibilities and patterns of thought that animate modern humanism. Berlin, however, overdraws the antagonism between positive and negative liberty. Positive liberty dwells on the strong consequentiality of personal identity for the highest good, while negative liberty is more concerned about the fragility of life and thus highlights the need for continuity of identity. They are different species, but of the same genus. Proponents of both positive and negative liberty seek to do justice to the singular importance of personal identity, however differently they understand that importance.

cultural uniqueness. However, across this range, a common judgment predominates: that the definitive and dogmatic form of Christian teaching assaults, rather than reinforces, human dignity. The unmoving and rigid particularity of Christian life and doctrine—"*This* is the truth about God . . . *This* is right and wrong . . . *This* is how you should live . . ."—yields a crushing authoritarianism.[7]

The range of criticism suggests a number of important critical threads, each of which leads to the conclusion that fixed statements of truth and required ways of life are inhumane. These critical threads have exerted tremendous influence over the modern mind, disposing us to regard the classical forms of Christianity as authoritarian. The first is based on the assumption that the human condition is irreducibly diverse, yielding a deep suspicion of truth claims that have hard particularity and singular focus. The second judges human progress primarily as a matter of unchaining the future from the burdens of the past. This makes inherited Christian teaching part of the problem to be overcome rather than the indispensable source of truth, as classical Christianity assumes. The third thread of criticism regards human fulfillment as a formal process rather than a particular state of affairs. For example, "informed and critical assent" is the distinguishing mark of truth, not a set of doctrines; "free association" characterizes humanizing community, not obligatory rituals or imposed standards of behavior. These three critical threads animate innumerable criticisms of Christianity, and we do well to consider them.

Diversity Rather Than Singularity

"Celebrate diversity!" This moral intuition is so ubiquitous that it has taken on the status of self-evident imperative. Some people are tall,

---

7. Part of a long tradition of thinkers who have sought to save Christianity from the dogmatic form of its traditional teaching, John Locke criticizes authoritarian narrowness and its debilitating moral consequences. Urging the cause of a more precise moral science, Locke catalogues a host of hindrances to rational progress in the affairs of men: the vagaries of ordinary language, the lack of clear algebraic formulae for moral reasoning, the perennial temptation toward promoting one's own self-interest, and so forth. Prominent in this list is the danger of dogmatic fervor: "Whilst the Parties of Men, cram their Tenets down all Men's Throats, whom they can get into their Power, without permitting them to examine their Truth or Falsehood; and will not let Truth have fair play in the World, nor Men the Liberty to search after it; What Improvements can be expected of this kind?" (*An Essay Concerning Human Understanding*, 4.3.22). This identification of the dangers of dogma and the proposed remedy of "fair play," and not Locke's defense of a "reasonable Christianity," have had enduring influence. We now presume that religious doctrine stifles the intellect, generates fanatical violence, and disrupts valuable social practices.

and others are short. It would be absurd to require all people to be the same height. Just as people are different heights, so also do they have different sensibilities, responsibilities, and life experiences, and it would be just as absurd to require them all to have the same beliefs or to conform to the same moral rules. Only a violent attack upon the bodies of individuals could produce a world of people the same height; so also does conformity of belief and practice require violent and inhumane assaults upon conscience, intellect, and will. Since classical Christianity requires doctrinal and behavioral conformity, it promotes exactly this inhumane assault upon our distinctive and unique lives.

When focus falls on the personal, this line of criticism develops as follows. As persons, each of us is unique. That uniqueness can be identified with particular powers of creativity, decisions and actions, or experiences, or some combination of them. The particular source of uniqueness, however, is not crucial. The decisive point rests in the irreducible distinctiveness of each individual. Though we might all follow the same rules of grammar, a poem is unique to its creator and cannot be explained by general principles of rhetoric or theories of language. We might conform to a common communal standard of behavior, but unique combinations of motivation and judgment animate particular moral decisions. However much we might share in a common culture or community, even in the genetic unity of paternity and maternity, our inner lives are necessarily distinctive. In this respect, then, we are intrinsically different from each other. From this fact, the critic concludes that any truth that speaks to our souls, to our creativity, our experience, our moral sensibilities and judgments, must have room and scope for our uniqueness. We must conceive of human flourishing as something that flows from individuality.

Here, the rigid form and fixed content of Christian teaching are judged wanting. Christianity, the critic argues, does not seek to cure the soul; it seeks to melt down our distinctive identities so that we can be pressed into a universal and singular mold. Since people rarely fit the mold, no small amount of energy goes into reshaping and reforming. Where actual flesh and blood is unwilling, severe measures follow. The critic of Christianity reads the warnings of John the Baptist as all too prophetic. "Even now the axe is lying at the root of the trees," John announces, "every tree . . . that does not bear good fruit is cut down and thrown into the fire" (Matt 3:10; Luke 3:9). The theme is repeated and reinforced with another image: "His winnowing fork is in his hand, and he will clear his threshing floor and will gather his wheat into the granary, but the chaff he will burn with unquenchable fire" (Matt 3:12; Luke 3:17). At every turn, metaphors evoke purification. Irregularities are purged, imperfections melted away, cancers excised, contradictions resolved. The result is a stream of blood flowing through Christian history: burned heretics and pogroms, crusades and sectarian warfare.

Critics can be both friendly and unfriendly. The friendly critic is disposed to assign blame to certain forms of Christian teaching and traditions of ecclesial practice. The critic deems these as inessential but champions the kernel of Christian truth as properly open to the diversity of unique individuals. For example, a friendly critic might say that the particular dogmatic form of Christian teaching and the ecclesial practice of requiring confessional conformity are features of institutional religion in general rather than Christianity in particular. The critic suggests that institutional forms are culturally necessary to maintain religion as a socially influential force but are inessential to, perhaps even antagonistic toward, the inner spiritual purpose of the Christian message. Ecclesially defined orthodox belief, then, is set aside as socially mandated conformity. "Authentic existence" is held up as the true message of the gospel. In this way, the friendly critic has redeemed Christianity, properly understood, from the charge of crushing authoritarianism.

The unfriendly critic has no interest in redeeming Christianity. This might stem from a commonsensical focus on Christianity as it is actually practiced rather than as it might be understood by progressive theologians. Perhaps the essence of Christianity is, indeed, a form of "authentic existence" that expresses, rather than compresses, human diversity, but as a social reality, the unfriendly critic observes, its requirements of conformity are what exert real influence. Those requirements of conformity necessarily constrict the full range of human thought, action, and experience. If the unfriendly critic does not emphasize the institutional form of Christianity, attention falls on its theistic content. Faith is intrinsically incapable of allowing for the full expression of diverse human uniqueness. The very idea of God creates a psychic shadow that darkens the plain of human life. We fear our uniqueness, some might argue, and we exploit any suggestion of greater power and higher truth to create for ourselves objects to propitiate and to which to submit. Human beings

fear their freedom to such a degree that even the slightest hint of divin-
ity becomes an irresistible temptation.

The concern about diversity has a cultural as well as individual
dimension. Impressed by the power of a common language and tradition to form human character, we might be less sanguine about individual uniqueness. Yet, however dismissive we might be about the
individualistic assumptions of modern Western culture, we cannot
help but acknowledge the uniqueness of diverse cultures. With this
affirmation, our concern about the homogenizing force of Christianity
shifts registers but remains essentially the same. The particular linguistic code, ritual enactment, and behavioral patterns of Christianity
conflict with other cultural systems. The missionary imperative of
Christianity guarantees that this conflict will reach a white heat of
intensity. Therefore, the evangelical success of Christianity is always
at the cost of the alien culture it encounters. A Jewish Christian, a
Japanese Christian, a Tanzanian Christian, is always someone who
has submitted the richness of his or her indigenous culture to the colo-
nial forces of Christianization. The many unique ways of other peoples are suppressed as Christianity seeks to force its particular cultural
matrix onto all others.

Friendly critics may advance revisionary hypotheses about the
nature of Christian truth, this time to avoid the charge of cultural
imperialism. Fundamental distinctions might be advanced between
the "spirit" of the gospel and the "letter" of its expression in Western
culture, which then allows for very different expressions of that spirit
in non-Western cultures. Unfriendly critics may ignore such revisions
as irrelevant to actual missionary practice; it is, indeed, difficult to
communicate a "spirit" without recourse to the culturally conditioned
"letter" that does the damage of cultural imperialism. Unfriendly critics may also question the capacity of Christianity to revise away its
offensive cultural heft. Speech and action, these critics might argue,
are effective only as embedded in a determinate cultural form.
Therefore, successful missionary activity is necessarily an activity of
"the letter" and never merely "the spirit." The only question, then, is
whether or not Christianity will repent of its aspiration for converts,
not whether it might pursue conversion in a nonaggressive, "spiritual"
way. But whether friendly or unfriendly, this concern about cultural
imperialism joins hands with a concern about personal uniqueness.
The particular truth claims and determinate ethical system of
Christianity diminish the diversity of the human condition. Like any

set form of life advanced as authoritative and obligatory, Christianity sands down the texture of human life.[8]

Openness to the Future Rather Than Dependence upon the Past

"Respect individuality" and "celebrate diversity" are watchwords of our age. The second set of intuitions about the prospective orientation of human flourishing rarely takes such slogan form, but it exerts just as great an influence over our assessments of classical Christian teaching.[9] The basic pattern is simple. The past necessarily influences present existence; however, the power of the past is a burden, and we must continually create a critical distance. We cannot escape the power of the past, but we can guide and direct that power toward the formation of a more humane future. As such, our vision must be directed forward rather than backward. To be sure, we need to be clear-minded

---

8. In an evaluation as forceful as any postmodern critique of the "metaphysics of presence," William James links the monistic impulse with a dogmatic, exclusivist sensibility. "The temper of monists," he writes, "has been so vehement, as almost at times to be convulsive. . . . The theory of the Absolute, in particular, has had to be an article of faith, affirmed dogmatically and exclusively." This convulsive determination to force a singular vision, no matter how recalcitrant the plurality of existence, stems from the very logic of monism. According to James, "The One and All, first in the order of being and knowing, logically necessary itself, and uniting all lesser things in bonds of mutual necessity, how could it allow any mitigation of its inner rigidity?" For James, the monistic urge is implicitly violent. He continues, "The slightest suspicion of pluralism, the minutest wiggle of independence of any one of its parts from the control of the totality would ruin it. Absolute unity brooks no degrees—as well might you claim absolute purity for a glass of water because it contains but a single little cholera-germ." The venture of monism is so grand and so comprehensive—all things find their fulfillment in a single form—that it is, finally, extraordinarily vulnerable. Within the logic of a monistic scheme, "the independence, however infinitesimal, of a part, however small, would be to the Absolute as fatal as a cholera-germ" (all quotations from *Pragmatism* [Cambridge: Harvard University Press, 1975], 78). This logical vulnerability produces a practical determination to prevent diversity from emerging. The cholera-germ of independence from the Absolute must be eradicated. For critics of Christianity, the claim that Jesus is the Alpha and Omega, the singular Son of God who dies for the salvation of the whole world, produces just such a vehement suppression of independent thought, independent spiritual experience, independent moral existence.

9. See John Dewey, *Reconstruction in Philosophy* (Boston: Beacon, 1948). For Dewey, new times demand new methods, and one of the primary tasks of philosophy is to turn forward: "The problem of reconstruction in philosophy . . . turns out to have its inception in the endeavor to discover how the new movements in science and in the industrial and political human conditions which have issued for it, that are as yet inchoate and confused, shall be carried to completion." This will lead to a "new moral order" (xxxix). For Dewey, then, philosophy is "true" only insofar as it is midwife for the future. That task of thinking is not to question the "confused" state of varied modern projects. Instead, we should devote ourselves to carrying the confusion "to completion." The future will forgive all, even the illogic of the present.

and informed about the past, but our devotion should flow toward the new possibilities of the future, not the imperfect actualities of the past.

Just as the concern about singularity is founded on a moral commitment to the unique dignity of individual persons and culture, so also does this distrust of the past have its basis in moral concern. Societies are shot through with injustice; institutions are as likely to undermine as promote well-being; families exhibit dysfunction; even the wealthiest, the most beautiful, and the most talented individuals seem unable to attain happiness. We want to understand these failures and diagnose this recurring, seemingly inevitable, inability to live up to the full potential of our humanity. To the extent that modern thinkers have wished to retain the hope that things might be changed, that the world might be made better, that the human prospect might improve, they have shunned naturalistic explanations for human failure and embraced explanations that depend upon contingent facts. After all, what is contingent might be otherwise, so if we think poverty, for example, is a consequence of particular economic arrangements, we can retain the hope that we might change those arrangements and alleviate poverty. In this way, our current dilemmas are explained as the consequences of the past. Something about the way in which we have lived—our culture, our family histories, our psychic makeup—is the source of ill. The past is part of our problem, and as such, we should view our inheritance as something to be overcome.

Christianity is inevitably caught up in this suspicion of inherited forms of life. The most powerful shaping force in Western culture, Christian thought and practice become prime suspects in the search for the causes of human misfortune. If contemporary culture is afflicted with enduring divisions of race and ethnic loyalty, then surely Christianity must have a hand in causing this evil. If Western societies subordinate women and deny them public roles, then again Christianity is the first place to look for the source of such injustice. If middle-class Americans continue to impose moral constraints upon sexual behavior, constraints unwarranted by science and judged unnecessarily repressive by enlightened moralists, then Christianity is the obvious impediment to progress. The list of particulars is endless, varying in focus according to the interests and commitments of the critics, but the basic logic is always the same. Our past is as likely to diminish us as enliven us, and positive personal and social change is only possible through an ever deepening critical stance toward inherited ways of thinking and acting.

Throughout the modern engagement with Christianity, criticisms have been advanced from within as well as without, and here we find no exception. Friendly critics of Christianity's dependence upon inherited teaching work hard to show how a faithful embrace of the tradition need not entail uncritical acceptance. Theories of religious language that distinguish between the essence of faith and its historical expressions abound. With this distinction, friendly critics can argue that the faithful must abandon themselves to the essence of faith (Holy Mystery, the kerygmatic "Christ event," the infinite in and through the finite, and so forth) but adopt an appropriately critical stance toward the particular formulations and teachings of historic Christianity. In this way the essence of Christian faith, which is necessarily eternal and timeless, frees us from the burdens of the past. We need not form our lives around the limitations of prior dogmatic formulations. In fact, demanding this freedom is actually a duty of faith, for otherwise one is idolatrous, worshiping the finite words and traditions of the past rather than the infinite God beyond time. Thus does the friendly critic show that true Christian faith takes the same form as modern critical consciousness.[10]

Unfriendly critics are divided into two camps. Some may have sympathy for the modern theologian's division of religious essence from traditional expression but are less optimistic about the value of historic Christianity. The classical formulations of dogma are simply too alienated from the timeless truths of faith. The language of divine lordship is so woven into the fabric of historic Christianity, the unfriendly critic might argue, that it cannot help but entrap believers in antiquated ideals of hierarchy and encourage dispositions of subordination. Other

---

10. The Enlightenment treatment of Christianity's relationship with Judaism illustrates this friendly emendation. David Hume expresses a critical commonplace when he draws attention to Christianity's designation of the Pentateuch as Scripture. Hume observes that this guides us backward toward a primitive past rather than an enlightened future. After all, Hume notes, the Pentateuch is "a book presented to us by a barbarous and ignorant people, written in an age where they were still more barbarous" (*An Inquiry Concerning Human Understanding* [Indianapolis: Bobbs-Merrill, 1955], 140). In Hume's day, the anti-Catholicism that fueled a Protestant antipathy for the economy of ritual made the Jewish element of the Christian inheritance an easy target for criticism. How, critics asked, could one take seriously a theological proposal that is implicated in something so painfully archaic and so obviously antithetical to true religion? As Enlightenment criticisms gained momentum, the question expanded until the entire inherited language of Christianity came to be thought of as a "mythological" impediment to the attainment of a truly "contemporary faith." See Rudolf Bultmann's programmatic essay "The Idea of God and Modern Man," *Translating Theology into the Modern Age* (New York: Harper & Row, 1965), 83—95.

critics are less concerned about the status of traditional language in relation to the essence of faith. They focus on the dynamics of Christian faith rather than the material content. Here, the unfriendly critic casts doubt on the ability of modern Christianity to disengage itself fully from a primitive loyalty to the past. However much scriptural texts and creedal formulations might be brought under critical examination, the unfriendly critic observes, theologians inevitably protect some aspect of the past from critical assessment. Faith necessarily looks backward rather than forward.

Formal Process Rather Than Material Claim

Anxieties about the closed circuit of dogma, the burdensome weight of tradition, and the crushing force of institutional authority bear witness to a general modern concern about material claims, specific commands, and particular states of affairs. The world is awash with aspirants to supreme authority, and they constantly seek our submission. In this atmosphere of threat, a defensive posture develops, one that tries to redirect human loyalty away from these vying material claims and toward a universal and formal process of deliberation, judgment, and assent.[11]

---

11. This turn away from particular questions of what constitutes human flourishing to that of how we might construct our beliefs and practices has been much observed. Alastair MacIntyre's *After Virtue* (Notre Dame: University of Notre Dame Press, 1984) pursues an analysis of the moral aphasia of modernity under these terms. Karl Barth's description of the essence of the Enlightenment in *Protestant Theology in the Nineteenth Century* (Valley Forge, Pa.: Judson Press, 1973) adopts similar patterns of analysis and draws a similar conclusion. The Enlightenment is, for Barth, a will to absolute form, a desire to find the encompassing framework for all material features of human life: intellectual and moral, personal and political. Erich Auerbach's investigation of the career of literary realism follows this path and draws the same conclusion in *Mimesis: The Representation of Reality in Western Literature* (Princeton: Princeton University Press, 1953). The archetypal literary form of the Enlightenment is, for Auerbach, Racine's neoclassical dramas. They represent the triumph of universal form over historical particularity and serve as the paradigmatic modern will to absolute form. Auerbach suggests that this will to impose a supervening form upon particularity lies at the root of the ideological brutalities of the twentieth century. In his sketch of the history of modern political theory, *An Intellectual History of Liberalism* (Princeton: Princeton University Press, 1994), Pierre Manent describes the change from material deliberation to formal procedures. According to Manent, in premodern thought, the wisdom of the participants in public life—their knowledge of the proper ends of human nature and their prudent judgments about what is feasible—was central. Modern political theory, according to Manent, changes this. In place of the substantive vision of wise leaders, modern thought seeks to define a just procedure for political deliberation. Representative government, an independent judiciary, a constitutional executive: these and other structures and formal systems of governance guarantee legitimacy and secure justice, not the material wisdom of the participants.

The idea is simple. To the extent that we must engage others, both as individuals and as institutions, we should do so on terms that preserve our unique dignity as persons. We must, of course, develop friendships, pursue romance, establish professional expertise and acquire new beliefs, but we should not do so under the influence of inherited patterns and ethnic loyalties, or according to family custom and cultural pressure. Instead, we should navigate our personal lives by the compass of some formal feature. Sometimes this formal feature is free and informed consent; other times we focus on a feeling or state of mind like "love" or "authenticity." For example, in seeking knowledge, we should strain all beliefs through the experimental method. Similar formal procedures are advocated as the proper foundation for institutions. Notions such as "majority rule" or "individual rights" command our loyalty. In each case a similar pattern obtains. We are guided by a disposition, a quality of experience, a procedure of decision rather than any particular outcome or material claim.[12]

The shift from material claims to formal criteria dominates modern concerns about knowledge. The medieval mind was profoundly concerned with logical forms, and the power of well-crafted rhetoric was well known. However, in that world, neither the logical consistency of inferences nor the immediate plausibility of certain statements constituted the bedrock of knowledge. The revealed Word of God and its ecclesially authorized tradition of interpretation served as the foundation for discerning true belief. To be sure, this foundation was an

---

12. In *On Liberty,* John Stuart Mill wishes us to shift both our social analysis and political loyalty from material claims to formal processes. Previously, notes Mill, social critics have focused on the specific social norms, arguing whether this or that inherited pattern of life ought to be revised or even dismissed. For Mill, this material analysis has been misguided. Critics should attend to the process of socialization and to the violations of human freedom entailed in the very notion of obligatory beliefs. "They have occupied themselves rather in inquiring what things society ought to like or dislike," writes Mill, "than in questioning whether its likings or dislikings should be a law to individuals" ([Everyman's Library; New York: Knopf, 1992], 10). Even the most heterodox thinkers in the past have assumed that their heterodoxy ought to become tomorrow's orthodoxy. For Mill, then, only a shift away from particular questions of morality and belief and to the question of how social custom relates to the individual will advance the cause of humanity. This shift, and not Mill's particular proposals for human flourishing and his thoughts about how to finesse questions of legitimate social obligations and personal freedom, makes *On Liberty* a truly revolutionary book and constitutes his lasting influence. However much critics might chuckle at Mill's residual nineteenth-century pieties and show the inadequacy of his arguments for the modern liberal distinction between private freedom and public obligation, on the central shift from material to formal analysis Mill is triumphant. Few now doubt that the essential personal, moral, and political question revolves around how we acquire and act upon our beliefs, not what we believe or do.

internally complex network of particular statements that defied epitome and resisted systematic display; nonetheless, premodern thought
found this unruly but concrete foundation for knowledge sufficiently
perspicuous to serve as a material basis for the justification of true
belief. Here, as elsewhere, modernity has undertaken a revolution.
Whether "clear and distinct ideas" or "experimental method" or
"immediate sense impressions," modern strategies of justification are
formal. They shift cognitive loyalty away from substantive claims and
particular practices that defend, extend, and apply those claims and
direct us toward various qualities of experience, modes of perception,
and procedures for acquiring beliefs. What the medieval *doctore*
would have thought important, but subservient, the modern thinker
treats as decisive. Intellectual responsibility now turns on *how* we
believe, not *what*.[13]

   Classical Christianity collides with this formal turn. Whereas
Christianity conceives of personal formation as the incorporation of
the individual into a divinely mandated pattern of life, modernity
treats all particular patterns as threatening diminishments that can
only be brought to humane form through some additional and supervening method of discernment. Christianity proposes the particular
shape and purpose of God's will, manifested in Scripture, common
worship, and service, as the determining force that gives health to a
person's life. In contrast, for the modern, this projection of humanizing power onto God is intrinsically debilitating, all the more so
because divine power is, according to Christianity, mediated through
temporal instruments such as Scripture and ecclesiastical structures.
Inevitably, the human person comes into orbit around an alien center. The only way to make Christianity humane is to shift the center
of gravity, to make Christian teaching into a potential aspirant for our
loyalty that must submit to our discriminating judgments (or sponta-

---

   13. Mill offers a classic statement of this shift. "Truth gains more," writes Mill in defense of
the freedom to be passionately wrong, "even by the errors of one who, with due study and prepa-
ration, thinks for himself, than by the true opinions of those who hold them because they do not
suffer to think" (*On Liberty,* 34). Although Mill does advance the argument that the freedom to
hold unpopular beliefs creates the conditions for the discernment of truth through the competition of ideas, the issue is not strictly one of testing ideas through open debate. Instead, Mill argues
that our mode of belief is even more important than the content of belief. "However unwillingly
a person who has a strong opinion may admit the possibility that his opinion may be false," Mill
observes, "he ought to be moved by the consideration that, however true it may be, if it is not
fully, frequently, and fearlessly discussed, it will be held as dead dogma, not a living truth" (35).
The crucial distinction is between "dead dogma" and "living truth," not between simple truth
and falsity. How we hold a belief is more decisive than what we believe.

neous intuitions). Christianity, like all material features of human life, must orbit around us.[14]

This third thread of criticism is often put to friendly use. Modern theologians are quick to embrace the move from material content to formal process. Jesus becomes the embodiment of inclusive love, the symbol of liberative praxis. At a more sophisticated level, attention turns to certain formal elements of the Christian presentation of Jesus. The gospel stories reveal the importance of narrative and contribute to the emergence of humanistic literary realism. The redemptive achievement of Christ might be translated into "acceptance of the unacceptable." The basic plot of Jesus' life, death, and resurrection can be recast as the manifestation of the fundamentally generative dialectic of presence and absence. Some of the most creative and intellectually ambitious initiatives in modern theology stem from these attempts to translate the Christian insistence upon material claims and particular practices into a formal process. Theologians seeking faithful witness to the apostolic tradition probe the structures of doctrine, the logic of divine encounter, the hermeneutics of proclamation. At every turn they seek the presumptively more significant, more universal, and more humane *form* embodied in the distinctive *content* of the Christian tradition.

Whether emphasizing diversity, progress, or process, these three strands of criticism circle around a common theme: Christianity proposes a life that diminishes our humanity. However internally complex the Christian tradition, the sheer fact that it has boundaries and is expressed in a finite cultural and historical register seems an inevitable constraint and diminishment of the diverse desires, aspirations, and experiences of the human race. Enduring dependence upon apostolic teaching cannot help but conflict with the modern desire to disentangle our humanity from its bondage to a fallen past. A recalcitrant particularity at the center of the Christian message puts it on

---

14. See one of the epigrams for Matthew Tindal's deist tract *Christianity as Old as Creation.* He quotes the following sentences from Samuel Clarke, Isaac Newton's apologist: "God does nothing in the government of the world by mere will and arbitrariness.—The will of God always determines itself according to the eternal reason of things.—All rational creatures are oblig'd to govern ALL their actions by the same eternal rule of reason." From these premises, Tindal is able to deduce the conclusion that all particular Christian claims must be judged by the universal rule of reason, which, for him, has a moral dimension. Tindal's rationalism no longer persuades, but the basic relationship between specific Christian teachings and whatever is substituted for universal reason (utility, feelings, intuition, authenticity, free and open debate: the list goes on forever) remains the same.

a collision course with the desire to discern a supervening formal matrix for humane belief and action. At every turn, Christianity limits and restricts. Instead of facilitating our full and unique participation in the project of being human, Christianity treats our unique identities as persons as raw material to be shaped toward a higher purpose. Our inner lives, the contingencies of the present age, the diversity of the human condition—these constituting features of our personal identity are subordinated to the machinations of priests and the constraints of archaic codes of conduct. Under the impress of faith, our unique identities are not consequential. Therefore, the humanistic critic cannot help but conclude that salvation, within the Christian frame of reference, is a vision of the relationship of personal identity to the highest good that leads to deadening conformity.

Vain Overreaching

Whereas one pole of criticism is animated by a concern about the crushing and constraining force of Christian claims to truth and righteousness, the other pole is motivated by worries about the stretching power of those claims. The critic of authoritarianism worries that inner potential and personal dignity are compacted by dogmatism, but the critic of vain overreaching sees other dangers—centrifugal ones. The disruptive redemptive ambition of Christianity shatters the fragile human condition. Supernatural claims, ambitions, and ideals test the limitations of human knowledge, endurance, and community. For these critics, the fragmenting force of Christian ambition produces two pathological forms of otherworldliness: quietistic retreat and fanatical agitation. Both threaten the continuity of our identities.

Quietism involves treating the disjunction between Christianity and ordinary life as sanction for passive acceptance of the present as a shadowy anticipation of coming glory. For the critic, this makes Christianity the opiate of the masses. Pie-in-the-sky faith in a heavenly reward allows us to separate present suffering and injustice from future blessedness and righteousness, and across that division we reassure ourselves that ordinary life is but a passing moment. As a consequence, we stretch our loyalties, our hopes and aspirations, toward eternity, accepting without passion our current state. We invest ourselves in life as we imagine it might be, draining all color from life as it must be led. However this disjunction is understood or achieved— as a mystical meditative practice or as a self-protective turn away from debilitating circumstances—the dynamic is constant. Faith greases the skids of otherworldliness. Our eyes turn upward, and we lose our ability to see and respond to the real blessings and challenges of our humanity. Who we really are—rational and embodied persons living in the world of flesh and blood—becomes discontinuous with the fantasies and illusions about who we might become.[15]

For the critic, fanaticism runs on the same rails as quietism, but with a different intensity and consequence. Fanatics have their eyes turned upward, but instead of accepting the world as a temporary way station, they are determined to restructure life so that it corresponds to the extraordinary vocation of faith. We should not wait for the heavenly kingdom; we need to get on with the business of building the kingdom of God out of the raw material of everyday life. This divinely appointed task produces a restless energy and unbounded zeal. As the critic observes, dogmatic truths give believers an unnatural confidence. The faithful are all too willing to slash and burn their way through the ambiguities of life. So, Bibles in hand, believers dictate to scientists what can and cannot be taught in biology classes. The faithful ring doorbells for political candidates, hold rallies in front of abortion clinics, and in an escalation that critics suggest is inevitable, they eventually become frustrated with worldly resistance to the voice of true righteousness and begin to throw bombs and shoot doctors. "Fundamentalist" becomes synonymous with "extremist."

Concerns about quietism and fanaticism are not simply worries about apathy and extremism. The real issue is deeper. Many critics of Christian otherworldliness are preoccupied with the ways in which Christianity undermines our solidarity with other human beings. Christianity provides an escape from the mundane. This may give the appearance of

---

15. On the venerable status of this objection in modernity, see John Keble's "On the Mysticism Attributed to the Early Fathers of the Church," *Tracts for the Times, No. 89* (New York: AMS Press, 1969). Keble opens his defense of patristic exegesis with a survey of the negative connotations that make "mysticism" an effective epithet against ancient Christian religious sensibilities. As Keble reports, as a term of derogation, "mysticism implies a sort of confusion of the physical and moral, visible and spiritual agency" (3). It "conveys the notion of something essentially and altogether remote from common sense and utility," suggesting "mere religious dreaming, indistinct fanciful theory," implying "a disposition, first, to regard things as supernatural which are not really such; and secondly, to press and strain what may perhaps be really supernatural in an undue and extravagant way" (4). Finally, Keble notes that "mysticism" parallels "asceticism" as a term of abuse. Both suggest religious excess at odds with the real interests of a responsible intellectual and moral life: mysticism is a dreamy quietism, and asceticism a severe fanaticism.

grandeur, but such otherworldly aspiration is but a pose, a psychic dodge by the faithful to excuse themselves from the hard work of being merely human. To the extent that Christians avoid complacency, they overreact with extreme and unrealistic projects of intellectual, moral, and political transformation. The faithful impose rigorous moral expectations upon the uncertainties of their own lives, always whipping themselves forward toward unrealistic goals. Many therapists cringe at the thought of all the repressive energy let loose by Christianity. Guilt is the bomb we throw at ourselves. Countless social critics decry the enduring cultural influence of these repressive mores. No matter how much energy progressive leaders put into demolishing inherited moral beliefs, people continue to feel inadequate. Here, the worry is not that Christian otherworldliness encourages us to check out of life. Instead, critics are preoccupied with the ways in which Christianity tries to make saints out of just plain folks—and in so doing makes us despair of our common humanity.

Criticisms of vain overreaching focus on three areas: intellectual life, moral ambition, and political participation. The basic claims are straightforward: (1) Christianity is unhealthy for the mind because it proposes beliefs that outstrip the powers of reason. (2) Christianity proposes an inhumane morality by advocating conversion and disjunctive change that turn the believer toward the impossible project of pure righteousness. (3) Christianity seeks to found a new community, the Church, which aspires to do justice to its role as a heavenly city. This new loyalty cannot help but cause Christians to forsake their proper roles as citizens. In each way—epistemically, ethically, and politically—Christianity stretches its adherents, jarring them out of the ordinary constraints of life and guiding them toward extraordinary possibilities. The result is fragmentation, division, and dismemberment.

Overbelief and Critical Lassitude

For the Enlightenment critic, Christian supernaturalism is the paradigmatic case of irresponsible faith. Larder loaded with reassuring beliefs about the origin of the cosmos, morality, and human destiny, the religious believer is short on reasons. How is one to justify the belief that Jesus is the Son of God? If we appeal to Scripture, then we are using the testimony of the credulous as evidence for the truth of the incredible. Do we justify belief by the miracles performed by Jesus? To do so entails believing something contrary to our own experience. By appeal to religious experience? The very notion of religious experience begs the question. At every turn, then, the critic of Christianity finds the believer overreaching. The content of Christian faith seems radically different from the sort of things that human beings can hold as justified beliefs.[16]

The crucial issue is not the cruelty of a great soul imprisoned in the small world of dogma, which is the concern of those preoccupied with crushing authoritarianism. The critic of overbelief is not inclined to view reason as a potent force straining against limits; instead, he views reason as inherently weak and easily derailed. Passions and prejudices inevitably corrupt our intellectual judgment. Against these perennial enemies of objectivity, modern gains in rationality have been hard won. Progress is slow, tentative, and reversible. In order to sustain rational practices, we must constantly rally our energies and focus our commitments. We need to discipline our arguments by open debate in order to resist the temptations toward sloppy thinking. We need to exhort ourselves and others toward increased devotion to empirical investigation. Otherwise, we fall before pleasant fantasies and self-serving prejudices, and we are vulnerable to the cynical manipulations of the worldly wise.

In view of these assumptions about the fragility of reason, this critic of Christianity is not likely to focus on fanatical overreaching. To be sure, scientific spokesmen decry outward attempts to force modern science to conform to revealed truth. For example, evolutionary biologists warn against the dangers of creationism. However, these public interventions can be beneficial. Blatant threats to the authority of science wake us from the stupor of blasé acceptance of science and its technological fruits. And this stupor, which encourages no real commitment to science and its demanding method and discipline, is the real danger. One need spend little time teaching undergraduates to be very impressed by the weakness of our scientific culture of experimental method. Students seem innately disposed to treat theory as dogma. Their instinct is, not to investigate and test, but to memorize

---

16. John Locke defends Christian belief but clearly expresses the judgment that Christianity overreaches the epistemic equipment of the human mind. However sympathetic Locke might be to Christianity, his ethics of belief make faith irresponsible. As Locke exhorts his readers, "It becomes the Modesty of Philosophy, not to pronounce Magisterially where we want that Evidence that can produce Knowledge" (*An Essay Concerning Human Understanding,* 4.3.6). For subsequent thinkers, Locke's restriction of philosophy to the sphere of human competence came to mandate a rejection of Christian supernaturalism.

and regurgitate, and the critic of Christianity fears that faith reinforces this tendency by distracting us with promises of salvation. Quietistic retreat, not fanatical resistance, is the threat that Christianity poses to science.

At best, the critic might say that Christianity offers no aid in the ongoing effort to defend intellectual curiosity and rigorous analysis against a lazy acquiescence to prevailing opinion and a determined desire to know nothing more than whatever will "be on the test." This critic might point to the authoritarian form of Christian teaching and suggest that it trains students to receive passively rather than investigate critically. However, this passivity has a deeper source. Christianity offers itself as sufficient for the salvation of our souls. As such, the critic fears that faith encourages a sated complacency. We have all we need in faith; everything else is a matter of indifference. This cannot help but lead to disaster. The vulnerable bulwarks of experimental method and critical analysis require all the concentrated passion of our souls. As soon as we stretch toward some otherworldly way of knowing, our commitment to the strenuous worldliness of reason is diminished. For the critic, the upshot is clear. Christianity cannot help but wrench our epistemic lives out of their rightful this-worldly context. Believers can remain scientists in practice, but not in passion.

Modern theology's predominant strategy for handling the conflict between science and religion exacerbates the underlying concerns of critics. The modern apologist perceives that the scientific endeavor creates cognitive discomfort for educated believers who feel stretched between the obligations of strict experimental discipline and the commitments of faith. To alleviate this discomfort, the apologist eliminates the tension by separating the epistemic practices appropriate to faith from those appropriate to reason. Reflection on faith falls into the domain of "meaning," while science and its intellectual practices are concerned with "facts." With this distinction, cognitive loyalties are parsed, since the domains of "meaning" and "fact" do not overlap. However successful this might be in reducing the outward conflict between science and faith, this distinction produces a quietism that is the greater threat to science and its strict intellectual discipline. Science cannot give "meaning" to the believer; it is simply a technical expertise. "Meaning" floats free from "facts," and the divided mind accepts science without resistance, but also without passionate commitment. This quietism draws us away from our duty to cultivate and promote a properly worldly form of inquiry. Overreaching may satisfy our need for "meaning," but it violates our obligation to contribute to the common human project of defending and extending reason.

Torture of the Soul

Whereas the critic of epistemic overreaching typically fears quietism, those who worry about moral overreaching focus on fanatical efforts to reshape the raw material of our humanity. To be sure, just as fanatical interventions into scientific instruction worry the defender of modern intellectual practices, so also does the irrelevance of certain kinds of Christian spiritual ecstasy worry the contemporary moralist. The idea that we can "move in the Spirit" on Sundays while relentlessly pursuing middle-class security and leisure the other six days a week troubles the moralist. However, this concern is not typical. Instead of worrying that we will go slack across the difference between spiritual ecstasy and everyday life, moral critics of Christian overreaching worry that we will intervene to reshape our lives to a higher calling. This reshaping, thinks the critic, will inevitably have a sharp, cutting edge.

No critic counsels complacency. Modernity seeks personal changes of many sorts. Yet the cautious humanist fears overreaching and seeks to rein in extreme and unworkable attempts to become different. We should beware aspirations that require radical surgery. If the human creature is constituted by mean desires, then wholesale attempts to purify the soul necessarily entail the death of the creature. Few will their own demise, but moral critics are quick to point out that Christianity has encouraged many lacerations, wounds, and amputations: "If your right eye causes you to sin, tear it out and throw it away. . . . And if your right hand causes you to sin, cut it off and throw it away; it is better for you to lose one of your members than for your whole body to go into hell" (Matt 5:29–30). The clay of our humanity must be reworked, and as the critic observes with dismay, that reworking is a profoundly painful and violent enterprise.

Few modern critics of Christianity have neighbors who wear hair shirts or know friends who crawl on their knees to the Church of the Virgin of Guadalupe. These outward displays of ascetical self-denial are easily explained as archaic religious forms; they may even be celebrated as expressions of folk religion. However, the critic knows and feels the pervasive atmosphere of spiritual self-doubt that obscures the landscape of realistic human expectation like a terminal smog.

Even though contemporary Americans go off to college and learn about the arbitrary nature of socially constructed sexual taboos, they continue to find their lives disrupted by repressive guilt. In spite of the ubiquity of economic theories based upon the inevitability of self-interest, the well-off seem unable to still an unsettling guilt about their ongoing desire for even more wealth. Regardless of reassurances from armies of therapists, social workers, and theorists of self-actualization, divorced parents have difficulty quieting the fear that they should have stayed married for the sake of the children, or even for the sake of the institution of marriage.

At every turn, the critic of Christianity sees an unnecessary assault upon our fragile, fallible nature. Is not divorce bad enough without adding layers of guilt and remorse? We feel our failure when we measure ourselves against ideals, and all the more so when those ideals are tinged with supernatural aspiration. Surely we cannot expect ourselves to sacrifice happiness—career, self-esteem, sexual satisfaction, security—to an institution ("Absurd!") or even to another human being ("Unfair!"). We might admire those who have the unique psychological makeup that allows for heroic sacrifice. Mother Teresa was very admirable, but she was also lucky that she could "be herself" by serving the sick and poor. But most of us are not so lucky. We are constructed out of the ordinary timber of humanity, and for us, these ideals are unrealistic. Self-sacrifice would entail the death of our all-too-natural desires, and that would be neither bearable nor possible. To live against ourselves would entail too much violence to the brute limitations of who we are.

For the moral critic of Christian overreaching, the basic objection is repeated again and again: Christianity promulgates a vision of human life that assaults the realities of our humanity. The material focus of this basic objection can shift. Countless modern prophets of therapeutic self-acceptance have decried Christianity as puritanical. The popular culture of success constantly seeks to reassure the well-born that they deserve their beauty, wealth, and power. "These are the facts of life," they insist. "To rebel against these limits is futile and will only create the unnecessary suffering of guilt, self-doubt, and self-mortification. We must, of course, try to be better, but always with a realistic sense of what is possible. Surely our lives are difficult enough. We should not add the burdens of otherworldly aspiration." For the critic, the modest zones of sanity we so painstakingly carve out of this painfully hostile world must be guarded against the assaults of a fanatical desire. We must be protected against ideals. We must be saved from the illusions of saintly transcendence. We must be delivered from the false promise that we can be fundamentally different.

Whereas the common strategy of modern theology has been to separate Christianity from science by creating two domains, an opposite tack has been taken when treating the otherworldly moral ambition of Christianity. At every turn, modern theologians have sought to show that Christian morality is not as disruptive as it appears. Optimists argue that the higher ideals of Christian love are coordinate with our own best impulses. We are all constituted from the same auspicious human material as Mother Teresa. The less optimistic among modern theologians may decry this as naïve humanism, but they are just as eager to reduce the stretching force of Christian moral ambition. The superhuman is recast as "eschatological." The threatening violence of self-sacrificial commandments is translated into sensibilities. We are to do everything from a disposition of love, but always with a vivid awareness of the limitations of a fallen world, always with a "dialectical understanding" of the "impossible possibility" of genuinely self-giving love. However executed, modern theology has sought a word of reassurance: "Fear not, Christian moral aspiration does not rend and tear the fabric of our humanity."

The Political Dangers of Overreaching

Whereas the rational critic worries about quietism and the moral critic focuses on fanaticism, the political critic of Christianity focuses on both quiescent neglect of social responsibility and extremist disruptions of social peace. Sectarian retreat and fundamentalist assault seem twin dangers of Christian otherworldliness. In both cases, the pattern of analysis applied to overbelief and moral overreaching obtains. The discontinuity between Christianity and worldly reality creates problems. Christians either check out of the world or rebel against its inevitable defects. Christians display either too much patience with human frailty or too little, but never the right mixture of concern about suffering and tolerance for social imperfections.

Political quietism results from a mental withdrawal. As a happy-minded believer, the Christian sings hymns exalting the righteousness of God. The beloved Church is cherished as a sanctuary from a sinful society. Troubles and sorrows are left at the door as the faithful bask in the promise of deliverance. For the critic, these pious affirmations are blind

to the complicity of the Church with patterns of social oppression, ignorant of the subservience of church life to ecclesiastical politics, and obliv-
ious to the cynical use of church membership as a means for social
advancement. Far from a heavenly city set apart, the Church is simply a
cog in the machinery of social legitimation. The pious overreaching of
Christianity disguises this reality, and by casting this veil of sanctity over
the mundane and often mendacious social processes of which
Christianity is necessarily a part, injustice goes unchallenged. Fantasies
of holiness distract attention from the realities of human suffering, and
when Christians do recognize human need, they apply the Band-Aids of
charity and proclaim that God blesses the poor. This insouciance
before injustice infuriates the critic. A haze of incense clouds Christian
vision, and the result is a culpable neglect of social responsibility.

Not all critics think Christianity complacent; just as many find
Christianity restless. Instead of a pious haze, these critics worry about
the white heat and intense focus of righteous anger. The critic sees
faith as an energizing agent that infuses the believer with a dangerous
and otherworldly ambition on behalf of society. Faced with sin, the
faithful wish to destroy it root and branch. Soon, witches are being
burned and heretics tortured. Venial transgression is placed in stocks
in the town square, and society falls under the intensely repressive
governance of clerics eager to make a city of angels out of fallen flesh.
The fanatical efforts of an otherworldly faith will not rest until the
world is remade in its entirety. Crusades are launched; campaigns of
evangelism, undertaken. In this atmosphere of expectation, the faithful seek an ever more refined public righteousness. Factions form
around disputes about just how and how much to make all things
new. Faction leads to conflict, and crusaders turn to sectarian warfare
without a moment's hesitation. At every turn, then, the critic sees faith
as gasoline on the fire of human passion. Our already dangerous dispositions toward violence, hatred, and dominion are sanctified and
intensified by a holy cause.[17]

---

17. In his assessment of the background for the French Revolution, the great nineteenth-century historian Jules Michelet voices a common modern view: "Pagan antiquity" certainly knew
murder and destruction, but "you do not find in her grand immolations so much passion, invet-
eracy, or fury of hate, as characterize, in the middle ages, the combat and the vengeances of the
religion of love." The proper explanation for the redoubled viciousness of Christendom, observes
Michelet, "is the prodigious intoxication of pride which [Christian belief] gives to its elect."
The conceit of transubstantiation is typical: "Every day, to make God descend upon the altar,
to be obeyed by God!—Shall I say it? (I hesitated for fear of blaspheming) *to make God!*" This

Whether voiced by the urban activist frustrated by Christian good-will that refuses to see the need for systemic change or the ACLU lawyer fighting Christian efforts to regain control of the public square, the basic concern about overreaching is the same. The quietistic tendency that transfers loyalties from this world to the next yields irresponsible indifference. Levered out of the everyday by faith, the Christian lacks a proper solidarity with common life, and without that solidarity, commitments to society are diminished. The earthly city is under constant attack from impersonal nature without and human moral failures within, and this vulnerability means that the earthly city cannot afford the luxury of allowing dual citizenship. It needs the hearts and minds of all in order to flourish. In a very different way, the fanatic is disloyal as well. Involved in political struggles, the fanatic appears as a dedicated reformer, but he is, in reality, a dangerous foreign agent. One must work within the laws of the earthly city, and the Christian violates this sacred principle when he seeks to replace the laws of men with the laws of God. In both cases, the overreaching otherworldliness of faith renders believers unfit for citizenship. Christianity produces either the decay of neglect or the deformations of foreign domination.

Whether happy-minded deception or iron-willed rigorism, for the critic of Christianity the upshot is the same. Christian overreaching leads to an inhumane form of life. Quietism renders the Christian unreflectively complicitous with prevailing injustice. The redemptive promise is so different from the facts of life that faith is always looking elsewhere. The fanatic is honest about the problems that the deceived believer never sees, but the result is, in some ways, even more troubling to the critic. Precisely because Christianity overreaches, its aspirations are unrealistic, and the rigoristic decision to win the prize through redoubled effort produces an assault upon ordinary life. The naive believer lives in the golden haze of piety; the rigorist is constantly doing emergency surgery on either society or the soul. The costs are steep. In neither case does the Christian put her shoulder to the wheel of human solidarity.

---

overreaching ambition gives the priest a dangerous illusion of omnipotence: "You may be sure that if, to maintain his position, he can destroy the world by a gesture; if he can exterminate with a word what God created with a word"—that is to say, to change the bread and wine into the body and blood of Jesus Christ—"the world will be exterminated" (all quotations from *History of the French Revolution*, 31).

An Analytic Statement of the Criticisms

To immerse ourselves in the range of criticism, to become familiar with typical critical tropes, is not sufficient. We must do more than simply breathe the air of modernity. If we are to avoid floating aimlessly in the atmosphere of criticism, then we need to bring the concerns about crushing authoritarianism and vain overreaching into sharper focus; only then can we undertake critical assessment. I propose to do this by stating the objections analytically. I will do so in terms of the relationship between personal identity and the highest good. My goal is to construct a logical artifact: we-matter-most humanism. In so doing, I hope to articulate the underlying vision of redemptive change that gives the two poles of criticism their electrical charge.

We may sacrifice a certain rhetorical immediacy and descriptive accuracy as we press toward a logical statement of the criticisms and the vision of moral change that animates them. The criticisms of authoritarianism and overreaching are rarely stated in pure form. This or that dogmatic claim falls under suspicion, not all dogma and all external authority. This or that supernatural claim is attacked, not each and every human ambition. Moreover, criticisms of crushing authoritarianism and vain overreaching are not necessarily linked to an underlying modern humanism. Concerns about human vulnerability are not uniquely modern. Ancient anxieties about the rending force of change can motivate criticisms of overreaching, a concern that has nothing to do with modern humanism and its characteristic preoccupations.[18] Late antiquity also knew and feared the dogmatic confidence of Christianity. Defenders of pagan thought and prac-

---

18. Even though Stoicism teaches a rigorous asceticism and indifference to death, both Epictetus and Marcus Aurelius reject Christian martyrdom as a self-denying fanaticism. Marcus Aurelius argues that we should all be ready to face death without fear, but "such preparedness must be the outcome of its own decision; a decision not prompted by mere opposition, as with Christians, but formed with deliberation and gravity" (*Meditations* 11.3). Whether Marcus is referring to a Christian willfulness in refusing to perform the civic obligations of cultic sacrifice, or is thinking more generally of the militant Christian rejection of the finality of physical death in the proclamation of the resurrection of the body, is unclear. However, both "oppositions"—to prevailing social expectations and the fatalism of the classical world—are tinged with fanaticism. Epictetus reinforces this suggestion when he commends fearlessness before suffering and death but notes that such fearlessness may stem from an undignified source, either madness or the ethos of the Galileans. Neither path is grounded in that noble human capacity for reason and demonstration. As such, though the Christian might give the appearance of a Stoic sage courageously facing death, the disposition is a false imitation of virtue, for the courage results from the hot enthusiasm and collective mentality of a sect rather than the cool deliberations of reason (see *Discourses* 4.7.1—8). At issue, then, for a Stoic criticism of Christianity, is not the severity of the Christian path of discipleship. Rather, the criticism focuses on the reasons Christians accept suffering and death, reasons that overreach the domain of the properly human.

tice could express a concern about crushing authoritarianism that seems to presage modern worries.[19] Furthermore, even though it advocates faith in divine revelation, Christianity itself can motivate forms of the two poles of criticisms. Submission to false gods is decried; the dangers of idolatry are noted; paradox that destroys reason is rejected.[20] The

Lucian's satirical account of the career of the charlatan Peregrinus exploits just this presumed uncritical vulnerability of Christians. A seducer of young boys and murderer of his father, Peregrinus flees into exile and takes up with a Christian group. Exploiting their trust, he sets himself up as a leader of the cult, making the followers "all look like children" as he "interpreted and explained some of their books and even composed many." This quick rise to prominence among Christians was by no means cut short by imprisonment. In jail, he is visited by all manner of Christians, "grey-haired widows and orphan children" as well as "bigwigs of the sect" who spend the night with him in jail. As Lucian paints the scene, other communities from as far away as Asia Minor send committees "with advice and consolation," and especially money. Indeed, Lucian anticipates any number of modern satires of the revivalist preacher on the make when he notes that Peregrinus "picked up a nice income in this way." The very indoctrination of the Church that leads Christians to "scorn all possessions without distinction and treat them as community property" makes them easy marks for a hustler like Peregrinus. "If a professional sharper who knows how to capitalize on a situation gets among them," Lucian observes, "he makes himself a millionaire overnight, laughing up his sleeve at the simpletons" (*Peregrinus* 9—13). Though others have shifted the drama away from enrichment to the darker themes of power and domination, the scene is essentially the same. Christians are simpletons easily exploited.

19. See Symmachus's plea for the restoration of the altar of Victory in Rome in 384. The model of epistemic modesty, Symmachus makes no claim that Victory is the only or supreme God. Rather, he argues that the long history of Roman prosperity should provide sufficient reason to preserve the altar of Victory. "Here the proof from utility comes in," observes Symmachus, "which is our best voucher with regard to the Deity. For since our reason is in the dark, what better knowledge of the gods can we have than from the record and evidence of prosperity?" Surely the cult has proven effective; after all, "this worship reduced the world under my laws; these sacred rites repulsed Hannibal from the walls, and the Gauls from the Capitol." However, Symmachus is aware of the aggressive exclusivity of Christianity, and he shifts from an argument in favor of the presumptive truth and effectiveness of traditional Roman practices to an argument in favor of tolerance. "Permit us," Symmachus pleads, "to transmit in our old age to our posterity what we ourselves received when we were boys." After all, Symmachus writes, "As each man that is born receives a soul, so do nations receive a genius who guards their destiny," and there is no good reason to suppress this diversity. "We look on the same stars," Symmachus observes, "the heaven is common to us all, the same world surrounds us. What matter it by what arts each of us seeks for truth? We cannot arrive by one and the same path to so great a secret" (all quotations from *Creeds, Councils, and Controversies* [ed. J. Stevenson; London: SPCK, 1966], 121—22). Thus does Symmachus, with arguments commonplace among modern cultural pluralists, try to prevent Christianity from wiping away the entirety of classical religious practice.

20. In *An Essay in Aid of a Grammar of Assent*, for example, John Henry Newman renounces all efforts to overreach. Newman writes with urgency, "My first elementary lesson of duty is that of resignation to the laws of my nature, whatever they are; my first disobedience is to be impatient at what I am, and to indulge an ambitious aspiration after what I cannot be, to cherish a distrust of my powers, and to desire to change the laws which are identical with myself" ([Notre Dame: University of Notre Dame Press, 1979], 273). For Newman, impatience with our humanity leads in two directions, first toward rationalist overreaching and then, by counteraction, toward skeptical inertia. Neither serves the proper ambitions of reason and faith.

friendly critics find ample resources within Christianity to formulate warnings against false authorities and improvident overreaching. All this is very true. Yet, no matter how diffuse and logically independent the particular criticisms of Christianity might be, I do not wish to treat symptoms and trace divergent sensibilities. I want to uncover the source of the overwhelming cultural *power* of the two poles of criticism as they function within our lives, a power that stems from the humanistic vision of our destiny.

The concerns about crushing authoritarianism and vain over-reaching do not just float freely. However much material overlap might obtain, with ancient worries or Christian critical traditions, their urgency and purpose stem from neither antique nor Christian sensibilities. These concerns are motivated by a modern conviction about the central importance of persons as supremely consequential and continuous in the changes necessary to achieve the highest good. We should not depend upon divine revelation; we should not even submit to the teachings of others. We should not believe in miracles; we should not seek an otherworldly habitation. There is a more humane way to pursue the highest good, one that affirms our identities more fully. The cultural power of the two poles of criticism stems from this confidence, and I wish to give that confidence explicit form.

What, then, is the logic of the modern cure of the soul? Stated programmatically, the vision is straightforward. Moral change must serve the realization and flourishing of persons. Who we are must matter most of all for the highest good that we seek. This positive vision, and not the particular lines of criticism, interests me. Of course, we cannot make much headway if we rest with a programmatic statement such as "We matter most for the highest good." To affirm that we matter is insufficiently precise. In order to push toward greater clarity, I propose to begin by identifying two moral prejudices—horror of dependence and fear of difference. They animate the poles of criticism, and together these two moral prejudices give distinctive shape and purpose to modern humanism. They give modernity its ambition and its claim upon our souls.

Horror of Dependence

The critic of authoritarianism is committed to the unique and unsubstitutable value of our personal distinctiveness. We are individuals with our own projects and purposes, agents who make unique and irreducible choices; we are unique and unrepeatable instances of our cultural and historical milieus. The critic of authoritarianism may affirm any or all of these descriptions of the sources of our personal identity, or another set entirely. However, the particular characterizations of our distinctiveness are not decisive. The question "What makes us unique?" operates within a consensus that whatever might be the source of our personal identity is to be cherished above all else. In this sense, the crucial commitment is formal, not material. Our individuality, however conceived, matters most. Our identities as persons are consequential, and to the greatest possible degree. Thus, our vision of the highest good must ensure the realization of our uniqueness; the moral project must grow out of our identities as persons.

The judgment that our personal identity matters most would seem necessary for fully and finally caring about human beings for their own sakes. How can one be "for another" if one is looking beyond him or her toward some higher, more important end? How can one love another if the reason for that love is not, finally, the particular person? How can one be a humanist without privileging concrete human beings above all else? For the consistent humanist, then, the violence of inhumanity has a single root: the failure to recognize the value of human beings for their own sakes, the failure to see that persons are unsubstitutable and irreplaceable. No cause, however highly prized, can justify the destruction and subordination of discrete and irreplaceably unique lives. Each and every one of us is consequential for the highest good, not as instances of the generically human, but as discrete and irreplaceable persons.[21]

---

21. Though written against the background of modern moral theory rather than Christianity, Susan Wolf's discussion of moral saints identifies precisely this concern. For Wolf, the intense focus of the moral saint—it is always better to be morally better—inhibits the development of "a healthy, well-rounded, richly developed character" ("Moral Saints," *Journal of Philosophy* 79, 3 [August 1982]: 421). Because the commitment to right action is both omnipotent and infinitely demanding (one can always be better), someone truly committed to the project of always doing what is morally best is absorbed into righteous aspiration. The upshot is a "fanatical" focus of the moral saint's attention and energy on the singular goal of goodness, and as Wolf accurately reports, common intuitions regard this maniacal focus as unattractive. Indeed, more than just unattractive, moral sainthood seems inhumane, for the repression of diverse desires to pursue nonmoral projects appropriate to the individual (she gives examples such as athletics, gourmet cooking, literary interests, music, and so on) seems to deny "the existence of an identifiable, personal self" (424). The project of being morally perfect eclipses the project of being. Here, Wolf gives clear expression to a perennial suspicion about Christianity. The intense focus and demands of the Christian life seem just such a reduction of the full range and texture of our distinctive individuality to a narrow path of discipleship.

I can express this commitment more precisely: *Who we are is a sufficient condition for what is best.* In this formulation, personal identity is supremely consequential. If individuality flourishes, then the highest good obtains. We have the basis, by virtue of the intrinsic dignity of personal identity, for making life worth living. The more we are true to ourselves, the better things will be. This moral faith is more than enough to motivate the most thoroughgoing critic of crushing authoritarianism. To say that something besides me is necessary for what is best—a dogma, clerical authority, divine intervention—entails denying that who I am is sufficient. Authoritarianism, then, is any account of human flourishing that proposes something besides discrete human individuality as necessary. Against this authoritarianism, the critic wishes us to recognize our supreme consequentiality for the highest good.

Fear of Difference

The criticisms of Christian overreaching are motivated by a cautious humanism of an emotional coloring different from the expansive faith that animates the criticisms of authoritarianism. Even though both seek to secure our full participation in the highest good, the fear of difference need not emphasize individuality and our intrinsic potency for the highest good. Instead, emphasis rests on solidarity and connection. For the critic of overreaching, the fragile community of persons engaged in responsible patterns of reflection and action must be protected against the seemingly perennial desire to transcend limitations. The vulnerable coherence of our lives must be guarded against disruption and disjunction. We need to build a protective fence around our lives, not to keep out the alienating deformations of dogma, but to keep in our cognitive loyalties, to maintain our mutual commitment to each other, to keep our aspirations without the bounds of our finitude. Both quietism and fanaticism overleap this protective fence, and the consequent betrayal of our ordinary humanity debilitates our ability to live well. We rend and tear at the fabric of life. We seek what we cannot have rather than cultivate realistic projects of moral amelioration and reform. We chase dreams of reason rather than discipline ourselves to join the battalions of science. This fear of difference can often conflict with protagonists of individuality. The glorious blaze of personal uniqueness can disrupt human solidarity just as dramatically as dreams of salvation.[22] A faith in unbounded human potency for the highest good can produce fanaticism. Indeed, the critic of over-reaching might countenance, even advocate, social practices that ensure a modest degree of conformity. Nonetheless, the root affirmation that energizes the criticisms of overreaching is the same as that which fuels the criticisms of dogmatism: we matter most; therefore, personal identity must be connected to the highest good.

Without a faith in human potency, the critic of overreaching is not committed to the proposition that each individual is sufficient for the highest good. Nonetheless, the critic does claim that each must have an ongoing role. Pursuit of the highest good can never be detached from our identities as persons. We matter most in our commonality, in our shared humanity, and not in some state of solidarity above or beyond the condition we all share as individuals. For example, the principle of utility, especially in its negative form as the alleviation of suffering, is a form of moral reasoning and practice that drives us inwards toward our shared condition as embodied beings. Such a moral commitment is compelling because the experience of pain is both deeply personal and ubiquitous. I am drawn into the circle of common humanity not only by virtue of counting in the moral calculus as one who feels pain but also in my efforts to identify and respond to the pain of others. Thus, the imperative to alleviate suffering operates within, rather than beyond, our shared humanity, causing us to change our attitudes and behaviors by an ever greater commitment to the everyday realities of sentience.

The principle of utility, either in its positive or negative form, is not beyond criticism. The critic of overreaching may worry that

---

22. Judith Shklar writes eloquently against the overreaching impulse in public life. As a political theorist with a keen eye for redemptive excesses of modern politics, Shklar urges modesty. "Liberalism," as she understands the tradition of modern humanism, "owes a deep and enduring debt to misanthropy, or to be exact, to a suspicious temper that does not think that any set of officials is fit to do more than inhibit, within strict legal limits, the grosser forms of violence and fraud" (*Ordinary Vices* [Cambridge: Harvard University Press, 1984], 3). Suspicious of over-reaching, "liberal democracy becomes more a recipe for survival than a project for the perfectibility of mankind" (4). Against fanatical efforts to reshape human life according to abstract ideals, the first virtue of the liberal soul is "a self-restraining tolerance" that accepts the difficulties of life amidst "contradiction, complexity, diversity and the risks of freedom" (5). For Shklar, this self-restraint does not stem from epistemic doubts, though such doubts are justified. Rather, her defense of modesty grows out of the recognition that "nothing but cruelty comes from those who seek perfection and forget how little good that lies directly in their powers" (39). We should avoid overreaching, not because it is unreasonable, but because it tempts us to become inhumane.

utilitarianism is dangerously reductive. We matter most, but we are
not simply instances of sentience. The higher aspirations of life are,
perhaps, worth the pain of their achievement: our pain and even the
pain of others. On just this issue, John Stuart Mill broke with his
Benthamite upbringing. However, the particular debates about how
broadly or narrowly to construe proper boundaries of personal identity do not define the fear of difference any more than debates about
the source and consequence of intrinsic human potency define the horror of dependence. Theories abound, and humanists often engage in
bitter argument. Instead, for the critic of overreaching, the decisive
question is whether an epistemic, moral, or political vision can support the continuity of human lives. At the minimum, such a vision
must be able to give a coherent account of how our ideals are properly human. I must be able to see myself connected, somehow, to the
highest good.

In view of this need to show the fundamental and enduring connection between our humanity and the ideals we seek, this species of
humanism seeks to defend the continuity of personal identity in moral
change. Transcendent aspirations inspire a fear of difference, and
against this tendency to want too much, the consistent critic of overreaching establishes a clear standard: *Who we are must be a necessary condition for what is best.* The critical intuition is clear: if
nothing distinctive to one's identity as a person is a necessary condition for the highest good, then moral aspiration is disjunctive. In personal terms, I am not connected to what I seek. The ideal may be
glorious, but it is not human, and I cannot participate in that ideal as
the finite and limited person that I am. Therefore, any account of
what is best that does not identify something about me as necessary—
my choices, my feelings of pain, my experiences, my biography—is an
instance of vain overreaching.

Modern Humanism Defined

I propose to use my analysis of the two animating moral prejudices
of modernity in order to create a logical artifact that I call "we-matter-most humanism." The two moral prejudices are motivated by
underlying assumptions about the relationship between personal identity and the highest good. We must be consequential in the strong
sense of being sufficient for whatever we seek as our moral end. We
must be continuous in the straightforward sense of being necessary

for that moral end. So, to conjugate in a formulaic mode, I offer the following definition: We-matter-most humanism is committed to the proposition that *who we are is necessary and sufficient for the highest good.*

The formulation sounds absurdly simplistic. I must admit that when I first undertook this project and developed this formulation as an initial, orienting thought experiment, I was skeptical. Surely the crude logical tools of necessary and sufficient conditions could not capture the nuances of modern humanism's defense of our lives as consequential and continuous! Well, yes and no. Of course, this logical artifact turns a rich tradition of critical thought and polemic and moral striving into a pale and rigid formulation. Yet, this simple statement of the relationship between personal identity and the highest good provides remarkable insights into the rich tradition of modern humanism. Moreover, the logical artifact has heuristic usefulness, which is not surprising. After all, modern humanism is concerned with human persons and wishes to affirm the critical transformation of society, of morality, and of personal hope in such a way that personal identity is consequential and continuous. Therefore, even though the proponents of modern humanism never articulate their convictions in this way, for all its complexity and nuance, their thought is shaped by the logic of we-matter-most humanism.

In the following chapters, I will talk about how Jean-Jacques Rousseau, David Hume, and especially Immanuel Kant are constrained by the logic of we-matter-most humanism. I will argue that we-matter-most humanism leads to contradiction over the question of atonement. Of course, I do not imagine that these modern thinkers had the bare-boned logical formulation that *who we are is necessary and sufficient for the highest good* in their minds. They sought to defend individuality and freedom. They wished to guard against disorienting intellectual, moral, and political overreaching. Their felt constraints were complex and heterogeneous. Their actual intentions were shaped by the very particular nature of their projects. Nonetheless, I beg the reader's indulgence. Allow me the conceit of we-matter-most humanism. It pays dividends.

The abstract formulation of we-matter-most humanism clarifies the true cost of theological accommodation to modern criticisms of Christianity. Christianity will run afoul with the cure of the soul that animates modern humanism, for a fundamental contest exists over what is the necessary and sufficient condition for the highest good.

Modern humanism says you and I fill that role. Christianity says Jesus. Defining we-matter-most humanism in a strict fashion forces the issue and blocks the illusion that Christianity can join hands with the animating moral vision of modernity. In faith, Jesus Christ matters most in the specific sense that he is the necessary and sufficient condition for the highest good—salvation. If Jesus does so matter, then no mediation of Christianity with modern humanism can succeed.

Although we-matter-most humanism is a logical artifact rather than a fully developed humanistic proposal, it helps us navigate the twists and turns of argument in the thought of Rousseau, Hume, and Kant. And clarity exposes failures of thought. None of these great thinkers can both advocate change and show how we are consequential and continuous in that change. None can affirm that the highest good must be sought and that we are necessary and sufficient for the highest good. Tracing the logical failures of we-matter-most humanism trains us to see the moral failures of modern life, which allows me to risk generalizations about the real consequences of the distinctively modern way of thinking about human destiny. As a way of thinking and living, the animating moral vision of modernity is irrational and inhumane.

Ultimately, seeing what cannot be said or lived without contradiction is insufficient. Little is humane in mere contempt for folly. Some account must be given of how you or I can matter in and for the highest good. The logical conceit of we-matter-most humanism has full and final value because it helps me articulate the Christian understanding of how we are taken up into the necessity and sufficiency of Jesus Christ. Beaten and betrayed, Jesus of Nazareth has everything to do with the crushing forces that make dependence upon another such a frightful prospect. Broken on the difference between life and death, he exposes, rather than disguises, the fragility of our common humanity. Thus, by using the artifice of we-matter-most humanism to examine the contradictions entailed in modern humanism, we can look again and more closely at the consistency of Christianity's account of how we matter in the necessity and sufficiency of Christ for salvation.

–Chapter 2–

REDEMPTION WITHOUT CHANGE

Each individual, by virtue of his inclinations, has a right to principles which do not destroy his individuality. Probably the origin of all philosophy is to be sought from here or nowhere.
— JOHANN WOLFGANG VON GOETHE, *GOETHES GESPRÄCHE*

In this chapter and the next, I hope to take the first step toward showing that a horror of dependence and fear of difference, the two critical prejudices that combine to drive the logic of we-matter-most humanism, cannot take on cogent form. We cannot affirm that personal identity is both consequential and continuous and, at the same time, affirm the modern critical project and its devotion to effecting morally meaningful change. For this reason, modern humanism cannot rationally justify the necessity of tearing down the citadels of dogma and restraining the pervasive hunger for the supernatural. It cannot make sense of the urgency of its moral criticism of Christianity. This is a bald claim, and I think it worthwhile to anticipate the logic of the matter before embarking on the close readings that will occupy us in these chapters, for the difficulties of change will emerge again and again.

First, consider this fact. You and I are already part of the world constrained by our dependence upon structures and necessities, be they religious, moral, or economic. Dependence seems to form our identities as persons. To a great extent, critics of crushing authoritarianism presuppose the widespread reality of this dependence. After all, their exhortations and reforms are animated by a profound dismay born of a vivid sense of our implication in structures of domination. Precisely because the tendrils of dogma and superstition are so strong, modern humanism attacks with ferocity and advocates change. However, this polemical drive exposes the problem of the gap between who we are and the highest good, and this gap threatens to subvert the strongly consequential role of personal identity.[1] If we are part of the world of crushing authoritarianism and vain overreaching, then in what sense can we be sufficient for the highest good that we seek? Or, if we are sufficient, then how can we even admit that there is any difference at all between who we are and how we ought to live?

The disjunction creates serious difficulties. If my mere identity is sufficient for the highest good, then there is no moral reason for me to criticize and seek to transform the world; I will simply "celebrate diversity!" The reason for criticizing authoritarianism—its failure to recognize and cherish the supreme consequentiality of personal identity—obscures the need for criticism at all. After all, you and I exist. The sufficient condition for the highest good is in place, and so it necessarily obtains. Indeed, the more our moral prejudice against authoritarianism is grounded in the consistent conviction that each person should live according to his or her individuality, the less sensible are calls for change. The greater the moral depth of the prejudice, the less rational the demand. If one wishes to criticize authority and change social practices on the basis of a humanistic commitment to the singular dignity of the individual, then this is a very odd and unfortunate outcome. As a consequence, the underlying logic of the moral prejudice against authoritarianism either backslides into dependence or renders change otiose.

Bedeviling difficulties emerge when we turn to vain overreaching as well. Consider this further fact. You and I are precisely those people who wish to believe what is comforting rather than what is warranted, what is ideal rather than real. We are credulous and weak-minded. Excess seems embedded in persons, and clear thinking requires a great deal of effort. Scientists are not born; they are formed through educational discipline. Since criticisms of vain overreaching express, at root, a concern about the continuity of personal identity, the gap problem emerges here as well. How am I—the person so

---

1. I take the notion of gap from John E. Hare's treatment of moral change in *The Moral Gap: Kantian Ethics, Human Limits, and God's Assistance* (Oxford: Clarendon, 1996). I drop his qualification of the gap as "moral" because I wish to maintain a broader frame of reference for the problem of change. There are personal, historical, and metaphysical ways to formulate the gap problem, as well as the moral form of the problem so effectively explained by Hare.

deeply vulnerable to salesmen and card sharks—continuous with the prudent and rational person that I seek to become? How can I be necessary for the highest good if I am so deeply implicated in the beliefs and practices that are being criticized?

Here again the gap challenges the critic. Surely, I cannot be too deeply imbedded in the tendency to overreach; otherwise, my identity is part of the problem and not the solution. But if I am not so deeply embedded, then criticism is not urgent, and perhaps the psychic benefits of credulity outweigh the limited liability. For this reason, the strenuous critic of overreaching faces the difficulty of explaining how any significant critical agenda is not a covert form of overreaching. The critic seeks to discipline our transcendent longings and convince us to reside at our properly human address. But to the extent that we leave behind desires and habits of mind that constitute our ordinary existence, we overreach and, in overreaching, breach the boundaries of our identities.

Unlike the horror of dependence, this critical sentiment presents no immediate logical difficulties. Critical urgency is a matter of degree, and changes urged may be partial rather than radical. However, the intensity of the criticism depends upon the perceived dangers of overreaching. The more the critic thinks persons tend toward overbelief, the more energy the critic puts into buttressing the disciplinary practices of scientific method. The more the critic fears moral zeal and political fanaticism, the more emphasis falls upon a pedagogical emphasis on tolerance and the social legitimacy of democratic processes. The urgency of criticism is directly proportional to the perceived ubiquity of the tendency to overreach. That much seems clear. Yet, the perceived ubiquity is evidence that the desire to transcend everyday humanity is, somehow, normal. This places the critic of overreaching in the contradictory position of advocating a humanism in which you and I—creatures with the pervasive and potentially destructive tendency to overreach—are not necessary for the highest good. Indeed, this "normal" desire is antithetical and must be repressed. The ardent critic of overreaching tells a story of moral change that involves precisely the denial of the constraints of common humanity that the critical principle forbids. In this way, the moral prejudice against overreaching implies a covert form of overreaching. The fear of difference creates a desire to become different. Again, this is a very odd and unfortunate outcome for a humanist who wishes to defend the continuity of personal identity in our quest for the highest good.

These brief anticipations allow me to state the problem facing modern humanism in programmatic form. Without a gap between who we are and the highest good, change is not morally necessary. And if change is not morally necessary, then the modern critical project has no moral basis. Yet, if we acknowledge the gap, then we seem to deny the proposition that expresses the supremely consequential role of personal identity: "My identity as a person is sufficient for the highest good." Once denied, we have no clear reason to be motivated by a horror of dependence, at least no good reason based on the relationship of personal identity to the highest good. Furthermore, the wider the gap, the more urgent the modern critical project and the more compelling its demands for change. Yet, if the gap is too wide, then we seem unable to affirm the proposition that secures the continuity of personal identity: "My identity as a person is necessary for the highest good." Again, we have no clear humanistic reason to allow our critical sensibilities to be agitated by a fear of difference. This, then, is the conundrum. Modern humanism, at least as I have conceptualized it in the form of we-matter-most humanism, must affirm change and, at the same time, affirm the consequentiality and continuity of personal identity for and in the highest good. This seems impossible.

Stated so starkly, the problems facing modern humanism seem like abstract logical puzzles. I need to give the difficulties flesh. To do so, I propose two engagements. Jean-Jacques Rousseau exemplifies the conundrums facing a thoroughgoing critic of authoritarianism. He will not backslide from the humanistic commitment to the supremely consequential role of personal identity in our quest for the highest good. Indeed, he expressly affirms the logical sufficiency of personal identity. To do so, he drives the gap out of the moral project and makes change unnecessary. Rousseau *is,* and that is enough. This chapter will analyze this remarkable claim.

David Hume illustrates the difficulties encountered by a clear-minded critic of overreaching. He embraces change. A gap definitely exists between who we are and how we ought to live. But his commitment to the continuity of personal identity creates difficulties. To avoid these difficulties, Hume proposes a mitigated moral urgency, a modest degree of change that avoids endorsing too much overreaching. But it is not at all clear that such a strategy will work. The change he advocates tends in two directions, neither satisfactory. The change he endorses either entails a covert overreaching, or it cannot be understood as morally meaningful change. Chapter 3 contains a careful exposition of Hume's mitigated and modest humanism.

Rousseau and Hume do not exhaust the possibilities for modern humanism. More cogent and successful theorists of the underlying rationale for urgent moral criticism of crushing authoritarianism and vain overreaching may very well exist. Indeed, as I will argue in chapters 4 and 5, Kant offers a more promising approach. He does not modify the strict logic of we-matter-most humanism, however great the difficulties seem. He tries to affirm (1) morally meaningful change and (2) the necessity and sufficiency of personal identity for the highest good. Nonetheless, Rousseau and Hume are particularly pure types, and they have been extremely influential in shaping modern attitudes. As a consequence, their thought throws the moral geography of modernity into sharp relief, and their failures mark boundaries.

Rousseau and the Gap

Reading Rousseau is difficult because his solutions to the taxing problems of life are so strikingly simple. As he insists in his self-imposed examination and trial, *Rousseau, Judge of Jean-Jacques,* all of his work is animated by a singular commitment, "a doctrine that [is] as healthy as it [is] simple."[2] Discerning this overriding conviction and simple doctrine is not necessarily easy. Relentless consistency creates optical illusions that easily exasperate.[3] Nonetheless, I will venture a claim about Rousseau's fundamental principle. In *Émile,* Rousseau puts the following hope of salvation into the voice of the freethinking

---

2. *The Collected Writings of Rousseau* (ed. Roger D. Masters and Christopher Kelly; Hanover, N.H.: University Press of New England, 1990), 1:209.

3. Ernest Barker's assessment of Rousseau in his introduction to *Of the Social Contract* (Oxford: Oxford University Press, 1947) testifies to the difficulties of navigating through Rousseau's hall of mirrors: "You can find your own dogmas in Rousseau, whether you belong to the Left (and especially to the left of the Left) or whether you belong to the Right (and especially to the right of the Right" (xxxix). The only dogmas you cannot find in Rousseau, claims Barker, are the normal and sane dogmas of English liberalism. See also John Plamenatz's assessment in volume 1 of *Man and Society* (London: Longman, 1963). According to Plamenatz, instead of precise (Plamenatz emphasizes this often) English categories of political theory, "Rousseau was obscure . . . because he failed to make his meaning plain" (392). This obscurity emerges because he too often used metaphors "to give vent to his feelings rather than to help make his meaning plain" (406). Certainly these two sensible Englishmen testify to nothing if not the vertigo induced by Rousseau's singularity of purpose. For a synopsis of the extraordinary variety of interpretation that Rousseau stimulates, see Peter Gay's survey in his introduction to Ernst Cassirer's *The Question of Jean-Jacques Rousseau* (trans. Peter Gay; New York: Columbia University Press, 1954), 3–32.

Savoyard vicar: "I long for the moment when, delivered from the chains of the body, I will be myself without contradiction, without division, and I will only have need of myself to be happy."[4] This vision is the driving principle behind Rousseau's humanism: to be oneself without interruption, division, or contradiction, in short, to be the God of the philosophers, the One beyond the many. This should be our aspiration, and such a vision expresses the humanistic truth that personal identity is sufficient for the highest good. Rousseau never gives arguments to support this faith. He champions the pure, simple, and primitive reason that clings to what is true rather than constructs gothic structures of argument. An exhortation of the Savoyard vicar to Émile strikes this note. Émile should set aside "vain and subtle arguments."[5] Against deceptive intellectual sophistication, the vicar advises, "Let us be simpler and less pretentious; let us be content with the first feelings we experience in ourselves."[6] For Rousseau, then, nothing he could say is more perspicuous than the simple truth that being oneself is sufficient. Rousseau orders both his life and his thought around this ideal.

The extremism of Rousseau's political philosophy stems from this redemptive vision. If we allow that social relations are intrinsic to who we are, and Rousseau insists that we must, then working out the implications of a blessedness in which each of us is sufficient requires a radical convergence. You and I, as individuals, must be joined so closely to the collective life of society that the sentence "In my inner-most being I choose to live in such and such a way" has precisely the same content as the sentence "Society, as a whole, requires me to live in such and such a way." In *Of the Social Contract,* Rousseau postulates this convergence as the highest good, both for persons and societies. The general will is a sufficient basis for justice, and under conditions of justice, my will is identical with the general will. Only in such a society do we rise to the heights of moral dignity. Only by such convergence of personal identity and social purpose does a society achieve virile harmony and common purpose. In this way, the Savoyard vicar's vision is fulfilled. We are *at one* with all, and therefore every law is an expression of our personal identity, and every feature of our personal identity is an expression of law. We live as we

---

4. Jean-Jacque Rousseau, *Émile* (London: Everyman, 1993), 307. I have altered the translation for accuracy.

5. Ibid., 278.

6. Ibid., 304.

ought to live: with other people and according to the inner springs of our very selves.

However, life does not cooperate. Our social formation does not take place in harmony with our personal choices. In all existing societies, laws and social mores flow from the self-interest of the powerful. They are not the perfected expression of the human dignity of all. As a consequence, whether or not Rousseau's social ideal is possible, it is not, he insists, actual. The upshot is a gap between who we are, our desires and projects, and how we ought to live as social animals. In a society in which we are obligated to live according to the prerogative and principles of others, our identities as persons become deformed. The yoke of duty is imposed rather than chosen. The obligations of social interaction reflect neither the interest of all nor the interest of any one person. The dead hand of conventional morality, social hierarchy, political power, and religious authority alienates us from ourselves.[7]

Such alienation leads to injustice, but a concern about injustice is not the "one great principle" that animates Rousseau.[8] Rather, the failures of social life throw into doubt the redemptive vision of the Savoyard vicar, the underlying humanistic commitment that fuels Rousseau's critical agenda. Unable to close the gap between the obligations that determine social life and the inner springs of individual personality, Rousseau faces a conceptual challenge. If our social impulses

---

7. Rousseau's *First* and *Second Discourses* are extended genealogies of alienation, and the upshot of these investigations is a despair about the possibility of closing the gap between the true dignity of our humanity and the ways in which we are required to live as members of society.

8. As Judith Shklar argues, Rousseau's social analysis yields no positive guidance toward the restructuring of society in order to create personal and civic integralism. She concludes that Rousseau counsels, far from reformist zeal, a resigned acceptance of the impossibility of achieving a seamless and humanizing integration into social life (*Men and Citizens: A Study of Rousseau's Social Theory* [Cambridge: Cambridge University Press, 1969]). From this resignation, Shklar draws a cautionary moral. We should not seek too much in public life. We should undertake modest reform as citizens, care for our souls as human beings, and be careful not to mix the two. This is a humane conclusion, one that commends Shklar to her readers, but I do not find it a persuasive reading of either the overall intention or actual impact of Rousseau on his readers. He never renounces his desire for the harmony of self and society, and the consequence is a profound restlessness in his soul, and an equally profound unsettling effect on his readers. Moreover, as my analysis of Hume will suggest, Shklar's counsel against political overreaching has conceptual problems of its own. Given the intensity and scope of his social needs, would not Rousseau, the great patron of an integrated inward and outward life, deny himself if he adopted Shklar's careful separation of the personal and the political as his own? My reading of Rousseau argues that he never adopts such a self-denying separation, even though he despairs of living in fraternity with others.

are frustrated, then we are not sufficient for the highest good. In light of this inference, Rousseau has three choices. Either we are not, finally, social beings, and therefore our social relations are inconsequential for the highest good. Or we are indeed social beings to the core of our individuality, and therefore we must acknowledge that the failures of justice and social harmony demonstrate that we do not suffice. Or, finally, Rousseau must argue that, contrary to first impressions, our social impulses are not, in fact, frustrated; we live with others just as we ought to live. Rousseau pursues the third option. A closer examination of life will show that Rousseau's redemptive hope may be combined with his conviction that we are social animals. However, Rousseau does not presume to examine our lives; he examines only his own.[9] In this self-investigation, he will not give up on the intense social needs he feels at the core of his being, and he will not give up on the humanistic faith that he is sufficient for the highest good.

Rousseau's commitment to this third option is not easy. Indeed, his autobiographical writings are important because they revolve almost entirely around this difficulty. His own life story turns on the same gap that dominates his social analysis, the gap between individuality and social existence. He is a good-hearted person who feels generosity towards others, but in the eyes of society he is a madman and misanthrope, an immoral scoundrel and atheist. A good man viewed by others as evil, Rousseau lives at odds with society, not in harmony. However, Rousseau's autobiographical writings do not simply describe his dilemma. They seek a solution. In accounts of his own life, Rousseau seeks to vindicate the third option. His life, even the social dimension that he experiences as adversity and rejection, is affirmed as sufficient for what is best. The world, however cruel and unjust, is not an impediment to an awakening realization that personal identity secures the highest good.

---

9. Rousseau consistently denies that we can have any knowledge of human nature, as such. For example, in his preface to the *Discourse on the Origins of Inequality,* Rousseau writes, "Like the statue of Glaucus, ravaged by time, the seas and storms, until it looked less like a god than a wild beast, the human soul, altered in the bosom of society by a thousand causes . . . has, so to speak, changed so much that it cannot be known." For further textual sources, see Christopher Kelly, *Rousseau's Exemplary Life: The Confessions as Political Philosophy* (Ithaca, N.Y.: Cornell University Press, 1987), 39–46. Kelly rightfully concludes that Rousseau will only define the needs and constraints of "human nature" insofar as he is its sole transparent manifestation. In this way, Rousseau shifts the ancient maxim—"man is *microcosmos*"—to a modern maxim— "I am *microcosmos,*" or more in keeping with his social interests, "I am *micropolis.*" For this reason, Rousseau's endless self-examination constitutes his "critical theory." I follow Kelly's lead in reading Rousseau's autobiographical works as perspicuous, and in many ways privileged, sources for Rousseau's humanistic vision as a whole.

Rousseau's preoccupation with the gap between who he is and what he knows to be the best way to live dominates his final work. Written in the last years of his life, *The Rêveries of a Solitary Walker* offers a seemingly pathetic description of his situation.[10] The first sentence of the First Walk captures his dilemma. "I am now alone on earth," he reports, "no longer having any brother, neighbor, friend, or society other than myself" (1). A deep chasm separates the social creature, Jean-Jacques, from the ordinary commerce of polite society, and throughout the various walks, Rousseau records his bitterness, disappointment, and frustration in loneliness. His public reputation inspires him with a baffled dismay. "Could I in my good sense have supposed," he questions, "that one day I . . . would . . . pass for and be taken as a monster, a poisoner, an assassin; that I would be the horror of the human race, the plaything of the rabble; that the only greeting passersby would give me would be to spit on me; that an entire generation would, by unanimous agreement, find delight in burying me alive?" (2).

An unsympathetic reader of Rousseau might find these outbursts amusing examples of Rousseau's afflicted self-involvement. To be sure, self-examination is a form of egoism, and Rousseau's more than others. However, Rousseau's genius rests in his ability to link his ideas to himself. In this case, the hyperbolic description of his rejection serves a conceptual purpose. The telling final clause of his tale of woe recapitulates the logic of *Of the Social Contract,* but now from the perspective of one who fears, rather than champions, the general will. The entire generation, *by unanimous agreement,* would like to destroy him. This evocation of the general will is no rhetorical slip. The second sentence of the First Walk uses the same formulation: "the most sociable and loving of humans [Rousseau] has been proscribed from society by unanimous agreement" (1). Rousseau does not live in a partial state, half in and half out, partially coordinated with society and partially at odds. Such a condition is prohibited by the theory of *Of the Social Contract,* and it seems existentially impossible for Rousseau himself. He either clashes with society, or he is entirely in harmony.

The echoes of *Of the Social Contract* in this account of his situation warn us that Rousseau will not treat his public rejection with nonchalance. In his political theory, the general will is necessarily tied

---

10. Throughout, I use the Charles E. Butterworth translation of Rousseau's *The Rêveries of a Solitary Walker* (Indianapolis: Hackett, 1992). The page citations in parentheses correspond to this edition.

to the will of the individual. The ideal society, writes Rousseau in *Of the Social Contract*, "puts justice as a rule of conduct in the place of instinct, and gives [man's] actions the moral quality they previously lacked." Thus, the natural egocentrism of the person is transformed, and in this way, "man acquires with civil society moral freedom" (bk. 1, chap. 8). As a result of this commitment to the necessary sociality of human dignity, Rousseau cannot simply dismiss his social role as, somehow, extrinsic and irrelevant to his personal identity. Quite the contrary, these two aspects of life must be brought together; otherwise, his nature is frustrated rather than realized, truncated rather than fulfilled. Because Rousseau feels the force of this *must,* both theoretically and existentially, his public rejection plunges him "into a delirium which has taken no less than ten years to be calmed" (2). And this disturbance is more than psychological. Dramatizing how deeply the social dimension penetrates into his character, Rousseau describes a physical reaction to his social isolation. "I still imagine," he reports, "that I am being tormented by indigestion, that I am sleeping badly" (1). The general will has an internal reality within him, even to the point of creating a physiological disturbance when it clashes with his own sentiments and feelings.

The gap between (1) Rousseau's desire for moral reciprocity and true fellowship and (2) his life as an outcast rather than a citizen sets the agenda for all the meditations he records in *The Rêveries.* He wishes to close this gap and show the convergence between his unique personality and the social existence he craves. Otherwise he cannot persevere in the redemptive faith in the sufficiency of personal identity for the highest good, a faith so clearly articulated by the Savoyard vicar. Who he is—and as I must emphasize again, this necessarily includes his social needs—must be enough for blessedness, which includes the blessedness of living in accord with others. Thus, the task of Rousseau's personal reflection is to show how he is enough, how he has triumphed and closed the gap in spite of his rejection by all others.

Rousseau begins this reflective exercise of self-justification with an apparent affirmation of Stoic withdrawal. He pronounces himself disinterested in those who have rejected him. "Dealing with them," he reports, "would be insipid to me and even burdensome; and I am a hundred times happier in my solitude than I could ever be living among them" (4). He claims to resign himself to his fate, to submit to his isolation "without railing against necessity any longer" (2). This resignation leads to a renunciation of worldly aspiration. As he reports, "the desire to be better understood by men has been extinguished in my heart, only profound indifference remains about the fate of my true writings and of the testimonies of my innocence" (7). Against social acclaim and acceptance, he contrasts his current life of isolation and affirms it. In a flourish worthy of Epictetus, Rousseau writes, "Everything is finished for me on earth. People can no longer do good or evil to me here. I have nothing more to hope for or to fear in this world; and here I am, tranquil at the bottom of the abyss, a poor unfortunate mortal, but unperturbed, like God Himself" (5). Self-caused, like God himself, the true humanist knows himself sufficient—invulnerable to external threat and indifferent to worldly concerns. Retiring from what does not matter, the sage lives in happiness.

With Stoic rhetoric so prominent throughout *The Rêveries,* it seems that Rousseau closes the gap between his inner life and outward life by rejecting the social realm as a mere appearance, as a passing play of shadows with no consequence. The only gap that matters is within, the gap between our voluble feelings and our vocation as rational beings. Therefore, cure of the soul involves attending to our unchanging vocation as rational creatures, not our entangling social needs and the world of passing fashion and public reputation. In this way, the gap is internalized, and the moral project requires renouncing the false affective and socially vulnerable self and conforming ever more closely to the true, rational self that cannot be disturbed by external events and the actions of others. We close the gap, then, by chiseling away the false self in order to cling to the unchanging true self that really is sufficient for the highest good.

It is very tempting to highlight the Stoic cure of the soul in our reading of *The Rêveries,* for a superimposition of classical ideals softens the distasteful features and apparent contradictions of Rousseau's meditations.[11] Students who read *The Rêveries* are nearly always disgusted by Rousseau's personality. They are repulsed by Rousseau's

---

11. Kennedy F. Roche considers Rousseau's autobiographical writings but emphasizes the political texts (*Rousseau: Stoic and Romantic* [London: Methuen, 1974]). He develops Stoic parallels, suggesting that the general will is Rousseau's transposition of ancient *recta ratio* into modern terms. Perhaps, but such a transposition is a fundamental divergence from the Stoic cure of the soul, not in the least part because, for Rousseau, the terrible fate of man is to live in a world of social divisions and competition in which there is no general will. How can one be a Stoic if one allows that *recta ratio,* or its equivalent, is contingent upon the decisions of others, so contingent that it does not exist in any actual society?

unending bitterness and relentless self-justification. He blames everybody but himself for his predicament. He insists that he has never
done anything wrong—ever! Why can't Rousseau just admit, students
ask, that he is an unpleasant man? More sophisticated readers raise
logical objections that amount to the same question. How can
Rousseau's tortured exercises in special pleading and casuistical eva-
sion be consistent with his proclaimed "profound indifference" to
society and his purported renunciation of "the desire to be better
understood"? How can the agitated emotion and almost frantic
urgency of so many passages of *The Rêveries* be consistent with the
"tranquility" and "resignation" Rousseau claims to have achieved?
Readers then answer these questions by dismissing the ranting denun-
ciations and tangled exculpations as Rousseau's own failure to be a
consistent Stoic.

These reactions fail to see the humanistic ambition of Rousseau's
project. The bile and exculpation are not mere outpourings of emotion but are intrinsic to who he is. If Rousseau is to sustain the
redemptive hope of the Savoyard vicar, then he must affirm his own
unique life as sufficient for the highest good, even his isolation, bitterness, and desire for approval. In view of this commitment to self-
affirmation, we should not read Rousseau disjunctively, as if he were
a Stoic in theory but a bitter old man who cannot control his emotions in practice. Ancient Stoicism advanced a general view of our
common humanity and argued that reason, which all human beings
possess, is a sufficient basis for living in accord with the cosmos. As
such, the Stoic sage treats feelings, sentiments, emotions—all that is
not reasonable—as potential impediments to living rationally. The
Stoic cure of the soul involves disciplining those feelings to correspond
to the dictates of reason. Here, Rousseau diverges radically and consistently. He is committed to the sufficiency of *himself*, not his reason.
Indeed, where ancient Stoicism sought to train emotion to obey reason, Rousseau treats argument and inquiry as widely shared human
practices that must be disciplined to serve his own unique sentiments.
Thus, Rousseau has no intention of renouncing his feelings, not even
his painful feelings of bitterness over his rejection and unrequited
desire for acceptance, for to do so would entail rejecting himself.[12]

---

12. See, for example, Rousseau's refusal to pursue a Stoic strategy of indifference to social
opinion in *Rousseau, Judge of Jean-Jacques*, in *The Collected Writings of Rousseau*, 1:234.

Rousseau will not hollow out his individuality by forsaking his feelings. Quite the contrary, he wishes to affirm his feelings, even in their violence and flux. To do so, Rousseau adopts a cure of the soul that moves in the opposite direction of classical Stoicism. Instead of internalizing the conflict between who he is and who he ought to be, Rousseau completely externalizes the gap between who he is and how he lives. The world, and not Jean-Jacques Rousseau, has caused the gap between his personality and society.

Draining the Gap of Moral Significance

Rousseau pursues this strategy of externalization throughout *The Rêveries*. He has not been cast out of society because of any defect of character or transgressive act. Rather, his fate is the result of malicious and evil sentiment. As he explains in the opening paragraph: "In the refinements of their hatred, they have sought the torment which would be cruelest to my sensitive soul and have violently broken all the ties which attached me to them" (1). The gap is completely "their" responsibility. As Rousseau protests, "I would have loved men in spite of themselves" (1). His impulse toward others is so healthy, so just, that even the worst of men could be the objects of Rousseau's affection. Yet, this is not possible. Not happy to simply be bad, "they" have chosen the greatest evil; "they" have cast out an innocent man. Society has not simply failed to appreciate his love; "they" have rejected him.

When Rousseau evokes the evil "they," readers tend to dismiss such passages as exaggerations born of incipient madness and a paranoid personality. Indeed, the sheer ubiquity of the pronoun "they" throughout *The Rêveries* and the absurd speculations about conspiracies that mark any number of episodes encourage us toward just such a dismissal. Yet, we should beware easy disregard for the omnipresent "they." However much Rousseau might have been emotionally unbalanced, he was never intellectually unstable. His explanation of the gap between his better self and the social world depends upon a universal evil force, a "they," a power active and malevolent. Only by explaining his dilemma in this way can Rousseau externalize the gap between who he is and how he lives, and this externalization is integral to his humanism. It cannot be ignored as paranoia.

A calm depiction of his separation from society illustrates this. In his Sixth Walk, Rousseau tells of his habit of making a certain detour, during which he encounters a lame child who approaches him and asks for alms. Rousseau reports that his initial reaction to these entreaties was positive. "At first," he observes, "I was charmed to see him; I gave to him very good heartedly and for some time continued to do so with some pleasure, quite frequently even prompting and listening to his little prattle which I found enjoyable" (74). Here, a human relationship seems to blossom, and Rousseau enjoys a "good heart," unified in sentiment and action, a foretaste of the redemption hoped for by the Savoyard vicar. He finds the child's company agreeable, and gives alms out of the bounty of his soul, uncoerced by conscience or social expectation. But innocence is fragile, and all too soon the relationship darkens. Expectations and obligations intrude. "This pleasure," Rousseau continues, "having gradually become a habit, was inexplicably transformed into a kind of duty I soon felt to be annoying" (74). "Le petit babil" of the lame child becomes a harangue, to which, reports Rousseau, "I had to listen and in which he never failed to call me Monsieur Rousseau many times to show that he knew me well" (75). Impersonal and practiced speech corrupts the spontaneous relation of the man and boy. Ingratiation replaces genuine encounter. However much the child might wish to show he "knows" Rousseau, his use of convention proves just the opposite. The little child's "Monsieur this" and "Monsieur that" lead Rousseau to conclude "that he knew me no more than those who had instructed him" (75). The lame child had become a mouthpiece of "them."

Here, as elsewhere in *The Rêveries,* the conspiracy against Rousseau comes to the surface. The formalities and manners that "they" have taught the innocent child transform Rousseau from an intrinsically good-hearted man into the social role of beneficent sponsor, a role that could be played by anybody, and as such by nobody in particular. A unique relation between persons has been changed, by "them," into an entirely typical relation according to a set and impersonal pattern. His initial convergence of sentiment and existence is destroyed. Who he is—a good-hearted man who loves children—is separated from the patterns of life forced on him by society. He soon goes out of his way to avoid the lame child.

This episode and Rousseau's explanation of the cause of his separation from free and spontaneous intercourse epitomize his general theory of the human predicament. Instead of doing what our hearts tell us is good, we do what is expected, and this necessarily corrupts. His good deeds, with respect to the child and with respect to others, are burdened "by the chains of duties they later entailed" (75). The spontaneity of love becomes a premeditated fulfillment of obligation. The child becomes a placeholder; he is The Needy Supplicant. Rousseau is similarly objectified. He becomes The Gracious Benefactor. The gap opens up between who Rousseau and the child are, as individuals, and how they must behave as social entities caught up in a system of obligations and expectations.

The importance of this episode does not rest in its illustration of Rousseau's general theory of society and his distinction between *amor propre,* the destructive impulse to compare ourselves with others, and *amor de soi,* a healthy instinct of self-regard. Instead, the crucial point is Rousseau's portrayal of his own role and how this shapes his cure of the soul. He is a passive victim of "them." Whether active in conspiracy or omnipresent as parents who instruct their children to use polite forms of address when soliciting alms, "they" cause the gap between Rousseau's feelings of affection and his social relations to others. As either immediate or underlying cause, "they" have destroyed Rousseau's ability to live in integral harmony as himself and as friend to others. For Rousseau, then, the word "they" is not a personal pronoun at all. The pronoun denotes the corruptive influence of society, and this corruptive influence transforms intrinsic goodness into extrinsic civility. "They" want to make him into a mask, a role, a placeholder in the dance of civility.

Not only do "they" represent an external demand upon Rousseau; "they" are also all-powerful. Just as the lame child becomes a mouthpiece of false and manipulative manners, nearly everyone Rousseau encounters becomes "their" pawn, transformed from individuals into creatures of society. In another spontaneous encounter with a child, Rousseau recounts the same pattern. The beauty of the moment is corrupted when "an evil looking man," whom Rousseau assumes is "one of those spies they keep constantly on my tail," approaches the child's father and whispers in his ear. This intervention causes the father to cast a disapproving glance at Rousseau (127). "They" have gained control over the situation, and in so doing, "they" dehumanize. The evil spy has, no doubt, whispered Rousseau's reputation, and as a consequence the father sees Rousseau only in his social role as outcast and misanthrope. Here, as elsewhere, Rousseau's paranoia is an expression of his sociological insight. "They" are all-powerful and everywhere because social convention penetrates every aspect of human life. "They" drive a wedge between Rousseau's intrinsically virtuous personality and the kinds of social relations he has with others. "They" whisper in everyone's ears, and in so doing turn innocence into guilt, genuine encounter into anxious social relations, the benevolent glance of the father into the dehumanizing gaze of reproach.

For Rousseau, the proper cure of the soul involves resisting the transformative power of "them." He can acknowledge the gap between who he is and how he lives as a problem, but he must deny that the solution rests in the social conformity imposed by the reproach of moral judgment. Against the shaping power of convention, he consistently insists that he already is "the most loveable and sociable of humans" (1), *yet* he has become a "solitary person" (6). Rousseau affirms his intrinsic sociality—he need not change in order to live well with others—*and* his lack of meaningful social relations. He asserts his love of all men *and* his bitterness and hatred of "them." These conjunctions are possible because his separation from others is not his fault; society causes the rift. "They" have caused the gap between his inner goodness and the unhappy course of his affairs. As Rousseau states at the outset, "I would have loved men in spite of themselves" (1). His love is unconditional. He is entirely willing to merge his will into the will of all, but the opportunity for selflessness has been taken from him: "Only by ceasing to be men, have they been able to escape from my affection" (1).[13] Social conventions have transformed "them" into "strangers, unknowns, in short, nonentities" (1). He loves everyone who lives as a human being. Unfortunately, other than Rousseau himself, no one does.

Elsewhere in *The Rêveries,* Rousseau repeats the reduction of all others to the status of nonpersons, and we cannot treat it as hyperbole. Rousseau's humanism requires this reduction. As Rousseau reports, a life of persecution has focused his mind. "For ten years," Rousseau sought "for a man in vain," and he reports, "I finally had to extinguish my lantern and cry out: 'There are no more!'" (114). The world seems full of people, but, as Rousseau concludes, "in relation to me my contemporaries were nothing more than automatons" (114). Unable to renounce his love for others, he has been forced to engage and understand the world of social automata, even in the blizzard of their hatred of him. In this "long and vain research" Rousseau achieves clarity. He sees "them all, without exception, participating

---

13. Here, I alter the Butterworth translation in order to clarify the fact that Rousseau thinks the world is populated by sub-human creatures.

in the most iniquitous and absurd system an infernal mind can invent" (114). Because he understands the great power of society to destroy humanity, Rousseau can see that he is the only human being left in the world. Everyone else has become an empty suit, a mere echo of the social system.[14]

Rousseau loves every human being, even the worst. However, since all others are mere mechanical expressions of social convention, they are not available for love and affection. The consequence of this conclusion is delightfully and paradoxically reassuring to Rousseau. In a world depopulated of genuine human beings, Rousseau's self-love is coextensive with his love of humanity. Everyone else has become a nonentity, and therefore the way is clear for Rousseau's very desires and sentiments to merge with the general will. After all, the general will is the will of all men. All others have ceased being men. Therefore, Rousseau's will is the will of all men.

Rousseau's remarkable and convenient syllogism allows him to see how his alienated existence fulfills his earlier teachings about the ideal social order. In *Of the Social Contract,* he writes of civic relations that the relation of one citizen to another "should be as limited, and the relations to the entire body as extensive, as possible in order that each citizen shall be at the same time perfectly independent of all his fellow citizens and excessively dependent on the republic" (bk. 2, chap. 12). In *The Rêveries,* Rousseau is the only man worthy to be a citizen of a republic of virtue because he is the only man who seeks the good of all rather than his own advantage. Although this isolates him from others, it does not prevent him from entering into a compact with himself. In the self-recollecting dynamics of *The Rêveries,* he sustains himself in a reciprocity of experience and recollection. Explaining his purpose, he writes, "No longer finding any food here on earth for my heart, I gradually became accustomed to feeding it with its own substance and to looking within myself for all its nourishment" (12–13). In his dialogue with his own soul, Rousseau creates an internal society: farmer, baker, and consumer of true nourishment. Totally dependent upon the compact that he has made with himself, he is positively obliged to remain properly detached from the fragmented pieces of his life, which he recalls in his memory and places before his readers. He can examine the many

---

14. For parallels, see the polemic against medicine and its ability to "make the dead walk" (*Émile,* 24–26). The arts of men hollow out life even as they sustain it and make it more comfortable.

aspects of his personality at a distance.[15] But he is utterly dependent upon his identity that holds all the fragments of his life together. Therefore, he is *micropolis.*

Rousseau's decree that none but he possesses humanity may seem perverse. It certainly is implausible. However, the purpose of my presentation of Rousseau was neither to defend his moral vision nor to soften the sharp edges of Rousseau's relentlessly consistent reflections. Instead, I want the reader to see the logical beauty of Rousseau's solution to the difficulty of living well. It is a solution that, no matter how bizarre in final form, is at least consistent with the conviction that I or you are sufficient for the highest good. As such, Rousseau's solution, however strange and unappealing in his relentless loyalty to its logic, defines one boundary of the logic of we-matter-most humanism.[16]

The horror of dependence that rebels against authoritarianism finds lucid expression in Rousseau's account of his own moral vocation. Instead of interpreting the gap between himself and others as his problem, Rousseau makes it their problem. For some reason, others refuse to enter into the nobility of his social compact with himself. Rousseau regrets this, but it does not alter the dignity of his life. He has resisted the temptation to enter into the alienating conventions of society and the temptation to make his moral life contingent upon the acceptance of others, and in so doing, he has preserved a faith in the surpassing worth of his unique personality. He has remained true to the belief that he is sufficient, true to the redemptive vision of the Savoyard vicar.

The final walk of *The Rêveries* epitomizes Rousseau's achievement—his self-acceptance—and the moral irrelevance of a thoroughly externalized gap. He reminds himself that, fifty years before, he had loved Mme de Warens, and in the spontaneity of that love, he says, "I did

---

15. The adoption of the legal device of self-trial in *Rousseau, Judge of Jean-Jacques* further reinforces the social dimension of Rousseau's self-relation, which culminates with a fantasy of social union. "Rousseau," the alter ego of "Jean-Jacques," says to the "Frenchman" (Rousseau's detached reading of himself), "If we write to form a social group with [Jean-Jacques] that is sincere and without fraud, once he is certain of our rectitude and our esteem, he will open his heart to us" (244).

16. I take this solution to be the "magical act of clarifying transmutation" that Jean Starobinski proposes as the overall tendency of *The Rêveries* in *Jean-Jacques Rousseau: Transparency and Obstruction* (trans. Arthur Goldhammer; Chicago: University of Chicago Press, 1988), 352–64. Intransmutable personal identity—the sheer fact of being oneself—is the beginning and end of Rousseau's thought. It brings about "the feeling of an unalterable and limpid presence" (364) that is the godlike state of perfect self-sufficiency.

what I wanted to do, I was what I wanted to be" (141). Those few years
with Mme de Warens were, for him, a century of life. Repeating the
coda of self-sufficiency, he exults, "I was perfectly free and better than
free, for bound only by my affections, I did only what I wanted to do"
(141). True to his innermost sentiments, he was the best of men. He was
free, indeed, freer than free. He was devoted and committed to Mme
de Warens, indeed, more than committed since his devotion came from
his soul rather than social convention or the dead hand of obligation.
At every turn, this eternity in time was entirely the result of Rousseau's
own transparent life—he did only what he wanted to do, not what
"they" expected him to do. Everything was right and pure; there was
no gap between Rousseau's identity and his life with Mme de Warens.
He was sufficient for the highest good, and on the eve of his death, in
the power of memory, he remains sufficient. All subsequent failures to
realize his love in relation to others, and his consequent unhappiness,
fall finally outside the realm of this moral achievement.

Rousseau's life with Mme de Warens came to an end, and this
prefigures Rousseau's adult life and his attitude toward the events
that afflict him. Rousseau reports that he, evidently, did not "suffice for her heart as she sufficed for mine" (140). She rejected him
as he never did her. This very pattern obtains in his old age. He is
rejected by society, even though he never rejected the humanity of
others. He could not prevent fate from taking Mme de Warens from
him, nor could he prevent "them" from absorbing all others into
the cruel machinery of polite society. In the face of these disasters,
Rousseau could not help but feel unhappiness and despair. But his
duty was to the highest good, and since the highest good only comes
about through being true to himself, his first and last duty had
always been to himself, the *micropolis*. And this duty he discharged
without a blemish.

Readers may react with horror. How could this lonely, bitter, and
paranoid old man think he lived a flawless life? Could everyone else
have so misjudged his character and motives? Readers may rebel.
Rousseau's cure of the soul seems so pat, so simple, so insanely self-
absorbed. His vision does not seem moral at all. It seems complacent
and self-congratulatory. Perhaps, but this underestimates the strenuous difficulty of simply being oneself. As Rousseau knew so well, the
relentless pull of social expectation interacts with our always restless
desire for genuine human fellowship. This interaction should not be
regretted. Rousseau is always clear that sociality is the key to human

dignity. Social relations raise us from instinctual to moral existence. As a consequence, when surrounded by immoral people, we may find self-affirmation the most difficult task of all. They tempt us to join them in base living, and our own best instincts make us vulnerable to that temptation.

Moreover, to judge Rousseau with categories of conventional morality—self-discipline, cooperative sociality, catalogues of duty— is to judge him according to principles that diminish. Just such an approach absorbs his unique life into prevailing social standards, making the success of his life dependent upon achieving a higher good of "normalcy" or "social acceptance" or "good citizenship" or "proper manners" that precedes, conditions, and constrains his personal identity. This Rousseau always refuses to do. But above all, our rebellions against Rousseau's self-exculpation, self-aggrandizement, and self-confidence cannot be logical.[17] Guided by the faith of the Savoyard vicar, Rousseau relates to himself in a way that suffices for the highest good. Rousseau is utterly consistent in shaping his own assessment of his life around this faith, and if we do not follow in his lead, then he can only regret that we lack real confidence in the supreme value of personal identity.

A vivid scene emphasizes Rousseau's confidence and consistency. In his imagination, he puts himself before the Eternal Judge and recapitulates in a single sequence the logic of his humanism. He asks, "What have I done here-below?" That question brings the problem of his social dereliction to the fore. "I was made to live," he acknowledges, "and I am dying without having lived." Rousseau was born to live with others, yet his old age is one of solitude. He is animated by desire to love his neighbors but feels little besides bitterness, hatred, and resentment. At just this point, however, Rousseau externalizes the gap. "At least," he says, "it has not been my fault." Because "they" caused the gap, Rousseau can, in good conscience, affirm himself and his life. He pledges to offer a vigorous defense of his life before the Eternal Judge (and his readers). "I will carry to the author of my being," he promises, "if not the offering of good works which I have not been permitted to perform, at least

---

17. As the "Frenchman" declares in *Rousseau, Judge of Jean-Jacques*, although he was warned that Rousseau's writings were filled with contradiction and paradox, when he actually read the books, he found "things that were profoundly thought out, forming a coherent system which might not be true but which offered nothing contradictory" (209).

a tribute of frustrated good intentions, of healthy feelings rendered ineffectual, and of a patience impervious to the scorn of men" (14).[18] What he has done is horrible, a failure in every respect. But that is irrelevant. He may have behaved like a scoundrel, but he succeeded in being himself. In the depths of his soul, he never changed; he never became a civilized automaton; he remained true to himself. That achievement makes Rousseau the best possible man who ever lived.[19]

The Price of Consistency

In his earlier, programmatic writings on social power, education, romance, and religion, Rousseau suggests a theory of alienation in which we can distinguish between our "true self" and "false self." With this distinction, we might make sense of the idea of moral change. Something about the world perverts and distorts our true humanity, and we ought to oppose it and restore the conditions for being true to ourselves. We should change the structures of social relations; we should reform educational principles; we should reconceive our expectations for love and marriage. In sum, we should seek authenticity in all things.

Rousseau is often read as making such proposals, and readers want him to pick up the critical tools he has forged and cure himself of false consciousness. Why does he pen a long and tortured justification of a clearly unjustifiable lie? Doesn't Rousseau see that morality is socially constructed? Why does he denounce his detractors? Doesn't Rousseau see that reputation is a tool for maintaining hierarchy? Why does he seek acceptance? Doesn't he see that his felt need for social approval is merely an internalization of social expectation?

---

18. A parallel scene of divine judgment opens Rousseau's *Confessions*. "Whenever the last trumpet shall sound," Rousseau proclaims, "I will present myself before the sovereign Judge with this book in my hand, and loudly proclaim, 'thus have I acted.'" This scene ends with a striking image. Although Rousseau may have done wicked deeds, before the Eternal Judge he challenges all humanity to affirm his life: "Let them listen to my confessions; let them blush at my depravity; let them tremble at my suffering; let each in his turn expose with equal sincerity the failings, the wanderings of his heart, and if he dare, aver, *I was better than that man*." Thus was born the modern conviction that one is superior for parading one's failures in public. He who is most willing to bear his soul before others proves himself shameless and, therefore, beyond reproach.

19. See Karl Barth's treatment of this self-evaluation as fundamental to Rousseau's project in *Protestant Theology in the Nineteenth Century*, 223–24.

But Rousseau always undercuts this reformist zeal.[20] When he turns to himself, he will not drive a wedge between the "true Jean-Jacques" and the "false Jean-Jacques." Rousseau feels what he feels; he wants what he wants; and either he is sufficient for the highest good, or he is not. No amount of conceptual smudge applied by distinctions between true and false self will obscure this choice. Since he affirms his sufficiency, Rousseau must deny that he needs to undergo any morally meaningful change. The gap must always be externalized, and the identity of the person affirmed, blemishes and all.[21]

Rousseau's autobiographical writings are important, then, because he follows this logic of self-sufficiency to the end. He will not apply the discipline of a theory of human flourishing to deform his sensibilities and desires. He will not allow the authoritarian diminishments of society to creep into his life, not even in the faux benevolence of a substantive ideal of authentic existence. One must seek simply to live according to the moral faith of the Savoyard vicar. In the Fifth Walk, Rousseau recalls a moment of contemplative bliss at an earlier time in his life. Rousseau asks, "What do we enjoy in such a situation?" In other words, what constitutes the highest good that redeems us from the burdens and afflictions of life? His answer reiterates the one great principle of his life. The highest good depends upon "nothing external to ourselves, nothing if not ourselves and our existence. As long as this state lasts, we are sufficient unto ourselves, like God" (69). Our goal should be to make this state of self-sufficiency everlasting.

---

20. For example, the pathos of the final scene in *Émile* is striking. Émile has been educated to be a new type of man, untainted by social convention and unimpeded in the expression of his inner sentiment. However, as the novel ends, Émile is an expectant father. He turns to the tutor, who has trained him to be utterly himself, and expresses this final hope: "Teach me to follow your example." Training in authenticity becomes, itself, a convention and pattern of imitation. Such an ending is dictated by the logic of Rousseau's humanism. No reformist program will work. Men cannot be trained to be themselves.

21. Whereas I have traced the logic of Rousseau's autobiographical self-affirmation, Pierre Manent shows how Rousseau's social philosophy as a whole cannot motivate moral reasons for change. Because Rousseau defends individuality in the strongest possible sense of sheer uniqueness, ordinary normative appeals to "human nature" or even "authentic existence" get no traction. Manent observes: "This is Rousseau's problem. Rousseau's thought incarnates the paradoxical moment when man's nature is most vehemently appealed to in political debate, and when it ceases in fact to serve as its regulator and criterion" (*An Intellectual History of Liberalism*, 74). For Manent, the consequences are clear. The modern demand for change cannot be tethered to any moral or principled claims about human flourishing. These demands can only reflect discontent (I would add "historical necessity") and will submit to no moral limits.

The goal is purely formal, which explains why Rousseau offers no material vision of the highest good, no substantive theory of human flourishing, no positive doctrine of authenticity. The relationship between personal identity and the highest good is fixed before any consideration of particular persons.[22] Who one is rests in the sheer givenness of one's individuality. If Rousseau is partially caught up in the cogs of social machinery, if his feelings and intuitions are at least partially shaped by convention, then so be it. He lives as he does, and that is really for the best. Indeed, no one has ever led a better life. He has made a compact with himself, and he remains always loyal. He has fulfilled the sufficient condition for the highest good: he *is*.[23]

Rousseau's moral vision may seem a bizarre megalomania, even worse than his perpetual complaint and relentless exculpation. I am inclined to agree, but I warn the reader that the megalomania follows from Rousseau's humanism. It does not stem from a senile madness we might imagine overtook him in old age. Consider the logic of Rousseau's situation. Either the social alienation we experience threatens our souls, or it is, finally, morally insignificant, a blemish and imperfection of finite life but inconsequential to our ability to live in accord with the highest good. Rousseau cannot take the first side of this disjunction, for allowing something to emerge as necessary calls into question the moral faith of the Savoyard vicar and the logic commitment of we-matter-most humanism to the supreme consequentiality of personal identity for the highest good. If we freight the need for social recognition with moral weight, then we contradict the hope that our identities as persons are enough; we deny that truthfulness to oneself is sufficient. Rousseau sees this contradiction, which leads him to drain moral significance from his

---

22. The Savoyard vicar expresses this formal relation clearly. "What I do know is this," proclaims the voice of humanistic faith, "my personal identity depends upon memory . . . , and I have no doubt that this remembrance will one day form the happiness of the good and the torment of the bad" (*Émile*, 295). In short, our presence to ourselves in memory will be our own reward and punishment.

23. In this way, Rousseau seems to return to the ancient cure of the soul. We should cling to that which abides. However, there is a crucial difference. For Rousseau, the "I am" abides, and nothing else matters. Ancient philosophy would regard such a claim as ridiculous. Death proves that neither you nor I abide. One may either search for the universal and unchanging source of being that will save us from this horrible fact, or one may join with the Skeptics in accepting that nothing abides. However, for the ancients, one cannot just assert that personal identity, as such, abides. Only modernity has made such a counterfactual belief seem plausible.

alienation. For this reason, Rousseau concludes that his isolation from others was not, finally, consequential. He has engaged himself in the fraternity of true fellowship. He has been a friend to himself as no man has ever been to another. The upshot is a social compact with himself that gives him the greatest possible moral dignity. "I love myself too much," he asserts, "to hate anyone whatever" (81). Thus, his case before the Eternal Judge could be no stronger.

From Rousseau's consistent affirmation of his own sufficiency, an odd conclusion follows, one that undercuts modernity even as it seems to provide its strongest possible basis.[24] Because the deformations of society—the crushing authority of manners and moral conventions, the isolating and alienating power of "them"—do not prevent Rousseau from achieving the happiness envisioned by the Savoyard vicar, Rousseau has no moral basis from which to launch his criticisms of prevailing social relations. The world might be a better place psychologically, aesthetically, and sociologically, but it could not be better morally. Who he is suffices for moral triumph. There is no reason, morally, for change.[25] Authoritarianism is ugly, stupid, and reactionary, but Rousseau cannot say that it is wrong, for the demands of authority, the corrupting tendrils of social convention, and the evil "they" who lurk behind every door do not prevent him from living a morally perfect life. Thus, his prejudices against social convention are purely personal, an expression of the sentiments that are unique to his own psyche. His violent rebellions against authori-

---

24. That Rousseau undercuts, even as he supports, the modern project helps explain his falling out with the Enlightenment *philosophes*. Although Voltaire, Diderot, and d'Alembert agreed with Rousseau's judgments about the failures of society, they saw their role as reformist. They recognized that Rousseau's radicalism rebounded into an ineffective quietism. See Cassirer's discussion in *The Question of Jean-Jacques Rousseau*, 66–71.

25. Rousseau's repudiation of moral change in no way commits him to social or personal stasis. Rousseau rejects morally motivated change, not change in any other form. Judith Shklar points out that Rousseau, unlike classical figures, rejects all theories of stable personal identity. At the end of book 1 of the *Confessions*, Rousseau sees his own life as governed by the "fatality of my own destiny." If events had not conspired to drive him from Geneva, he could have been "a good Christian, a good citizen, a good friend, a good man." But such constancy was taken from him. He had to leave Geneva and entered into a lifetime of turmoil and flux. Just this feature of his life must be affirmed. For this reason, spontaneity supersedes *apathia* as the mark of the sage, and change is affirmed as a descriptive truth without normative consequence. As Shklar puts the matter, change "was for him a part of that restlessness which was the very mark of man's freedom, of his psychological development" (*Men and Citizens*, 11). Freedom is to have the psychic confidence to affirm whoever one is, or might become. One greets change, then, as a simple fact about our humanity.

tarianism can only be a consequence, not of his vision of the highest good, but of his personal identity.[26]

That Rousseau finds no cogent basis for his own moral prejudices against authoritarianism should not surprise us, for it follows from the logic of we-matter-most humanism. The sheer fact that a demand or an obligation has its power and purpose outside my distinctive identity makes it inhumane simply because it is not me. Any impulse toward living well that does not spring from within the unique individuality of our lives is wrong. All that is left, then, is my feelings and sentiments. However, this rebellion against that which is not me has no moral force. I have a psychic life regardless of what I do or what is done unto me. I am always in a position to be true to myself. Indeed, I cannot gainsay who I am. How could I? I am always exactly the kind of person I ought to be. That my psychic life might rebel against authority is just a fact about me. If I were the type of person who desired submission, then so be it.[27] I must be true to myself. Everyone lives as he or she should. Rousseau's achievement was to see that any consistent faith in the supreme consequentiality of personal identity entails this radical affirmation. Therefore, he resisted any moral reasons to change. As he says in the first line of *Émile,* "God makes all things good; man meddles with them, and they become evil." Rousseau will not meddle with himself. He will only embrace himself as good. If we are to follow Rousseau, we must refuse to meddle. Morally motivated change is unnecessary; we must embrace ourselves as sufficient for the highest good.

---

26. Even this formulation is absorbed into the megalomania of Rousseau's humanism. If personal identity is sufficient for the highest good, then the particularity of Rousseau's personality—his likes and dislikes, his anxieties and fears—constitutes the highest good. To tell his own story is to say all that needs to be said about truth, beauty, and goodness.

27. Rousseau so perplexes his readers because he combines both submission and rebellion. He professes a willingness to submit himself absolutely to a virile republic of like-minded men, but he rebels against the craven corruption and diminishing conventionality of every society he encounters. Thus, Rousseau can seem a collectivist in the morning and an individualist by sunset. If my reading is correct, then Rousseau's contradictory needs for both absorption into others and fierce independence cannot be dismissed as a contradiction. It did not matter whether his spontaneous passion took him from submission to rebellion and back again. The formal affirmation of personal identity remains constant, only the particular impulses and situations in his life changed. This constancy helps explain why Ernst Cassirer is correct when he makes the profoundly counterintuitive claim that Rousseau "eliminated feeling from the foundation of ethics" (*The Question of Jean-Jacques Rousseau,* 99). Personal identity is the sufficient foundation; the particular psychic makeup of a person is a matter of moral indifference. Rousseau is forever telling us how *he* feels, but it is only because he suffices for the highest good, not because he wishes to commend to us any particular kind of feeling or habit of mind as decisive.

–Chapter 3–

A Mitigated Humanism

> If the benefit of that which is newly better devised be small, sith
> the custom of easiness to alter and change is so evil, no doubt
> but to bear a tolerable sore is better than to venture on a dan-
> gerous remedy.
> —RICHARD HOOKER, *OF THE LAWS OF ECCLESIASTICAL POLITY*

Jean-Jacques Rousseau and David Hume are as different as night from
day. In style, Rousseau is hot and passionate, whereas Hume is cool
and measured. Rousseau writes endlessly about himself. Hume hints
at his life as a gentleman philosopher but consistently refers to patterns of thought and action people share in common rather than the
particularities of his circumstances. Rousseau provides epigrammatic
moments of luminous inspiration, compressing his most powerful
insights into paradoxical formulations. Hume's literary genius rests
in extended descriptions of enigmas and problems, outlining their
anatomy, providing a "mental geography" of ordinary practice and
habit.[1] The one philosopher inspires; the other clarifies. The one
focuses on the burning spark of individuality; the other, on the enduring forms of habit and sentiment.

---

1. The phrase "mental geography" is found in the *Enquiries Concerning Human
Understanding and Concerning the Principles of Morals* (ed. L. A. Selby-Bigge and P. H. Nidditch;
Oxford: Clarendon, 1975), 13. Page citations will follow this edition, indicated by the abbrevi-
ation E. I will also quote from Hume's *Treatise of Human Nature* (ed. L. A. Selby-Bigge and P. H.
Nidditch; Oxford: Clarendon, 1978), indicated by *T; The Natural History of Religion* (ed. H. E.
Root; Stanford: Stanford University Press, 1957), indicated by *NHR;* and *Essays Moral, Political,
and Literary* (ed. Eugene F. Miller; Indianapolis: Liberty Fund, 1985), indicated by *MPL*.

One can hardly imagine a more disparate pair, yet they were friends, at least as much as the volatile Rousseau could ever have friends. This friendship is not so surprising. Their differences did not produce contradictory, or even unrelated, projects. Day meets night at dusk and dawn, and Rousseau and Hume have two important points of contact. The first is a shared awareness of the existential disruption caused by the gap between who we are and how we ought to live. Life seems out of joint for Hume, just as it seems for Rousseau. The second point of contact is the proposed solution both give to this disjunction. Something deep inside of us, underneath our moral engagement with others and our rational engagement with the world, closes the gap. For both, who we are, inwardly, matters most for the highest good.

For both Hume and Rousseau, our moral aspirations and rational ambitions entangle us in dangerous falsehoods. Rousseau is clear that his own moral goodness makes him vulnerable to the artificiality of society. Only a man who loves others can be manipulated by the false manners of society. A misanthrope never allows himself to become alienated because he never vests any hope in the possibility of entering into the dignity of a compact with others. As we shall see, Hume identifies a similar link between our own best selves and our worst and most dangerous temptations. Our very identities as persons make us vulnerable to unhappiness and despair.

Hume shares with Rousseau more than a common judgment of the inner cause of our dilemma. His solution follows Rousseau's pattern. We should identify and recover the affective basis for our properly human lives. We should rest on reliable sentiment. In this way, Hume's mental geography, no less than Rousseau's spiritual autobiography, has a homeland. As a result, their humanistic cures of the soul will have important formal similarities. We must repent of a vagrant existence and return, via indefensible inner feelings, to our place of natural citizenship. For both, philosophical practice can help in this repentance and return; philosophy should bring us to ourselves.

We have seen how Rousseau understands this *metanoia*. We must embrace ourselves as sufficient for the highest good; we must establish an unbreakable bond of loyalty to our identities. Now we give ourselves over to the task of understanding Hume's cure of the soul, for the valences of his approach are quite different. Unlike Rousseau, Hume does not argue that we are sufficient for the highest good. That side of we-matter-most humanism holds no attraction for him.

Instead, Hume emphasizes the necessity of personal identity for the highest good. We must commit ourselves to forms of reflection and patterns of life that ensure our continuity, as persons, in the quest for the highest good. Yet, however much this may diverge from Rousseau's vision of self-sufficiency, the upshot is the same. Just as Rousseau can give no rational support to the modern critical agenda of personal and social transformation, Hume finds it very difficult to affirm morally meaningful change.

The Curse of Overreaching

Hume's cure of the soul is shaped by his decision to renounce the radical aspiration of speculation and embrace the more modest goals of informed inquiry. At the outset of the *Enquiries Concerning Human Understanding*, Hume identifies two approaches to questions of life, two methods of reflection. The first is an "easy philosophy" in which "striking observations and instances from common life" constitute the medium of expression (*E* 5). Remaining in the realm of everyday life, this approach applies distinctions where helpful, advances arguments where necessary, and examines evidence as appropriate. In contrast, Hume describes the "hard philosophy" of speculative ambition that seeks "the foundation of morals, reasoning, and criticism" and searches underneath or beyond common life for "hidden truths" (*E* 6). This ambition drives philosophers to search for certainties that are "beyond controversy" (*E* 6). Such philosophers wish to proceed "from particular instances to general principles" and thus secure truths that transcend the limitations of particular times and places.

Hume does not remain neutral in his contrast between easy and hard philosophy. Contrary to his reputation as a rigorous thinker who is tireless in his search for truth, Hume commends the former.[2] "It is certain," Hume observes, "that the easy and obvious philosophy will always, with the generality of mankind, have the preference above the accurate and abstruse" (*E* 6). This popularity is not a matter of regret. Rather, philosophy conducted with apt illustration and winning rhetoric gains Hume's approval because the preference for "the accurate

---

2. For a detailed account of Hume's distinction between easy and hard philosophy, and a clear case for understanding why he commends the former, see Donald Livingston, *Philosophical Melancholy and Delirium: Hume's Pathology of Philosophy* (Chicago: University of Chicago Press, 1998), 17–52.

and abstruse" that characterizes hard philosophy is profoundly dangerous. Understanding this danger is the key to understanding Hume's vision of the relation between personal identity and the highest good.

What, exactly, is the danger of speculative thought? How could the abstruse philosophy that "cannot enter into business and action" and "vanishes when the philosopher leaves the shade, and comes into open day" be a threat (*E 7*)? If, as Hume observes, the principles of hard philosophy cannot produce enduring influence, then why does he warn of its danger rather than merely reject it as impotent? Let us begin with Hume himself, for he, like Rousseau, presents himself as a case study of his own insights. His life manifests the positive dangers of a philosophical ambition that cannot "retain any influence over our conduct and behavior" (*E 7*).

Hume admits that he suffers from a temptation toward this dangerous ambition; that is, his mind tends toward the speculative and hard philosophy that leads toward hidden truths. Were our reflective practices inconsequential, then he might enjoy such speculations, perhaps fully acknowledging the superiority of a practical mode of life. He might affirm himself and his own reflective adventures as harmless diversions. However, the cultivation of philosophical inquiry is never innocent. For Hume, our mental lives have tendencies and patterns that color everything we believe and do. Here, the hard and ambitious philosophy that would seek first principles and final causes has an effect upon our lives, and that effect is negative, alienating. The dynamic is simple. The purpose of a speculative philosophy is to reach beyond the assumptions of common life to find a truer, more certain mode of reflection. Insofar as this goal is sought, the speculative philosopher drives a wedge between ordinary habits of mind and whatever is more certain and true about the world. Ambitious philosophers seek to see as God sees, which commits them to cultivate an absolute and fundamentally inhuman perspective. On this point, Hume stands as far apart as possible from Rousseau and the vision of the Savoyard vicar. For Hume, the desire for a divine perspective, however enticing, debilitates rather than redeems.

Book 1 of *A Treatise of Human Nature* is Hume's most sustained performance in the hard and ambitious mode of philosophy. Hume's skeptical conclusions regarding fundamental questions are well known. More important, for our purposes, is Hume's account of the moral consequences of such an inquiry. Many readers have followed with awe and admiration the relentless precision of Hume's treatments of causality, necessary connection, and personal identity, finding book 1 a model of exemplary philosophical honesty and commitment to the rigors of argument. Carried forward with a faith in naturalistic accounts of the cosmos, readers applaud Hume's demolition of the metaphysics of classical philosophy. They read his appeals to experience as warrant for scientific methods of experimental observation. Hume is championed as a patron of progressive and objective inquiry, with concomitant moral commitments to freedom of thought, personal liberty, and social reform. However, Hume draws a very different conclusion. Far from inspired and enlivened by his intellectual efforts, he reports that this venture into fundamental questions has left him demoralized and exhausted. Instead of energized with a vision of reconstructing philosophy, morality, and politics along experimental lines, he is overwhelmed by feelings of despair and melancholy.

Hume's description of where his sustained speculative efforts have taken him closely parallels Rousseau's self-description:

> I am first affrighted and confounded with that forelorn solitude, in which I am plac'd in my philosophy, and fancy myself some strange uncouth monster, who not being able to mingle and unite in society, has been expell'd all human commerce, and left utterly abandon'd and disconsolate. Fain wou'd I run into the crowd for shelter and warmth; but cannot prevail with myself to mix with such deformity. I call upon others to join me, in order to make a company apart; but no one will harken to me. Every one keeps at a distance, and dreads that storm, which beats upon me from every side. I have expos'd myself to the enmity of all metaphysicians, logicians, mathematicians, and even theologians; and can I wonder at the insults I must suffer? I have declar'd my dis-approbation of their systems; and can I be surpriz'd if they shou'd express a hatred of mine and of my person? When I look abroad, I foresee on every side, dispute, contradiction, anger, calumny and detraction. (*T* 264)

Honest thought about the reality of human life leaves Hume isolated, expelled from society. He undertook his fundamental inquiries in order to serve others, to contribute to the common human project of seeking truth. Yet, he has achieved the opposite. Far from appreciating him, others hate him. He wishes to draw others to him in the community of rational reflection, but none will come near. As happened to Rousseau, that part of Hume that seems most noble brings disaster. Rousseau sought to love honestly and freely, and it yielded calumny and conspiracy against him. Hume sought to think clearly and without prejudice, and it brought him melancholy and despair. For both Rousseau and Hume, a terrible gap opens between their quest for the highest good and the social life they seek.[3]

Hume's response to this gap does not follow Rousseau's solution. He will not externalize the gap and drive change from the relation between personal identity and the highest good. Instead, Hume explains that the danger rests in our very powers of observation and inference. These aspects of our identities, the best and noblest aspects, push us far from ordinary life. We take for granted that a swing of the golf club will be sufficient to launch the golf ball, but under the charm of speculative inquiry, we can come to the point of doubting that our belief in causality is justified. When we wake, we presume that we are the selfsame persons as when we went to sleep. Yet, the speculative impulse can carry us so far from common sense that we may find ourselves unable to account for continuous personal identity. Hume gives solutions to these two difficulties, and others, but these solutions are faint and make no impress upon the mind. They are vaporous and dissipate as soon as attention shifts elsewhere, providing no support for intellectual inquiry or practical affairs. "The understanding," Hume concludes, "when it acts alone, and according to its most general principles, entirely subverts itself, and leaves not the lowest degree of evidence in any proposition, either in philosophy or common life" (*T*267–68). Far from leading to more solid ground, the overreaching mind hangs in the air.[4]

---

3. The parallels extend beyond a shared alienation from society. Rousseau also uses the metaphor of lost and storm-threatened existence in order to express his sense of the human condition. "I pondered," reports the Savoyard vicar in his speech to Émile, "on the sad fate of mortals, adrift upon the sea of human opinions, without compass or rudder, and abandoned to their stormy passions with no guide but an inexperienced pilot who does not know whence he comes or whither he is going" (Rousseau, *Émile*, 275). The two authors fill the metaphor with different content. For Rousseau, social custom is a blinding fog, and an inner sentiment, however inexperienced, is the proper pilot. For Hume, speculative ambition leads astray, and as we shall see, common life guides us safely to shore. Nonetheless, the situation is similar. Demands for change— social conformity (Rousseau) and epistemic transcendence (Hume)—disorient and debilitate.

4. Hume reiterates this conviction in many places. For example, when discussing the practical consequences of speculative philosophy, Hume observes, "When we leave the closet, and engage in the common affairs of life, its conclusions seem to vanish, like the phantoms of the night on the appearance of the morning; and 'tis difficult for us to retain even that conviction, which we had attain'd with difficulty" (*T*455).

The isolation and vulnerability of understanding does not stem from confusion or paradox. Hume's analysis in book 1 of the *Treatise* is precise and cogent. The subversion results from the abstractive move itself, a move entailed in the project of foundational philosophy. The step back from ordinary life produces results; Hume has an explanation for our confidence in causal connection. However, this explanation cannot create strong convictions and forceful beliefs. In his essay on skepticism, Hume explains the ineffectiveness of the step back into abstract thought by analogy. "A man may as well pretend to cure himself of love, by viewing his mistress through the *artificial* medium of a microscope," he writes, "as hope to excite or moderate any passion by the *artificial* arguments of a SENECA or an EPICTE-TUS" (*MPL* 172). As soon as one looks up from the microscope or philosophical argument, ordinary perceptions and reactions regain their sway. The weakness, then, has nothing to do with the ability of the microscope or arguments to produce results. The problem rests in the artificiality of the results, not in the sense of illusion or falsity, but in the sense of detachment and remoteness. For Hume, then, "the reflections of philosophy are too subtle and distant to take place in common life, or eradicate any affection. The air is too fine to breathe in, where it is above the winds and clouds of the atmosphere" (*MPL* 172). We must hold our breath in order to see as God sees, and for Hume, sooner rather than later, we need to return to lower elevations in order to breathe.

If the step back yields no lasting results, then why do we ever leave the thick atmosphere of ordinary life? Hume asks this question, and his answer is central to his view of the human predicament and his own humanistic cure of the soul. The answer has two sides. We are tempted both by the way ideas work in our minds and by our very desire for knowledge.

Consider the way ideas work. They often detach themselves from everyday perceptions. We might collect fine coins and in handling them have a vivid impression of the gold from which they are minted. We might climb mountains and have a subtle and pleasant knowledge of their rugged shapes and arduous slopes. Ideas bewitch, and through a mental trick, we can produce a compound, the idea of a golden mountain. In itself, such a notion is innocent, even poetical. However, just the same process occurs elsewhere, and with deleterious consequences. We submit ourselves to the wise decisions of an experienced judge and champion the beneficence of the local magistrate. In these experiences of social relations properly discharged, we develop a vivid mental image of human virtues. Then, through the tendency of the ideas to solidify into mental objects, independent of their original contexts, we add superlatives and come up with the idea of a Judge and Lord who is an "infinitely intelligent, wise and good Being" (*E* 19). In this way, unhinged from everyday life, ideas compound and extend beyond everyday life, even to the point of generating the idea of a Supreme Being who enjoys ontological and moral perfection.

Ideas may tempt us, but Hume does not externalize the problem, as does Rousseau. Hume is clear that we are not victims of language. To be sure, the fact that concepts exist as mental objects draws us into the illusion that we can gain knowledge of reality by manipulating, analyzing, and compounding them, but our desire to see as God sees pushes us far more than the lure of detached ideas pulls. Human beings have a heroic temper, and therefore, instead of despairing over the conundrums that emerge when ideas are pressed beyond ordinary life, philosophers redouble their efforts and seek new solutions. "In vain do we hope," writes Hume, "that men, from frequent disappointment, will at last abandon such airy sciences, and discover the proper province of human reason" (*E* 12). Something inside us will not rest content with wise judges and good magistrates. We seek knowledge of absolute wisdom and perfect goodness. As Hume explains, "many persons find too sensible an interest in perpetually recalling such topics" (*E* 12). Indeed, the impoverished results of previous philosophers increase, rather than reduce, this impulse. "Each adventurous genius," observes Hume, "will still leap at the arduous prize, and find himself stimulated, rather than discouraged, by the failures of his predecessors; while he hopes that the glory of achieving so hard an adventure is reserved for him alone" (*E* 12). The difficulties of abstract thought are enticements rather than deterrents; the threat of disaster a cherished challenge rather than a feared fate. The impulse to step back and find the underlying or transcendent basis for common life seems intrinsic to our humanity.[5]

We might allow that speculative ambition is part of who we are. Yet, in what sense is such ambition dangerous rather than simply futile? An expedition is most vulnerable when farthest from home, and mental overextension, whether caused by the lure of words-

---

5. For a detailed account of the way in which our speculative impulse gains dominion over our reflective lives, see Livingston, *Philosophical Melancholy and Delirium*, 18–52.

become-concepts or by our own vain ambition, courts disaster. Hume feels this danger existentially. His own efforts to press beyond common assumptions produced a profound sense of isolation, affliction, and despair. However, for Hume, the dangers are not merely, or even primarily, personal. Our endeavors to "penetrate into subjects utterly inaccessible to the understanding" leave us unprotected against the blandishments and threats of those who practice "the craft of popular superstition" (*E* 11). After all, we do not live in isolation. No matter how alone Hume feels at the end of his effort to think through the fundamental question of what holds things together, the "cement of the universe" (*T* 662), he will walk out from his study and onto a street full of people. He may find nobody to join his community of philosophy, but many are eager for Hume to join their sects, eager for him to invest in their company or to vote with their party. To the extent that our abstract researches lack the power to create or alter strong passions, we are vulnerable to these efforts. "The passion for philosophy, like that for religion," Hume warns, "seems liable to this inconvenience, that, though it aims at the correction of our manners, and extirpation of our vices, it may only serve, by imprudent management, to foster a predominant inclination" (*E* 40).

The tendency to foster vice in spite of good intentions has two forms, tending in two different directions, both of which we have surveyed in our account of the modern criticism of Christianity as vain overreaching: quietism and fanaticism. In the emptiness of philosophical reflection, either we go slack in a "supine indolence" and "pensive melancholy," or we puff up in "lofty pretensions" and "rash arrogance" (*E* 41). Inconsequential, abstruse thought yields either a vulnerable despair or the illusion of real transcendence. These are the real dangers we face, and the chimerical consequences of heroic efforts, not only in speculative thought but in religion and morality as well, tempt us in both directions.

For Hume, "supine indolence" rarely takes the form of philosophical despair and true skeptical *apathia*. We wish to lead active and engaged lives and resist the conclusion that our overreaching leads to nothing of lasting import. Unable to find in subtle reflections a vivid and powerful spring for life, many people submit themselves to what Hume calls "superstition." When Hume writes about this tendency, the psychological atmosphere he describes is strikingly similar to his own mood, as he reports at the end of book 1 of the *Treatise*. In his essay "Of Superstition and Enthusiasm," he observes that "weakness, fear, melancholy, together with ignorance, are the true sources of SUPERSTITION" (*MPL* 74) and that "superstition is founded on fear, sorrow, and a depression of spirits" (*MPL* 75). The mental process is clearly articulated. The human creature wishes to know the whence and whither of the world, the inner springs of things and their final purpose. This very desire leads us astray, for as Hume so effectively shows, the more deeply we push such questions, the more isolated and lonely we become. Unable to endure an unknown world, we embrace explanations and purposes willy-nilly. If we cannot know the ultimate basis for things, at least we shall believe something. This will to believe makes us extremely vulnerable. We allow ourselves to be absorbed into theological systems of belief. In rituals and rites we seek to make cultic contact with the foundational truths that our understanding cannot make vivid and powerful in our lives.

The overreaching impulse leads to social patterns that are as debilitating as the mental process itself. Morally, Hume sees superstition as ascetical groveling before priests and blind obedience to prophets. Moral practices are enforced with clarity and vigor, even as the final goal of the moral life remains as chimerical as a "golden mountain." Politically, Hume associates superstition with political authoritarianism. Since we cannot form a vivid and affectively potent idea of God, social agents take God's place. A sophisticated system of ritual, social control, and hierarchy function as surrogates for the great divine power we seek to serve. In this way, superstition, Hume observes, "renders men tame and abject, and fits them for slavery" (*MPL* 78). Overreaching in our desire to see as God sees, we compensate for our inability by binding ourselves to some greater power. If we are unable to achieve our heroic ambitions on our own, then we shall associate ourselves with a force more powerful, more majestic, more divine.[6]

"Lofty pretension" and "vain arrogance" begin at the same point of overreaching but find power and purpose in a disposition Hume calls "enthusiasm." Instead of defaulting to an external, ceremonial, and priestly power, enthusiasts cathect their heroic ideals with internal sources of psychic potency. Natural human desires, desires that provide effective motivation for ordinary life, are deflected from their proper objects and redirected into the quest for ultimate truths. Our desire for power and our love of dominion mix with our impulse toward the ultimate source of all things. Charged with psychic force,

---

6. See *E* 342–43, where Hume identifies Pascal as the archetype of the superstitious personality.

the overreaching ambition becomes dangerously unhinged. "A full range is given to the fancy in the invisible regions or world of spirits," warns Hume, "where the soul is at liberty to indulge in every imagination, which may best suit its present taste and disposition" (*MPL* 74). Our vanity in ordinary life is checked by others. We may think ourselves surpassingly intelligent and good-looking, but the comments of our friends, not to say our enemies, mark a boundary of excess. However, should we redirect our vanity inward and toward spiritual things, we find no limits. How beautiful, perfect, and righteous we may judge our inward, spiritual selves! For this reason, Hume observes that "hope, pride, presumption, a warm imagination, together with ignorance, are, therefore, the true sources of ENTHU-SIASM" (*MPL* 74).

Like superstition, enthusiasm has a moral and political aspect. Morally, the enthusiast is a fanatic, straining against the constraints of ordinary life. Politically, the enthusiast is a rebel, quick to ignite flames of violence and bitter division among peoples. Across these different manifestations, the same pattern obtains. In overreaching ambition, the enthusiast supplements with passion what cannot be supplied by reason. The hero shall conquer the world on behalf of the truth, by whatever means are necessary.[7] Hume recounts the consequences: rivers of blood flow through history, instruments of torture seek to shape us into forms unknown in nature, the *auto-da-fé* consumes those unable to live in the kingdom of God. Whereas the overreaching soul who abandons himself to superstition can easily be made a foot-soldier in the war on ordinary humanity, the enthusiast is the commander, the strategist poring over maps of the soul trying to find ways to conquer the citadel of human life on behalf of "higher ideals."[8]

With his analysis of superstition and enthusiasm, Hume articulates the difficulty posed by our humanity. The problem stems from our identities as rational creatures. We seek more than we can have; we undertake a heroic quest for transcendent knowledge. In the desire to overleap the limits of our humanity, we venture into foreign regions

---

7. Hume identifies the ancient Skeptic Diogenes as the archetypical enthusiast. Denying a rational basis for life, Diogenes became a law unto himself: "The morality of the soul was his standard principle; and even his sentiments a divine providence" (*E*, 343). Licentious desires, always strong in the human psyche, substituted for the greater power that Diogenes was unable to find.

8. See Hume's assessment of the overriding religious motives for the destructive violence of the English civil war in *The History of England* (Indianapolis: Liberty Fund, 1983), 5:572.

where alien forces easily take us captive. Our heroic temper makes us vulnerable to both tendencies.[9] Exhausted by our attempts to secure speculative knowledge, we hear the voice of superstition beckoning: "Come, ye who seeketh after that which is before all things and that which shall endure forever. I know the answer to the riddle of the cosmos. Come, enter into the temple. Offer a sacrifice and a prayer, and God will reveal His hidden face." Should we lack the submissive disposition, the danger of enthusiasm emerges: "True, my arguments have failed to secure the hoped-for conclusions. My reflections have been dashed upon the rocks of epistemic limitation, but the Transcendent comes to me nonetheless, in a flash of insight rather than a careful inference. Yes, God has given me a voice with which to speak the divine word. I cannot prove God's revelations, but I know His glory. Follow, or be consumed by the fires of a coming judgment." Even if we avoid such unlucky fates, as Hume managed, we are still left with the void of speculative knowledge sought but not found. Our greatest hope, then, seems to be the quiescence of despair.

Salvation through Custom and Habit

Patrons of sober argument have celebrated Hume's criticisms of the overreaching impulse. However, to the extent that his readers remain satisfied by his critical project, they fail to understand Hume's cure of the soul. The *success* of his critical inquiries left Hume in despair. The results of that inquiry were largely negative, and where positive, they were vaporous and spectral. Demolishing false cures of the soul might be a helpful propaedeutic to this task, but Hume is not satisfied with a Socratic solution. To know that one does not know strikes him as false. We *do* know a great deal. We know not to exit a building by a third-story window. We know that the deliverances of our senses are more reliable than the testimony of witnesses. We know that a hot iron produces pain when applied to skin, and we pull our hand away without hesitating and thinking that we cannot know. Hume wishes to recover that confidence, to restore that immediacy of knowledge

---

9. Hume draws together Diogenes the philosopher and Pascal the believer at the end of the *Enquiry Concerning the Principles of Morals*. They both led "artificial lives," and, detached from common custom and ordinary constraints, "no one can answer for what will please or displease them. They are in a different element from the rest of mankind" (*E* 343). The heroic temper presses us beyond our proper boundaries and makes us imagine that we are beyond the praise and blame of ordinary human beings.

and action. We are meant to form judgments about the world. Speculative inquiry both excites and frustrates that desire by leading us beyond the proper realm for rational life, which leads to perversions of many sorts. Against this overreaching, Hume wants to have a philosophy that empowers us to undertake reasoned reflection and intelligent action. Whatever might constitute the highest good, surely such a philosophy and its use of human rational powers are necessary elements in achieving that goal.

Rousseau conceives of the gap similarly, although in a more fevered atmosphere of antagonism. And although he emphasizes our moral alienation rather than our epistemic alienation, the combination of seduction and well-intentioned vulnerability functions along the same pattern. For Rousseau, our native philanthropy impels us forward into social relations. We seek to love as Rousseau loved Mme de Warens, freely and out of the very depths of our being. Initially, society seems to offer institutions and structures in which to express this inner desire for noble relations to others. But just as Hume views the microscope and arguments of philosophy as "artificial," Rousseau sees society as transforming spontaneous goodwill into artificial forms of life. Society seeks to crush his love in the iron cage of manners and moral convention. The sweet taste of love turns sour in the heat of socially formed expectations and the judgmental gaze of others.

Rousseau wants to reconceive the basis of our lives so that we can cure the soul by healing this rift between our inner dignity and the way we actually live, between our intrinsic goodness and the hateful, spiteful reality of social existence. Reason cannot provide the leverage for escape; reason is implicated in the social perversion of our inner dignity. The forces of social influence corrupt our practical syllogisms by substituting premises based on social convention for those based on the reality of our unique lives. So Rousseau reaches more deeply into the raw particularity of life. His identity, his unique and undivided soul, manifest in sentiment and feeling, shall be his compass. The cure Hume proposes is similar. For Hume, sentiment and feeling provide what speculative philosophy cannot: a stable basis for intellectual, moral, and political life.

Hume's explanation of causality is typical. Although syllogism and inference based on incontrovertible first principles can give no explanation of how effect follows cause, the human mind connects cause to effect nonetheless. "This connection," Hume explains, "which we feel in the mind, this customary transition of the imagination from one object to its usual attendant, is the sentiment or impression from which we form the idea of power or necessary connexion" (*E* 75). A feeling anchors our ability to dwell in the world with cognitive confidence. Like Rousseau, Hume has found the feature of our lives that has the power to overcome our alienation. Sentiment saves Hume from his Rousseauian afflictions. He is not delivered from his "forelorn solitude" by the power of reason. Indeed, the overreaching impulse of reason has created his isolation and caused his despair in the first place. Instead, redemptive power rests in "a strong propensity" that he feels more vividly than the conclusions of any abstract arguments.

Hume's fundamental reliance on feeling brings him extraordinarily close to Rousseau, but Hume's understanding of the nature and source of his redemptive sentiments propels him in the opposite direction. For Rousseau, sentiments are strongest when they are most unique and spontaneous. For Hume, his "strong propensity" is most powerful when most ubiquitous and constant. Such sentiments arise, he argues, from experience and habit. Experience is the impress the world makes upon our minds. This weight of the world upon us has little to do with our individuality; it anchors us in the common world of physical and social events. No matter how weak our speculative powers, the world acts upon our minds and carves channels of mental habit. Thus, for Hume, the inner strength of habit and custom explains why we continue to think and act even though we lack a cogent philosophical account of the basis of our epistemic and moral practices. Habit and custom are the "cement of the universe," the *arche* that speculative thought seeks but cannot find.

As Hume describes his redemption from isolation and despair in the *Treatise*, he appeals to the enabling power of experience and habit. "Experience is a principle," he writes, "which instructs me in the several conjunctions of objects for the past. Habit is another principle, which determines me to expect the same for the future; and both form certain ideas in a more intense and lively manner, than others, which are not attended with the same advantages" (*T* 265). Experience and habit—sentiment reinforced by the constancy of sensation and buttressed by social practices—give vivacity to our thoughts and impel our wills. For Hume, then, just this feature of our identities has the power to bring us home to ourselves. "Custom is the great guide of human life" (*E* 44). We can live as cognitive beings, confident that the world is held together by connections we can analyze and anticipate in ordinary thought and scientific inquiry. We can live as moral agents engaged in society with others, assured that we are persons of continuous character and identity. In both instances, we should embrace experience in the form of habit and custom, for there we find the glue that holds our world together—a stable basis for the cognitive and active lives that constitute the human vocation. Experience, in the full social and historical sense Hume intends for this concept, connects personal identity to the highest good.

In view of this claim, Hume's cure of the soul commends loyalty to custom and experience. Against overreaching, Hume insists that a proper use of the mind involves submission to common patterns of thought and action. "Here then I find myself absolutely determin'd," writes Hume of his repentance from the speculative desire to see as God sees, "to live, and talk, and act like other people in the common affairs of life" (*T* 269). As if making a religious vow, Hume reports, "I am ready to throw all my books and papers into the fire, and resolve never more to renounce the pleasures of life for the sake of reasoning and philosophy" (*T* 269). His turn away from "reasoning and philosophy" entails neither misology nor laziness. Everyday intercourse requires analysis and deliberation, constraint of passion, and discipline in action. Anxiety about investments, the most natural of feelings, stimulates extraordinarily complex judgments about commercial interactions, as well as refined deliberations about the character of those to whom one entrusts one's savings. To repent of the heroic impulse thus returns Hume to the everyday responsibilities of thinking clearly and acting prudently in the affairs of life.

Hume's renunciation of philosophical ambition need not entail a rejection of all speculative inquiry. The cure of the soul he embraces renounces speculative illusions, not the human capacity for such mental operations. Indeed, in his famous commendation of "mitigated scepticism" at the end of the *Enquiry Concerning Human Understanding,* Hume observes that philosophical inquiry, properly subordinated to the power of sentiment and habit, may have a positive role. The disciplines of clarity in observation and cogency in argument enhance our everyday mental deliberation. More importantly, the search for the foundations, properly conducted and honestly acknowledged as futile, can have a humanizing effect. To know that one cannot know things in their universal and transcendent aspect undermines the tendency toward overreaching. For example, his specific inquiry into the basis for causal reasoning fails, but it fails in such a way as to direct his attention back to the ubiquity and fittingness of ordinary epistemic practices. So also does speculative philosophy, as a whole, fail, but in failing, it directs us back to the glue that holds our lives together, the impress of habit and the sustaining embrace of custom. Our desire to see as God sees cannot be satisfied, but as we reach beyond ourselves and fail to come to rest in anything other than our own solitude and isolation, we are chastened. Thus chastened, Humean philosophers "will never be tempted to go beyond common life, so long as they consider the imperfection of those faculties they employ, their narrow reach, and their inaccurate operations" (*E* 162). Reason, properly sensible of its limitations, has the power to cure itself and guide us toward our proper end—living with others in the shared world of connected physical events and morally governed human interaction. In this way, we "make a kind of merit of our ignorance" (*E* 32). The salvation we earn with this merit is deliverance from our isolation and a return to the solidity of everyday affairs. Thus, Hume offers us his governing motto: "Be a philosopher; but, amidst all your philosophy, be still a man" (*E* 9).

Hume provides a sophisticated justification for the fear of difference that animates one pole of the modern critical project. Something deep inside us—custom and habit—closes the gap between who we are and the highest good, a good that involves persons who think and act in the world. Indeed, so crucial is this power for closing the gap that Hume can say that this feature of personal identity, this sentiment of custom and habit, connects us to the highest good. Without the overwhelming force of custom and experience, the true source of stability, the "cement of the universe," we would be isolated and adrift in the world. Without our inner sentiments of habit, we would not be able to enjoy and contribute to common life. This aspect of our personal identities is necessary for us to live as rational, moral, and social agents.

Thus, even as Hume begins with the experience of social isolation and makes feeling the key to his cure of the soul, he endorses an approach to the relation of personal identity to the highest good that is at odds with Rousseau's approach. Hume marks a very different boundary of the logic of we-matter-most humanism. We are not sufficient. Hume sees very clearly that we need the world and its impress on the mind. We need culture and its socializing force. Nonetheless, this exterior force has an indispensable internal aspect. Custom does not alienate; it humanizes. Hume's speculative reflections have taught him that we need the vivacity and actuating power of sentiments that close the gap between our rebellious intellect and the everyday world in which we must live. However we might conceive of the human vocation, however far we may wish to push ourselves and our society to change toward a higher goal or greater ideal, we must never leave behind this sentiment, the impress of life burned into the raw material of our souls. It is the anchor of our humanity, and it is necessary for the highest good.

The Continuity Problem

Hume's cure of the soul appeals to common practices and powerful inner impulses. He closes the gap between who we are—our natural desire for the company of others, our own innate tendency to prefer the real over the ideal, as well as our odd and ambitious desire to transcend life in order to know its first principles and ultimate purposes—and how we ought to live by turning toward the sentiments that grow out of our participation in common life. This turn toward common life is necessarily a turning against the heroic temper we too often feel and obey. We are to repent of overreaching in order to dwell more fully in custom and habit. This philosophical therapy allows Hume to envision our discipline of change as a form of self-affirmation, not in the individualistic sense endorsed by Rousseau, but in a collective sense as persons embedded in a shared, human world. We cure our souls by embracing our common humanity, an embrace rendered effective in the psychic force of sentiment.

Hume's cure seems altogether sensible, but problems emerge. The very force that connects us to life—custom and habit—is the same force that alienates us, for the transcending desire does not come from outside. It emerges from the kinds of persons we are: the odd ways in which our ideas come detached from referents, the heroic temper of our minds, and the infinite variety of social practices that encourage speculation, superstition, and enthusiasm. As Hume notes, the "artificial lives" of the ancient philosopher Diogenes and the modern Jansenist Pascal both "have met with general admiration in their different ages, and have been proposed as models of imitation" (*E* 343). Philosophical and religious ambition are actively commended by our common life, and our own sentiments seem unfailingly attracted to this ambition. Hume knows this very well. After all, he embarked on the foundational project of book 1 of the *Treatise*. He genuinely wanted to know the real "cement of the universe," and he knew that success would win the approbation of his peers. Thus, Hume's cure of the soul seems to take a contradictory form. We must transcend that part of common life that encourages us to transcend, and we must do so by connecting ourselves more closely to common life. We are redeemed *from sentiment*—the heroic temper—*by sentiment*—by everyday habits and experience. Thus, far from affirming our humanity, Hume's cure of the soul seems to set up a conflict within us between the "bad habits" of speculative ambition and the "good habits" of everyday life.

To illustrate the difficulty Hume faces, consider his famous argument against the probative value of miracles. The details are unimportant. Crucial, however, is Hume's characterization of the disciplinary value of these arguments. He is convinced that his analysis of miracles is correct and suggests that it will "be useful as long as the world endures." And why will it be useful for the rest of human history? Because, he reports, "for so long, I presume, will the accounts of miracles and prodigies be found in all history, sacred and profane" (*E* 110). However, he also says that "custom is the great guide of human life" (*E* 44), the very basis for the active, reflective life. Thus a problem emerges. People seem to be in the habit of believing miracles—so much in the habit that Hume cannot imagine a society or cultural practice that does not involve this overreaching. Yet, we must extirpate this custom from our souls. But how? We do so by following the strength of our sentiments, themselves the affective form of custom and habit. How can such a strategy for living bring us back to what is normal, natural, and common in our lives rather than divide us in two?

Hume's treatment of miracles embodies his overall approach to what is best for human beings and our relationship to it. What is noblest about human life is the possibility of cogent thought and prudent action. Philosophical reflection tries to ground this nobility in transcendent knowledge. It cannot do so. Indeed, the ambition to do just that alienates us from what is noblest and best. Priests and prophets wait in the wings to exploit this alienation, generating social practices that intensify and solidify our overreaching impulse. The monk imagines that he is drawing nearer to the source of all goodness and truth the farther he retreats from ordinary life. The Puritan firebrand imagines that a reconstruction of civic life along theocratic principles will bring the populace closer to the revealed truths. In both cases, the general human tendency to overreach is reinforced, and our alienation is deepened. Against both the innate impulse to overreach and the social practices that nurture this tendency, Hume advocates discipline and change. We must extirpate transcending desire and the social practices that buttress and intensify it, even though that desire and those social practices are part of our mental constitution and common life. No wonder Hume thinks his cure of the soul difficult. To eliminate a transcending desire so deeply woven into the fabric of our humanity would seem to require suprahuman effort.[10]

Here, then, is Hume's problem. His commitment to an immanent explanation of human behavior prevents him from ascribing our over-reaching tendency to a "fall" out of the natural order of things. He will have no truck with speculative explanations of our speculative impulse.[11] As a consequence, Hume must allow that the tendency toward superstition and enthusiasm is descriptively "normal." Indeed, his concern rests on an awareness that these tendencies are all too normal. The intensity of his criticism of miracles is directly proportional to the ubiquity of our credulity and our desire to believe. The upshot is a vision of the highest good in which part of our humanity is conquered by another part. Personal identity is divided rather than continuous. We need to be a little bit divine in order to stop wanting to be divine. We must put our shoulder to the effort of recovering the properly human address for life. This effort requires resisting the powerful feelings and habits that lead to overreaching. Hume testifies to his own determination, even to the point of throwing the book and papers that tempt him into the fire. The strength of character necessary to resist overreaching requires transcending discipline. One

---

10. The war of self against self is also evident in Hume's *Natural History of Religion*. Insofar as Hume undertakes a naturalistic explanation of religion, he explains the emergence and development of religion in terms of basic human needs and tendencies. Hume observes that vulgar polytheism and vulgar theism are irrational and inhumane religious practices that stem from human fear and anxiety about unknown causes and an uncertain future. In fact, Hume views superstition as so deeply embedded in human nature that he cannot imagine a popular religion of reason and virtue that would not be twisted back into perennial patterns of irrational and vicious popular piety. "If we should suppose," Hume writes, "that a popular religion were found, in which it was expressly declared, that nothing but morality could gain favour; if an order of priests were instituted to inculcate this opinion, in daily sermons, and with all the arts of persuasion; yet so inveterate are the people's prejudices, that, for want of some other superstition, they would make the very attendance on the sermons the essentials of religion rather than place them in virtue and good morals" (*NHR* 70–71). Surely, then, any attempt to live without superstition entails the ambition to live against the grain of a ubiquitous and powerful human tendency, the ambition, in short, to live against oneself.

11. For an account of Hume's immanent and naturalistic explanation of our speculative impulse, see Livingston, *Philosophical Melancholy and Delirium*, 53–79.

almost needs a heroic temper to resist something so pervasive as the heroic temper.[12]

Hume is aware of this difficulty. He tries to mitigate the resultant intrapersonal conflict by adopting a modest heroism. We do, in fact, need to have the courage to renounce the heroic part of ourselves, but that part is neither attractive nor useful. We will not regret the change. The surgery will improve our lives.

Hume advances this modest heroism in two ways. The first involves dissecting selected social practices. Critical scrutiny, selectively applied, can cure souls. We can come to see that *certain* human practices are unappealing. The second method requires Hume to construct a progressive account of the development of human society. Even if critical renunciations detach us from part of ourselves and part of our social world, Hume reassures us that our modest heroism connects us to the emergent common life of modern society. Progress will repair any breach that our critical discipline and modest heroism creates. Let us look, briefly, at each strategy—critique and progress—for they loom large in latter attempts to make modern humanism seem cogent.

To a great extent, Hume (echoing Rousseau) trusts his own sentiments. He finds superstition and enthusiasm repugnant. "Parties of religion," he writes with uncharacteristic force, "are more furious and enraged than the most cruel factions that ever arose from interest and ambition" (*MPL* 63). He sets out to describe these forms of life with sufficient rhetorical skill to make his readers feel as he does. Not just

---

12. Bertrand Russell represents a twentieth-century tradition that is forthright. Our overreaching ambitions do, indeed, require an equal and opposite ambition. For Russell, like Hume, speculative efforts fail. Close attention to fact, conclusions based on evidence, theory governed by experiment: only these modest approaches will give us good guidance and genuine knowledge. Yet, Russell does preserve a special role for philosophy: "The essential characteristic of philosophy, which makes it a study distinct from science, is criticism" (*The Problems of Philosophy* [Oxford: Oxford University Press, 1959], 149). For Russell, critical thought enlarges our minds: "It removes the somewhat arrogant dogmatism of those who have never travelled into the region of liberating doubt" (157). We should step back from the mean limitations of common opinion and the all-too-natural tendency to remain "shut up with the circle of private interest" and "instinctive wishes" (157–58). The upshot of the step back is an "enlargement of the self." The "free intellect," liberated by the heroic endeavor of critical thought, "will see as God sees . . . without the trammels of customary beliefs and traditional prejudices" (160). With such soaring rhetoric, Russell demonstrates the instability of Hume's critical agenda. The heroic temper reemerges in philosophy, now in a critical, rather than speculative, mode. We will burst the bonds of ordinary humanity by throwing off the fetters of self-interest, prejudice, and dogmatic belief. For the first time, guided by the heroic achievement of critical thought, we will live as men were meant to live. Russell's backsliding into heroic rhetoric raises Hume's problem with clarity. How, exactly, is the Enlarged Self, unfettered from self-interest and free from prejudice, continuous with the ordinary person, who is typically altogether too parochial?

a matter of style, his rhetorical skill rests in Hume's ability to uncover the machinery of life. He shows us the habits of overreaching, and our instincts rebel against them. A great deal of his criticism functions this way. Hume exposes the inner workings of a bad human practice, and his readers recoil. Just as few can endure touring a slaughterhouse without misgivings about the evening menu, so also do Hume's readers find themselves disturbed by the tour he gives of the role of religion in society.[13]

Hume's *Natural History of Religion* is full of artful combinations of psychological and social analysis, innuendo, and mockery. For example, Hume articulates a theory of anthropocentric projection in religion (*NHR* 28). He explains the psychological dynamics by which local deities are elevated to universal status (*NHR* 43–44). The reader is brought to see that the Christian doctrine of the real presence is as absurd as any pagan piety and that a severe Christian monk is as bizarre a figure as a Turk (*NHR* 55–56). Hume suggests that religious faith is always empty and hollow; it has no traction in real life. As a consequence, zealous believers intensify dogmatic commitment and become fanatically intolerant in order to hide, from themselves, the emptiness of their own beliefs (*NHR* 60). In these and many other ways, Hume unveils the foolishness and conceit of religion. No particular claim that Hume makes need be compelling on its own. Hume seeks overall effect. He wishes to demystify traditional religion and inculcate his readers with a jaundiced, critical disposition toward the claims of religious doctrines and authorities.[14]

Hume's rhetorical strategy has proven massively influential. Critique exposes the organs and intestines of life; our sentiments rebel, and we cling to whatever remains hidden. Hume exposes what he dislikes, and he dis-

---

13. In *Religion and Faction in Hume's Moral Philosophy* (Cambridge: Cambridge University Press, 1997), Jennifer A. Herdt makes a strong case for reading Hume's *History of England* as a genealogical exercise designed to unveil the venality and cruelty of religious interests. "The *History of England* is," she observes, "an attempt to increase awareness of the hypocrisy and self-deception of religious belief" (14).

14. One of Hume's contemporaries, Bishop William Warburton, identified the intended purpose of *The Natural History of Religion*. Commenting on the title of Hume's study, Warburton observes, "Would not *The Moral History of Meteors* be as sensible as *The Natural History of Religion?*" ("Remarks on Mr. David Hume's Essay on The Natural History of Religion," *The Works of the Rt. Rev. William Warburton, D.D., Lord Bishop of Gloucester,* vol. 12). Warburton recognized that Hume's approach naturalizes our understanding of that which we are inclined to think of as supernatural. Religion becomes a human, rather than divine, phenomenon. Warburton vigorously rejects both Hume's approach and its consequent deflation of religious beliefs and practices.

likes traditional religion most of all. He keeps that which he cherishes properly veiled in the piety of devotion and loyalty. In this way, Hume shapes his readers to feel as he feels, and with striking success. More than two centuries later, more than just religion falls under the searching lights of social analysis. Vast stretches of culture are exposed as instruments for the preservation of power and status. The charms of literary genius fall before poststructuralist critical theory. Critique breaks bewitching spells, shows the ugly basements and subbasements that support the seemingly beautiful and transcendent architecture of human aspiration.

Hume shows more than ugliness; he also tries to show progress. Not only wanting us to rebel against bad habits, he wishes us to throw our loyalty behind good customs. In his discussion of miracles in the *Enquiry Concerning Human Understanding,* Hume undertakes to uncover the innate sources of credulity, pointing out how pleasant we find "the passion of *surprise* and *wonder,* arising from miracles" (*E* 117). However, this "strong propensity of mankind to the extraordinary and marvellous" (*E* 118) diminishes with the development of more sophisticated cultures. The tendency toward the marvellous recedes "in proportion as we advance nearer the enlightened ages," and even though the inclination toward overreaching in belief "can never be thoroughly extirpated from human nature," at least we can console ourselves that the prevailing customs of civilized society militate against the worst excesses of this tendency (*E* 119). Hume supports this progressive view by providing a sketch of the social conditions for credulity. Lack of extensive communication, uneducated masses, interpretations of social conflict as divine contestation—all these features of the past contribute to the human tendency to overreach. Hume has confidence that the material improvements of modern life alter these conditions, and therefore, the tendency toward belief in miracles is diminishing. Common life is developing away from simpleminded credulity.[15]

---

15. Hume uses the presumption of progress to harmonize his sharp attacks on heroic philosophy and his commendations of certain philosophical habits: "Among the ancients, the heroes in philosophy, as well as those in war and patriotism, have a grandeur and force of sentiment, which astonishes our narrow souls." Of course, we should beware this astonishment, for these heroes "are by far too magnificent for human nature." Our own tendency to overreach might become too warm if our admiration is uncritical. Against such a possibility, the models of the ancient philosophers should "be rejected as extravagant and supernatural." However, Hume thinks that we need not simply reject. We can admire and emulate without danger because "in modern times" the virtues of philosophy have become more generally diffused. The reflective life, properly modest and practical of course, no longer separates one from the commerce of society and the company of worldly men. Even the lawyers of Edinburgh are eager to engage in a little afternoon speculation (*E* 256–57).

Hume's reading of history encourages us to renounce the debilitating excesses of overreaching while remaining confident that our renunciations of the heroic temper do not alienate. The discipline of our soul helps usher in a new regime, a new pattern of custom and habit. By changing, we are keeping up with common life, not isolating ourselves. When we deny our inclination toward the extraordinary, we are not denying an important part of ourselves. We are cutting off the residue of the past and embracing the living vitality of an emergent and modern common life. We are disciplining ourselves to conform to the flow of history.[16]

Rhetorically, Hume's strategies of transcendence work. Since his time, the masters of suspicion have plied their craft, and we often feel impelled to change by the ugliness of what we see. Progress has entered into modernity as an unquestioned dogma and metaphysical principle. We can only be ourselves by changing. In spite of these rhetorical successes, the logical problem remains. Hume, and all those who follow him in the tropes of critique and progress, must give an account of how our identities are continuous across change. Hume must show how the mental habit that desires to see as God sees is connected to our mental habits that have renounced such a desire. He must show how a common life that so willingly embraces miracles and prodigies is connected to a common life that has purged this habit of mind. Hume must show how the person who goes wrong in enthusiasm and superstition is *continuous* with the person who has disciplined herself. To put the matter in the theological terminology that will emerge as decisive, Hume must show how we can be "at-one" across change.

Hume never establishes continuity. He cannot explain how the heroic philosopher renounces his transcending impulse without

---

16. Hume's contemporary Samuel Johnson offers less sanguine observations about the personal and social costs of progress. His *Journey to the Western Islands of Scotland* is full of apposite remarks about the disjunctions and discontinuities imposed upon the Scottish Highlands by English policies of pacification, as well as by modern economic changes. The ban of tartan was emblematic of the English determination to break the bonds of clan loyalty. The nascent manufacturing economy encouraged migration that depopulated the Highlands. Johnson does not take a reactionary attitude toward these changes. Later romantics will idealize the grinding poverty and rigid hierarchies of premodern society. Johnson, however, was too close to the world being eclipsed, both in time and personal experience, to regret its passing. Nonetheless, Johnson is less smug and cheery than Hume. Modernity may be very good for Edinburgh and its lawyers and people of commerce, but for many, the torn fabric of ancient habit and custom is never mended. In seeing that not everyone had the psychic or material resources for the careful adjustments in light of change, Johnson's humanism, more antique and Christian than modern and progressive, shines through. Johnson saw that the rustic men and women of the backwoods were led as lambs to the slaughter.

renouncing some significant part of himself. The genealogical efforts require either speculative judgments that certain features of common life are not properly human or the aesthetic judgment that what is ugly is not human, or they fall back to Rousseau's position in which the genealogies just reflect Hume's purely personal sentiment, his dislike of clerics and monks. The first is blocked by Hume's commitment to descriptive philosophy, the second is radically implausible, and the third, as we have seen, cannot give an account of morally meaningful change. Hume's account of progress is also unsatisfactory. To promise that the world will embrace the new, modest heroism of common sense and critical thought in no way shows continuity of personal identity. Wanting does not make it so. Thus, the genealogical and progressive rhetoric may ease the minds of readers, especially those already inclined to agree with Hume, but it does not solve the problem of continuous personal identity across the disciplines and renunciations necessary for change.

In the end, Hume cannot explain how his cure of the soul rests in the proposition that we are necessary for the highest good. *Part* of us is necessary, but another part is positively antithetical. Sentiments that attach us to everyday life should be affirmed, but sentiments that lead toward heroic overreaching must be denied. Therefore, instead of advancing a modest humanism concerned about the pervasive tendency to rend and tear at the fabric of human life, Hume reproduces the patterns of overreaching that he intends to criticize and restrain.[17]

---

17. For a close textual assessment of the difficulties facing Hume's cure of the soul, see Herdt, *Religion and Faction in Hume's Moral Philosophy*, 117–67. Herdt tracks the contradictory ways in which Hume seeks to both expand and constrain our sympathy for different ways of life. Her conclusion is telling: "His appeal to 'natural boundaries' of vice and virtue and to the regularity with which the natural principles of the mind play when left to themselves seems to lapse into a more substantial view of universal human nature, something which can be invoked in order to exclude certain things from the task of understanding, rather than as an assumption which guides interpretation along inclusive lines" (166). In other words, a speculative artifact—universal human nature—intervenes to show that "common life" is not necessarily what is commonly thought and done. Sentiment must be constrained and tutored by something other than sentiment.

Herdt's attempt to relax this difficulty involves trying to force Hume toward self-consistency. She exhorts her readers to refrain from Hume's judgmental dismissal of religious believers as superstitious bigots and dangerous enthusiasts. In her view, religion is just as much a part of common life as any other human impulse and practice. However, such an exhortation only compounds the problem Hume faces, for how can human beings, with moral interests and passions, adopt an "inclusive sympathetic understanding" of others without deeply disciplining those moral interests and passions? Only intensive and transformative socialization can create persons capable (or imagining themselves capable) of such a dramatic step back from judgment and disapprobation. What, exactly, is the power that effects such a change? After all, judgment and disapprobation are part of our humanity. Should we, then, enter into the paradox of denying ourselves (our judgmental tendencies that are so common and widespread among all human beings) in order to affirm our common humanity?

He takes a scalpel to the heroic impulse, and he cannot explain how such surgery serves, rather than bifurcates, our identities as persons. In this way, Hume anticipates the fate of the tradition of modern humanism that seeks to guard and protect our humanity. He either reverts to an overreaching funded by a presupposed universal theory of human nature (Auguste Comte), or he imposes the vagaries of his own sentiment (Friedrich Nietzsche), or he endorses change as a necessary fact (G. W. F. Hegel).

The Problem of Transformative Desire

Rousseau's redemptive project drives the problem of change out and onto society. He was perfect; everybody else conspired against him. Our transformative desire is, finally, a form of false consciousness, an echo of social convention, a consequence of *amor propre*. He may seem petty and bitter, but Rousseau's brilliance and achievement rest in his willingness to endure these negative impressions in order to remain fully and completely connected to the one thing sufficient for nobility and goodness—himself. In contrast, Hume seems far more normal, far more sane and appealing as a person. He made a mistake. He thought that he could find a way to live that depended only on the truths his mind could prove. But he failed, and in his honesty, he acknowledged that failure. Falling back upon the essential health of his soul, he returned to the common way of living. He disciplined himself to renounce the vanity of philosophical superiority, and he commends this path to us as well. We, like him, should repent of overreaching. Such a humanism may seem normal and sane, but it is not cogent, for Hume cannot account for the continuity of personal identity in this repentance.

Here, then, is our problem. Rousseau offers a self-consistent account of the horror of dependence, keyed to the unique dignity of each individual. He is able to motivate the prejudice against authoritarianism, but only at the cost of stripping that prejudice of moral significance. We are who we are, and that is enough. Any rebellion against dogma and social constraint reflects no more than the peculiar elements of one's individuality. It is just that person's way of being true to himself. Hume, in contrast, preserves the disciplinary logic of morally motivated criticism. Hume is able to provide winsome descriptions of a cure of the soul that avoids overreaching and stays connected to everyday life, but he cannot give a coherent account of moral change. The sentiments of transcendence war against the sentiments of common sense.

The soul is divided by critical discipline, with the desire for transcendence separated from the habits of everyday life. One sentiment must subdue another, but he cannot show how this discipline of one part of our identities by another can produce a form of life in which both parts are united. In this puritanism of common life, our identities as persons are not necessary for the highest good; only a part is necessary. The other part must be cut away. Therefore, we-matter-most humanism seems caught between Rousseau's implausible consistency and Hume's plausible incoherence.

Rousseau and Hume do not exhaust the humanistic agenda. Few are as relentless as Rousseau in reducing the project of living well to simple self-acceptance. Few are as pessimistic as Hume about our innate tendency to overreach. Most critics of authoritarianism and overreaching simply assume a moral justification for proposed reforms. They move forward in the strength of their convictions, confident that the morally charged atmosphere of critical demands for change can affirm the consequentiality and continuity of personal identity. We need to free people from the illusion that dependence is necessary for what is noblest and best. What could be more obvious? We should debunk zany schemes of salvation and reprimand credulous belief in miracles. Who could think otherwise? We need to restrain people from reaching beyond the realm of ordinary life. How could our humanity be served by something beyond ourselves? Thus does modern humanism preserve its animating moral prejudices. The horror of dependence and fear of difference are simply obvious and self-evident.

What is obvious is not always self-consistent, and as the prejudices of modern humanism seek theoretical justification, two approaches predominate. Against Rousseau, humanists internalize the gap by adopting a morally pointed distinction between the real identity of persons and socially constructed identity. The imperative "You must be true to yourself!" takes on normative significance. Authentic life has a certain shape, a determinate set of criteria, a visible form. It involves denouncing suburbia, condemning career for career's sake, worrying about whether or not one is still in love with one's spouse. Or, in more domesticated forms, it means shopping at the local independent bookstore rather than Barnes and Noble, patronizing the local potter rather than Pier One, and picking out one's own rugs and furniture rather than hiring an interior decorator. In any event, against this normative background, authenticity is not purely personal. Change makes sense because being a certain kind of person, *an authentic per-*

son, is sufficient for the highest good. There is a very good chance that neither I nor you are that kind of person, at least not yet. So, we change in order to become ourselves, our true selves.

To provide a cogent account of continuity, humanists take the opposite tack with Hume. They externalize the causes of overreaching. We tend toward superstition and enthusiasm, they claim, because a perverse social conditioning has distorted our essentially healthy mental organs. We have fallen victim to priestcraft and are manipulated by propagandists. If only our minds were not infected with the virus of faith passed on by nuns at the local Catholic school . . . Children would grow up into responsible natural scientists just as acorns grow into oak trees if only the debilitating poisons of false promises and threats of eternal punishment did not interfere. We are continuous in the transition from credulity to critical thought because our credulity was always artificially imposed. To renounce overreaching, then, does not require us to renounce anything about ourselves. To renounce overreaching simply involves putting off the false consciousness imposed from without in order to embrace the common sense and the experimental method encoded in our genes.[18]

Insofar as modern humanism sustains the moral prejudices against authoritarianism and overreaching with these two approaches, it does so by shouting "Rousseau" while whispering "Hume," or by shouting "Hume" while whispering "Rousseau."[19] Against the amoralism of a

---

18. I draw these formulations from the tract by evolutionary biologist Richard Dawkins, "Viruses of the Mind," in *Dennet and His Critics* (ed. Bo Dahlbom; Oxford: Blackwell, 1993), 13–27. Dawkins's use of the technological-medical rhetoric of "viruses" signals a classic modernist strategy. What is descriptively ubiquitous is redescribed as "abnormal" because it is "unhealthy" and "unnatural." Of course, Dawkins cannot assert what his rhetoric implies. As every evolutionary biologist knows, whatever obtains for a species, however debilitating and disadvantageous to species survival, is by definition natural. This must be so; otherwise, extinction could only be regarded as unnatural, and such an admission makes evolutionary theory absurd. Therefore, if Dawkins's use of "virus" is anything more than a rhetorical expression of his personal distaste for faith, it can only be a metaphysical statement about what inhibits the proper function of the mind. The antecedent hardly counts as a rational criticism of faith, and the consequent entails a normative view of proper species function that is an altogether scandalous transgression of the discipline of evolutionary biology.

19. Consider the clear examples of authoritarian criticisms of authority and overreaching criticisms of overreaching in Martha Nussbaum's propaganda for "progressive" higher education, *Cultivating Humanity: A Classical Defense of Reform in Liberal Education* (Cambridge: Harvard University Press, 1997). "All too often," Nussbaum reports, "people's choices and statements are not their own" (28), and the goal of education should produce students "who can think for themselves rather than simply deferring to authority" (10). She commends appropriate pedagogical methods of critique, shock, and challenge. Students should be forced to step back from their

fully consistent commitment to the principle that we are sufficient for the highest good, the patron of individuality insists that authenticity requires discipline and change. We must become ourselves through careful recrafting of our identities. In this way, the Rousseauian moralizes the existential tautology "Be yourself!" Against the incoherence of a program of reform based on the principle that we are necessary for the highest good, the patron of solidarity denies that overreaching is our fault. The gap is shifted out of personal identity. This approach allows the critic to advocate change, but only because a speculative insight has been achieved. Somehow, the critic has entered into the soul and separated the real, underlying natural me from the false, socially constructed me. In this way, the critic reassures us. The heroic temper is an unnatural and cancerous growth, not a vital organ. We should welcome the surgery. In this way, the Humean demoralizes the fact that human beings want very much to be otherwise than themselves. The problem is medical—a matter of viruses and cancers—and not moral.

Both strategies are forms of logical sausage making. To moralize authenticity entails backsliding into a modernist form of authoritarianism. The free and pure have consigned countless souls to the flames of inauthenticity. Modernity has nurtured a remarkable literature of denunciation. Jean-Paul Sartre can match any cardinal of the Spanish Inquisition for dogmatic confidence and ruthless judgment of others. Frothing with therapeutic language, the modern priests of self-realization put demands upon us: "You must overcome your tendency to feel guilty. Self-acceptance is a much healthier attitude. You really need

---

beliefs. The authority of the teacher and the power of the institution should be applied to prevent narrow-minded, dogmatic students from remaining who they are. And toward what end is this discipline applied? Nussbaum bows to ideals of self-realization, but she is honest enough to recognize that her vision of education will not permit dogmatic personalities to realize themselves as dogmatists. In the end, the educational system must shape students to meet "the altered requirements of citizenship" (6). Education should produce "citizens of [the] entire world" (7). The implausibility of humanistic overreaching rarely appears with such clarity. Teachers are to force their students to take a step back from inherited beliefs and practices—the very forms by which human beings are bonded together in solidarity—in order to create a new community, a global community. This dream of reason makes the faith of the Mormons of Brigham Young University—an institution Nussbaum finds deeply regrettable—seem worldly indeed. And Nussbaum's overreaching tends toward just the fanaticism and quietism that humanistic critics fear. Fanaticism: Hell hath no fury greater than the pedagogue whose students refuse to renounce inherited beliefs and take the "larger perspective." Quietism: The "world citizens" produced by elite American universities are the ideologically self-confident bureaucrats and sales managers of the American *Imperium*.

to work on this." In this and many other ways, a moralized agenda of self-affirmation can motivate change. Indeed, it can lash us forward with as much urgency as any project of salvation. However, it cannot claim to be humanism, at least not a humanism that treats personal identity as supremely consequential for the highest good. Instead, such a pseudohumanism treats our personal identities as raw material for the highest good. Such a cure of the soul contradicts rather than champions Rousseau's humanism of self-sufficiency.

To introduce a speculative theory of human nature into Hume's approach does not produce contradiction. Instead, it depends upon implausible assumptions. By what flash of insight can we discern that our heroic temper is a feature of our lives that should be cut away with the sharp instruments of critical philosophy, genealogical studies, and Whig histories? We are embedded in common life; yet, somehow, we are not embedded in ubiquitous practices of overreaching? Such a miracle stretches credulity. And the facts speak against such a miracle. Fantasy and wishful thinking remain a widespread feature of common life. Salesmen depend upon this seemingly inextirpable habit; lotteries exploit it. But critics soldier on, confident that they are liberating our humanity from an imprisoning cage of irrationality. The contemporary university is full of such servants of sober reason and critical thinking, ready to disabuse students of their prejudices, unmask their beliefs, show their moral habits to be elaborate systems of taboo. These critics are utterly innocent of the thought that a person might regard the loss of an ideal, however removed from ordinary life, more seriously than the loss of his or her hand. The critics imagine themselves servants of humanity, and they avert their eyes from the disciplinary overreaching of their approaches with the following inference: if something is not rational, then it is not human. Only an ideologue, deeply committed to the logic of we-matter-most humanism, can affirm such a counterfactual belief.

The affirmation that personal identity is both consequential for and continuous in the highest good turns out to be difficult to sustain, and wanting modern humanism to be a coherent critical project does not make it so. Some account must be given of how personal identity is both consequential for and continuous in the highest good, and in such a way that moral change makes sense. Otherwise, it is difficult to see how our individuality is affirmed rather than sacrificed, our humanity sustained rather than abrogated, in the quest for morally meaningful change. Immanuel Kant provides such an account. Kant links Rousseau's concerns about self-sufficiency with Hume's worry about staying connected with common life. Kant wishes to show how righteousness is only possible on the basis of a freedom that is utterly dependent upon the individual, and he intends that same righteousness to fulfill, rather than abrogate, our lives. Unlike Rousseau, Kant will not externalize the gap between who we are and how we ought to live. The gap is, finally, our fault. Unlike Hume, Kant will directly confront the difficulty of accounting for the continuity of personal identity. He will insist that we must join rather than divide the soul across moral change. His humanistic project, in short, wishes to vindicate our transformative desire by providing an account of change in which personal identity is both necessary and sufficient.

–Chapter 4–

VINDICATING CHANGE

If reality is not redemptive, it is not moral.
—P. T. FORSYTHE, *THE PRINCIPLE OF AUTHORITY*

Kant's humanistic ambition is direct: we need to change, and in such a way that we matter most. To realize this ambition, Kant must provide a cogent account of the two moral prejudices that animate modern humanism: the horror of dependence and the fear of difference. From Rousseau, Kant adopts the conviction that we rightly rebel against the diminishments caused by dogmatic authority. With Hume, Kant insists that we are justified in our critical efforts to restrain various forms of overreaching that lead to superstition and enthusiasm. Our revulsion against the dependence that makes us pawns of larger powers is legitimate, and our rejection of supernatural beliefs and ascetical practices expresses a proper concern about the integrity of our merely human lives. Both critical concerns are, for Kant, justified. Yet, against Rousseau and Hume, Kant intends to show that neither the horror of dependence nor fear of difference rules out dramatic personal change. At every turn our concern for change must be vindicated, rather than systematically renounced (Rousseau) or carefully managed (Hume), and vindicated in such a way that our identities as persons are consequential and continuous.[1]

---

1. I caution the reader that I do not intend these remarks as a causal explanation of Kant's account of human destiny, as if he read Rousseau and Hume with precisely these thoughts in mind. Kant's interest in Rousseau is well documented. A portrait of Rousseau was the only decoration in Kant's study, and his regular routine was famously broken only by the arrival of Rousseau's *Émile*. Kant's indebtedness to Hume is evident as well. He credits Hume with waking him from his precritical "dogmatic slumbers." Nonetheless, to trace the influences of Rousseau and Hume on Kant would be to undertake an exercise in the history of ideas, and this

This affirmation of our desire for change is necessary not just theoretically but practically, for the modern dissatisfaction with inherited forms of life is extraordinarily powerful. Both Rousseau and
Hume testify that our ordinary sense of self is heavily invested in dogmatic certainties and supernatural aspiration. Motivated by a horror
of dependence and fear of difference, a thoroughgoing renunciation
of traditional life undermines the stability of inherited social forms
that provide the underlying stability for our lives. Rousseau's efforts
to live outside the oppressive conventions of polite society contributed
to his mental instability. Hume's criticisms of miracles put him at odds
with the traditionally Christian aspects of the common life that he
affirmed as the basis of a stable intellectual and moral outlook.
Against this instability, Kant wants to bring order and purpose to the
inevitable changes wrought by the prejudices of modern humanism.
We should reorder personal and public life toward the highest good.
Kant never backs away from the intense desire for change that animates modern humanism. Yet, we must change in a fashion that reinforces our dignity and integrity as persons. We should change in such
a way that our identities as persons remain consequential and continuous, or to use the heuristic device of we-matter-most humanism,
according to principles of criticism and programs of reform in which
personal identity is necessary and sufficient for the highest good.

The long march through Rousseau and Hume has produced two
important results. A Rousseauian commitment to the sufficiency of
our individuality seems to drive change out of the moral universe. A
Humean commitment to the necessity of our common humanity
seems unable to encourage significant personal change without setting us against ourselves. In both cases, the transformative desire that
makes the two poles of criticism so urgent lacks a clear rational basis.
For Rousseau, that zeal has no moral motivation. For Hume, the zeal
curves back upon our common humanity in a paradoxical heroic
denial of heroic ambition. In neither figure does the full moral purpose of modern humanism find cogent support. Kant's goal is to give
precisely this support. He wishes to make sense of the moral project
of modernity. Here, my critical interests are obvious. Can Kant remain
loyal to the logic of we-matter-most humanism and escape the diffi-

is outside my competence. Therefore, I use Rousseau and Hume to illuminate the conceptual
issues at stake in Kant's moral vision rather than to identify specific contributions of either figure to Kant's project.

culties that afflict Rousseau's and Hume's cures of the soul? Can he give cogent support to the critical dynamism of modern humanism? Can he articulate a conception of the highest good that makes sense of this desire for change and, at the same time, confirms that we matter most for the highest good? Can he give an account of morally meaningful change in which our identities as persons are supremely consequential and continuous?

Kant's answers to these questions require patient development. They require us to understand his cure of the soul. I divide this task into two parts. First, we need to understand Kant's explanation of why we should want to change. To do so, we must gain some clarity about the nature and origin of the gap between who we are and how we ought to live, for it is in closing this gap that personal identity is so decisively consequential, and across this gap personal identity must be continuous. Once the terrain of moral engagement is established, we can turn to the actual drama of moral change. It must be fundamental and dramatic moral change that cuts to the quick of who we are, and in that change, we must be necessary and sufficient. This chapter focuses on establishing the exact nature of the gap; the next chapter charts the humanistic logic of Kant's story of moral change.

Under the first heading of this chapter, "Wanting to Be Different," I survey Kant's rejection of speculative metaphysics and eudaemonistic ethics, which reduce to forms of self-expression and self-discovery rather than self-wrought change. Neither can give theoretical form to our basic desire to live differently. Both are essentially stationary conceptions of human destiny, and neither can serve as the theoretical background for a story of deeply personal and morally significant change. The potency of philosophical insight and moral obligation must be dynamic and transformative, not static and confirmatory.

Under the second heading, "Moral Faith," I sketch the basic structure of Kant's moral vision, a vision in which Kant explicates what must be true about the highest good, ourselves, and the cosmos such that personal identity is necessary and sufficient. The key concept is the freedom that produces dynamism for change. The power of self-command allows us to realize a good will within ourselves by choosing duty for its own sake, and this power, far from a threat to who we are, serves as the anchor of personal identity. Thus, freedom is both the basis of personal identity, the "substance" that constitutes persons, and the necessary and sufficient condition for what is best. Not surprisingly, then, Kant proclaims that the concept of freedom "is the keystone of the whole architecture of the system of pure reason and even of speculative reason." [2] Indeed, the determination of both personal identity and the highest good through the concept of freedom gives "stability and objective reality" to the entire sweep of humanistic faith.[3] To shift from the *I am* of Rousseau to a dynamic *I can* allows Kant to vindicate the *I ought* that drives our desire for moral change. This provides a theoretical background against which Kant can tell his humanistic story of redemptive change. To the crucial notion of freedom, Kant adds God and immortality. These postulates ensure the continuity of personal identity across the changes wrought by freedom.

Finally, under the third heading, "Three False Views of Evil," I begin an extended examination of Kant's classic work in philosophy of religion, *Religion within the Boundaries of Mere Reason*. There, Kant describes the conditions under which morally meaningful change is both necessary and possible. That story of change must assume a doctrine of radical evil, which serves as a very powerful theoretical and existential explanation of why we need to change, and it marks the point of closest contact between the Christian view of redemptive change and Kant's version of modern humanism. Only after we see why change is necessary can I turn, in chapter 5, to a close analysis of Kant's story of how we do, in fact, change. In this account, Kant is at odds with Christianity. In the next chapter, I shall do more than show divergence. I wish to expose modern humanism's failure to affirm both consequential and continuous personal identity. The strict logic of we-matter-most humanism, a logic that Kant affirms far more clearly and directly than either Rousseau or Hume, leads to self-contradiction. Kant cannot affirm that we are both supremely consequential for the highest good and, at the same time, continuous persons across the moral transformations mandated by modern humanism.

My claim will be that this self-contradiction in Kant's story of the soul is not an isolated logical failure. It epitomizes the most painful failures of modernity—its assault upon the continuity of persons, its irreparable disjunctions and violent discontinuities, its torn tunic of

---

2. Immanuel Kant, *Critique of Practical Reason* (trans. Lewis White Beck; Indianapolis: Bobbs-Merrill, 1956), 3; Ak, 5:4. All further citations will be drawn from this translation, unless otherwise noted, and will be abbreviated *CPrR*. I will provide page numbers from this edition and also add the volume and page of the Akademie (Ak) edition.

3. *CPrR*, 3.

memory, in short, its inability to describe hoped-for moral change in which we can be "at-one" with the future we seek. But this is to parade conclusions before arguments. Let us turn to Kant and allow him to guide us toward a rigorous understanding of the role of personal identity in modern humanism, both as the theoretical condition for a morally charged imperative for change and as the fundamental logical constraint upon a humanistic cure of the soul.

Wanting to Be Different

Kant inherits two traditions of thought that seek to explain the proper basis for human dynamism. The first is rationalist, and the second is eudaemonist. Kant's rejection of both testifies to the centrality of transformative desire in Kant's philosophy. The details of Kant's arguments are not crucial. Instead, we need to survey the broadest outlines of Kant's analysis to see how both rationalism and eudaemonism fail to do justice to the human lean toward change. If we understand the central role of transformative desire in Kant's overall project, then we can see more clearly the importance of change in his cure of the soul and the high standards he raises for the success of his own redemptive project.

Speculative Self-Discovery

The metaphysical systems that characterize rationalism are diverse, but their basic answer to the question of change is simple. Reason has the ability to attain supersensible knowledge, and by virtue of our status as rational creatures, we participate in that power. Therefore, we possess the ability to transcend the constraints of ordinary life and dwell, through transcendent truths, in a fundamentally different realm. The engine of transcendence rests in our cognitive potency toward eternal truths. The precise mechanisms of rational transcendence are irrelevant. One might adopt a Platonic emphasis on contemplative insight or an Aristotelian emphasis on syllogism and inference. In spite of these differences, for the rationalist tradition, broadly conceived, the desire for something different is woven into the fabric of our cognitive powers. Change is both possible and humane because it flows from the innate dynamism of the human intellect. Transcendent knowledge, moral righteousness, and religious faith are properly human aspirations because our mental potency as rational creatures extends to include these possibilities. Our cognitive identities stretch upwards to include something greater.

Kant's critique of this rationalist tradition is telling. Like Hume, Kant thinks that the heroic ambition of speculative thought is futile. Far from an adventure beyond ordinary life, the speculative project curves back into the way things already are. Our habit is to assume that our ideas are connected to a world of objects, so we postulate the reality of substance as the power that binds them together. Our custom is to treat our conscious existence as continuous through time, so we assume that our lives are grounded in an underlying soul. We treat the world as intelligible, so we conceive of it as stemming from an intelligent cause, a supreme being. For Kant, critical philosophy recognizes that these concepts are conditions for the possibility of knowledge. That is to say, they express the structure of our thought, the ligaments and tendons of epistemic practice, giving metaphysical form to our mental stance in the world. As such, the upshot of speculative ventures, however well dressed in the finery of metaphysical concepts, confirms and reiterates who we are rather than secures a basis for change. What we take to be transcendent knowledge—our notions of God, substance, and soul—is simply a conceptual echo of the way we ordinarily think.

By analyzing speculative philosophy in this way, Kant eliminates the possibility of transformative knowledge. Metaphysics expresses who we are rather than provides leverage for transcendence. No matter how ambitious our efforts, the results of speculative inquiry cannot satisfy the hunger for change that fuels speculative desire and motivates the heroic impulse. As a result, the project of deploying the powers of the mind with ever greater effort cannot be the basis for change. We might know who we are in the sense of knowing the conditions for the possibility of thinking; however, we cannot know who we might become. We cannot stretch to forms of knowledge fundamentally different from our current way of being in the world. Speculative knowledge is, then, a form of self-discovery disguised as self-transcendence, and far from the engine of change, it pours the concrete of metaphysical rhetoric into the molds of everyday life.

For Kant, the impotence of speculative thought is not innocent. It leaves us vulnerable to fanatical commitments. In his preface to the second edition of the *Critique of Pure Reason,* Kant observes, "So far are the students of metaphysics from exhibiting any kind of unanimity in their contentions, that metaphysics has rather to be regarded as a battle-ground quite peculiarly suited for those who desire to exercise themselves in mock combats, in which no participant has yet succeeded in gaining even so much as an inch of territory, not at least in such a manner as to secure him in its permanent possession."[4] The inability of metaphysics to produce arguments with sufficient rational force to generate consensus shows, continues Kant, "beyond all questioning, that the procedure of metaphysics has hitherto been a merely random groping, and, what is worst of all, a groping among mere concepts" (*CPR* Bxv). This failure, however, is not the end of the story. Empty concepts are raw material for propaganda and irrational assertion. Because concepts without intuitions are empty, they may be filled with the content of prejudice and the supernatural claims of religion. In this way, the vain groping of speculative thought and the mock combat of the philosophical schools mirror the equally vain but tragically real combat of cynical manipulators of opinion and crusading true believers.

Our souls are restless, and the failure of the rationalist project breeds illusion and violence rather than sober modesty. "The natural consequence," writes Kant of inconclusive speculative inquiry, "is that if reason will not subject itself to laws it gives to itself, it has to bow under the yokes given by another."[5] The horror of a vacuum operates as a law of the soul. We are unsatisfied by the ways in which rationalism disguises our current epistemic practices with the trappings of transcendent knowledge, as if the dignity of the concepts were sufficient to transfigure their reality. Disappointed by speculation, our transformative desire seeks a basis for dramatic change, whether or not we can find a rational basis. Because this transformative desire is so fundamental to who we are, at a certain point, we will take orders from any quarter that promises redemptive change. Unable to bend the mental logic of self-discovery into self-transcendence—we cannot know more about "substance" or "supreme being" than the role these

---

4. Immanuel Kant, *Critique of Pure Reason* (trans. Norman Kemp Smith; New York: St. Martin's, n.d.), Bxv. All further citations are drawn from this translation and will be abbreviated *CPR*. Page numbers, however, will not follow the English. They follow the pagination of the Akademie edition (present in the margins of most translations). I conform to the standard citation method in which A signifies the first edition; B signifies the second.

5. Immanuel Kant, "What Does It Mean to Orient Oneself in Thinking?" included in *Religion within the Boundaries of Mere Reason and Other Writings* (trans. and ed. Allen Wood and George di Giovanni; Cambridge: Cambridge University Press, 1998), abbreviated *R*, with the Akademie citation following (*R* 12, Ak 8:145).

concepts play in the way we already think—we overreach; we pledge ourselves to occult and suprarational powers that hold out promises of genuine transcendence.

Kant directly follows Hume's analysis as he charts the two tendencies that stem from our unsated appetite for transcendent knowledge. "First," says Kant, "genius is very well pleased with its bold flights, since it has cast off the thread by which reason used to steer it" (*R* 13, Ak 8:145). Not able to navigate beyond common life by rational principles, our zeal for change leads us to follow the inner promptings of feeling. "We common human beings," writes Kant, "call this **enthusiasm**" (*R* 13, Ak 8:145). Kant thinks this rash subjectivism is merely episodic and fated to fall into a "confusion of language" that cannot be sustained. Blind spontaneity leads everywhere and nowhere, and as a consequence, "inner aspirations must ultimately be seen to arise from the testimony of preserved facts" (*R* 13, Ak 8:145). Our desire for change seeks a polestar that the flux of inspiration cannot provide, so we gravitate toward a fixed system of dogmas and rituals. Following Hume, Kant sees this satisfaction of transformative desire as a capitulation of reason to external authority. It is, to use Kant's description, "the complete subjugation of reason to facts, i.e., **superstition**" (*R* 13, Ak 8:145). The dictates of a supernatural authority, the sheer fact of "thus says the Lord," may violate our intellectual consciences and override our moral sensibilities, but at least such an authority drives us toward change, and this attracts our loyalty. Thus does rationalism lead, through its inevitable failure, to the very overreaching and authoritarian diminishments of human dignity that it seeks to escape.

Although Kant follows Hume's analysis of the inevitable failure of speculative thought and the perverse consequences of heroic ambition unfulfilled, he does not adopt a Humean cure of the soul. Kant considers the Humean strategy of life grounded in the stabilizing forces of habit, but he cannot affirm Hume's turn away from heroic ambition, no matter how well decorated it is with elegant argument and humane sentiment. Kant's critical injunctions against the speculative project do discipline our heroic ambition, just as Hume imagines that his own story of speculative disorientation will chasten readers of the *Treatise*. Nonetheless, we cannot overcome our vulnerability to enthusiasm and superstition by renouncing our impulse toward change. We cannot but take an interest in something beyond ourselves; the zeal for change is a living force within human beings. "Human reason," writes Kant in the opening sentence of the *Critique of Pure Reason,* "has this peculiar fate that in one species of its knowledge it is burdened by questions which, as prescribed by the very nature of reason itself, it is not able to ignore, but which, as transcending all its powers, it is also not able to answer" (Avii). We thrust against the boundaries of our identities, and insofar as reason is implicated in our impulse toward change, our thinking presses beyond its proper bounds. Even though speculative metaphysics cannot deliver us from this inner contradiction, for Kant, we cannot pretend that our heroic ambitions can or should be rejected as foolish or unnecessary. "It is idle," he writes, "to feign indifference to [metaphysical] enquiries, the object of which can never be indifferent to our human nature" (*CPR* Ax). To be human is to want to be more than one is. As a result, Kant is unwilling to take Hume's approach of trying to minimize heroic ambition through careful rhetorical management.[6]

For Kant, a proper renunciation of ambition applies only to the forms of rationalism that characterize classical metaphysics. "The loss," he writes, "effects only the *monopoly of the schools*" (*CPR* Bxxxii). The speculative path toward personal change is blocked, but, as Kant conceives it, this diminishes "in no respects the *interests of humanity*" (*CPR* Bxxxii). Here, the "interests of humanity" rest in a vindication of our restlessness and the consequent desire to find some footing for changing ourselves and the world. Once the deceptions of the speculative use of concepts are recognized, "immediately we are convinced that there is an absolutely necessary *practical* employment of pure reason—the *moral*—in which it inevitably goes beyond the limits of sensibility" (*CPR* Bxxv). The humanistic project of going beyond the constraints of common life by reforming society, morality, and spiritual life is legitimate and, once freed from the false promises of speculative justification, finds its proper basis. "I have therefore found it necessary to deny knowledge," Kant famously writes in his second preface to the *Critique of Pure Reason,* clarifying the constructive intent of his project, "in order to make room for faith" (Bxxx). We must renounce the speculative project so that our heroic impulse can find its proper expression in the transformative potency of a moral faith. Change does not stem from our quest for knowledge;

---

6. For an account of Kant's commitment to the human desire for transcendence, to which this account of the import of Kant's critique of speculative philosophy is indebted, see James Collins, *The Emergence of Philosophy of Religion* (New Haven: Yale University Press, 1967), 89–128.

it is bound with our desire for righteousness. In this way, the heroic ambition to go "beyond the limits of sensibility" remains, for Kant, an essential and fundamental feature of our intrinsic dignity as persons. Vindicating this ambition, now recognized as moral and not speculative, is the true vocation of philosophy.

Morality and Self-Love

When Kant turns from the speculative project to our understanding of moral obligation, he remains fiercely opposed to any view of the highest good that covertly confirms, rather than changes, our lives. We must not allow ourselves to become ensnared in a moral vision that parallels the illusions and failures of speculative thought. Moral obligation must drive us toward a new way of being. The felt "ought" must be transformative. Thus, in the realm of morality, Kant guards against a normative version of the rationalist solution to the problem of change.

One of the prevailing approaches to morality is eudaemonism. This approach invests human desire, in general, with the dynamism toward change. Our lives are filled with harms and hurts, and our natural desire for pleasure and comfort propels us forward. We are intelligent creatures, and our intelligence is shaped and stimulated by our desire to avoid pain. We reach into the fire to pull out the cooked food, and our fingers are burned. The next time, we use a stick. Of course, explanations of change need not be so simplistic. Psychological theories of moral formation may predicate a natural, inborn set of moral sentiments. Good behavior gives satisfaction, and bad behavior creates feelings of failure and shame. Moral development occurs, then, as a complex interplay of innate desire and social reinforcement. In still another approach, moral theorists might assign fundamental significance to a basic, amoral human need for social belonging. Moral development is, then, a self-motivated project for fitting into society. It is not so much that we naturally want to do our duty; rather, we want to be thought of as the kinds of people who do our duty. Across the many differing theories that privilege a variety of passions and desires, sometimes noble, sometimes base, the same solution obtains for the problem of change. We are restless creatures, always looking for a way to find fuller and more certain satisfactions for our tireless wants. Like water that always finds a way to run downhill, our identities as persons have a fall line. No matter how circuitous or multifaceted the path, we stretch toward satisfaction of our desires.

Kant advances a number of arguments against eudaemonism, but for our purposes, the crucial claim is that all moral reasoning based on the satisfaction of desire reduces to self-love. "All material practical principles"—by which Kant means all principles of moral action that depend upon some empirical fact about human desire and its fulfillment—"are, as such, of one and the same kind and belong under the general principle of self-love or one's own happiness" (*CPrR* 20, Ak 5:22). Defined this way, self-love is not merely an impulse toward self-preservation or tendency toward self-regard; it is an existential stance or moral framework in which the highest good remains enclosed within the magic circle of ordinary humanity. No matter how selfless the prudent man might be in practice, his moral horizon is defined in theory by the limits of our current ways of understanding, assessing, and living in the world. The consequence is a renunciation of fundamental change. The facts of life define the goal of moral striving, not the ideal of righteousness. Like rationalism, which satisfies our heroic ambition with conceptual echoes of mental habit and ordinary epistemic practice, eudaemonism curves us back into our particular ways of living in the world. Considerations based on human needs and desires might counsel any number of adjustments and modifications, but it always navigates in the enclosed sea of innate human desires. Prudence does not venture into the open ocean of fundamentally new possibilities.

Against eudaemonism, Kant argues that the foundation of morality is righteousness for its own sake. Duty is not the upshot of an all-things-considered judgment about how to attain happiness. Instead of filling out the potency of our natural desires, duty drives a wedge between who we are and how we ought to live. Duty is a hard taskmaster, and the demands of conscience, properly understood, require us to do our duty for its own sake, and not for the sake of any satisfying outcome. Here, Kant never compromises: the gap between who we are and how we ought to live is utterly real and central to our destiny. We cannot bridge this gap by translating obligation into the logic of normal life, reinterpreting the *must* of duty into the *want* of natural desire, for such a translation of duty into happiness eliminates the gap and dulls the transformative edge of change. Conscience becomes an echo of our present way of being in the world. Kant preserves the edge of difference by arguing that, properly understood, moral duty is formal rather than material, objective rather than subjective, noumenal rather than phenomenal. All these contrasts serve the purpose of preserving the urgency of transformative desire by expressing, in conceptual terms, the gap that conscience feels between our present way of living and the life of righteousness we seek. Only if duty is formal, objective, and noumenal can it retain the power to make us change.

Kant's repudiation of eudaemonism and affirmation of duty as the power of change separate him from Hume and Rousseau. So central is Kant's commitment to the sharp edge of redemption that, if forced to choose, he would align himself with the dogmatic enemies of both the Savoyard vicar and the Humean agnostic rather than renounce his transformative cure of the soul. Consider this passage from the *Critique of Practical Reason*. Kant's view of the highest good as duty for its own sake rules out both the "empiricism of practical reason, which bases the practical concepts of good and evil merely on empirical consequences (on so-called happiness)" and "the mysticism of practical reason, which makes into a schema that which should serve only as a symbol, i.e., proposes to supply real yet nonsensuous intuitions (of an invisible kingdom of God) for the application of the moral law, and thus plunges into the transcendent" (*CPrR* 73, Ak 5:70–71). Kant's tireless criticisms of eudaemonism show that he never intends to domesticate our transformative impulse by reducing duty to the project of living well amidst the constraints of current life.[7] Just as clearly, his criticisms of rationalism show that he does not wish to backslide into the enthusiasm and superstition of dogmatic conceptions of right and wrong. Nonetheless, Kant reveals a telling preference. "The protest against empiricism of practical reason is much more important and commendable," he reports, "because mysticism is compatible with the purity and sublimity of the moral law" (*CPrR* 73–74, Ak 5:71). In contrast, he rejects "empiricism allied with the inclinations, which, no matter what style they wear, always degrade mankind when they are raised to a supreme practical principle" (*CPrR* 74, Ak 5:71). Kant would rather ally himself with otherworldly divine commands than reduce morality to the intramundane enterprise of adjusting principles and practices to the perceived limitations of human nature.

---

7. See, e.g., *CPR* A555/B583. Kant insists that circumstances, however relevant and consequential, in no way shape, constrain, or color the "causality of reason," the source of moral character that is "complete in itself."

We can too easily read such a preference for "mysticism" as evidence of Kant's Stoic antipathy to passion and embodiment. But this reading fails to take seriously Kant's insights into the logic of we-matter-most humanism. He knows that people want to be different. This is a common experience, felt again and again in pangs of conscience. Moreover, proponents of progress are very aware of the need for dramatic change, not just in society but in the very sense of ourselves as persons. Kant's famous essay "What Is Enlightenment?" exhorts us to "think for ourselves," and he knows how deeply such a commitment will change the underlying basis of the lives of individuals. A peasant cannot imagine thinking for himself. A man habituated by a lifetime of deference is unable to speak his mind before his social superiors. Only an entirely new and fresh approach to life, a revolution in our souls, will allow us to live as we ought: as free and rational creatures who properly command respect.

An "empiricism of practical reason" cannot make sense of the dramatic disjunctions enjoined by the transformative ideals of modern humanism. Eudaemonism reduces to self-love. Moral judgments based on perceived needs and felt desires do nothing more than dilate and extend who we are; such judgments cannot change us. Of course, a "mysticism of practical reason" cannot provide a basis for we-matter-most humanism either, for it raises the danger of a lawless moral ambition that overleaps the proper purposes of morality, subordinating persons to the authority of purported prophecies and revelations. However, Kant sees that such a divine view of the moral vocation, in contrast to eudaemonism in its many forms, acknowledges and respects the fundamental human need for change. The mystical distortions of practical reason may implicate us in the dehumanizing excesses of superstition and enthusiasm, but these excesses do something that modern humanism seeks: they push toward that which is different. A successful explication of the moral logic of modern humanism must do the same.

Moral Faith

For Kant, we feel the sharp edge of our transcending impulse in the practical, moral potency of reason. The voice of conscience speaks, and our ability to heed its commands allows for both change and continuity. The moral imperative is so pure in form—duty for duty's sake— that we cannot bend it back into our many projects of self-discovery and self-love. The demands of morality cut into the way we live, and the rigor of duty resists domestication. But however sharp the edge of duty, in both its subjective form as conscience and its objective form as the categorical imperative, our moral vocations have a profound inner reality. We *want* to be righteous, and we *know* righteousness to be the highest good, and in our capacities as free moral agents, we *can* achieve the highest good. Thus, for Kant, these governing moral necessities are neither eudaemonistic nor speculative. Precisely as the force of the ever present "ought," conscience and duty freight our lives with transformative urgency. The goal of Kant's moral theory is to show how that transformative urgency serves, rather than oversteps or oppresses, our identities as persons.

In most of his practical philosophy, Kant focuses on the three postulates necessary to conceive of how we participate in the highest good as human beings and do so in such a way that the basic principles of we-matter-most humanism obtain. These three postulates—freedom, God, and immortality—establish the conditions for a humanistic vindication of the desire for change. Against Rousseau's worries, Kant conceives of personal identity as constituted by the power to become different, and as such, moral obligations need not undermine who we are. In freedom we are the sole consequential basis for morally meaningful change. Against Hume's worries, Kant establishes conditions for human life that permit a heroic ambition that does not rend the fabric of ordinary life. In a cosmos created by a morally motivated God, and as immortal beings, we can remain continuous persons, even across the most dramatic moral changes. The postulates, then, are necessary in order to set the stage for the redemptive drama of we-matter-most humanism.

Before embarking on this explication of the fundamental postulates of Kant's moral vision, I want to drive home to the reader my profound lack of interest in the specific and controversial ways that Kant formulates his account of the moral law and our relation to it. Perhaps Kant's formulations of categorical imperative are so formal that they cannot provide an adequate basis for social and personal ethics. Perhaps his account of freedom is inadequate, and his moral anthropology breaks apart on a sharp dualism of noumenal freedom and phenomenal passion. Perhaps his relentless perfectionism in ethics overrides the plurality of goods that constitute the life well lived. Perhaps Kant's individualism fails to account for the proper role of social institutions in moral habituation. These and many others are legitimate problems. They are worthy of investigation, but they are outside my interest. For the purpose of this inquiry, I want to understand whether or not we can cogently connect personal identity to the highest good under the strict logic of we-matter-most humanism.

To investigate this possibility, I need only establish the formal relations that obtain between Kant's account of the highest good and our identities as persons. I need not be concerned about the material content of the moral law and the cogency of the anthropology in which Kant explicates what it means to be free and rational. I will analyze the structural engineering, not the building materials, because if Kant cannot establish a cogent relationship between personal identity and the highest good, then the details of his moral theory are inconsequential. There is no reason to worry about the quality of the bricks and mortar when one knows that the building will collapse before it is completed.

Two logical requirements of we-matter-most humanism will guide this structural analysis: that personal identity is both consequential for and continuous in the highest good, or more formally that personal identity is necessary and sufficient. This approach, however removed from the standard interpretations of Kant, is a clearer guide to the larger significance of Kant's thought for the broad tradition of modern humanism than a mud-wrestling match in which we try to pin down the specific meaning of the tortured scholasticism of Kant's many and diverse formulations. The former admits to a degree of abstractive clarity. The latter involves a strenuous exercise in close reading and coordination of Kant's extensive writings that can be overwhelming in scope.

The Postulate of Freedom

For Kant, we are rational beings, and as such, we are capable of intellectual participation in the highest good. Constituted by the potency of pure practical reason, we can see duty as universal and unconditional. As Kant stipulates, "Respect for the moral law is a feeling produced by an intellectual cause, and this feeling is the only one we can know completely a priori and the necessity of which we can discern" (*CPrR* 76, Ak 5:73). Who we are includes the power to grasp the binding force of duty. No human mind is without this feeling of obligation. We cannot help but realize that our identities are defined in light of the moral law. We come to see that duty is the pivot on which the distinctive shape and purpose of our lives will turn. As a result, no matter how each of us might live, no matter how our identities might be distinct and plural, moral obligation does not come upon any of us as an alien intrusion. It is the polestar for our lives.

However, our rational nature is insufficient; we must be more than persons who can recognize the universality of the moral law. As persons, we must be constituted by our acts of freedom in light of our rational apprehension of the moral law; we must be able to navigate according to the polestar. Therefore, Kant insists that we have not only the power to affirm duty as a justified and binding demand but also the power to conform ourselves to our obligations. In so doing, we become righteous, not extrinsically as a quality or property that we add to our static identities as persons, but intrinsically, precisely as persons constituted by righteous wills. The moral law can become the basis for our lives because our identities as persons are, morally speaking, determined by our choices.

Although Kant does not use the language of personal identity, his account of freedom can be formulated clearly in such terms. Personal identity, for Kant, does not depend upon an enduring substance or the empirical features of a person's life. Metaphysical notions of substance have no role in Kant's critical philosophy. Empirical features cannot secure identity.[8] Instead, a man's personal identity is found in "a single phenomenon of his character, which he himself creates" (*CPrR* 101, Ak 5:98). As phenomena, we may well be bundles of habit, inclination, and memory, but for Kant, as noumena, we are exactly identical to that which we will. Viewed in this way, personal identity is vested in a dynamic power, independent of all empirical and sensual constraints. Kant calls this dynamic power "freedom." Personal identity may have other constituent factors, but throughout his moral reflection, Kant treats persons as defined by the power of freedom or becoming.

Our power of becoming is not exercised willy-nilly. For Kant, we are not free to be "anybody" or "anything" on the basis of a libertarian ideal of freedom. Freedom involves self-command not self-creation. Freedom is exercised with respect to the moral law. We are

---

8. See Kant's remarks about the instability of any conception of personal identity based on desire and inclination (*CPrR* 27–28, Ak 5:27–29). If we assume that some empirical feature of our subjectivity constitutes personal identity, then "each man makes his own subject the foundation of his inclination, and in each person it is now one and now another which has preponderance" (*CPrR* 28, Ak 5:28).

either righteous or not according to how each of us turns on the pivot of the moral law that we feel a priori and necessarily. As such, freedom is not originative; it is determinative. Our choice of the moral law (or failure to so choose) determines, at the most fundamental level, who we are. For this reason, Kant conceives of personal identity as vested in our moral identity. We are who we are in and through our relation to the moral law.[9]

On the basis of these key assumptions about our identities as persons—that who we are is found in our self-determination with respect to our always present knowledge of the moral law—Kant seems able to make short work of the task of explaining the logic of modern humanism. Our identities as persons are fundamentally consequential for and continuous in the highest good. The moral law needs no authorization other than its rational potency, and because we are rational, we can see the essential rightness of the moral law. That is enough to give the moral law its internal and personal character as obligation. Further, we have the power to be righteous through the free and unconditioned determination of our will toward duty for its own sake. The moral law demands nothing we cannot provide. As a consequence, the demands of duty, however stringent and overriding, can involve neither authoritarian oppression nor overreaching ambition. Freedom allows the dynamism of moral change to stand at the very center of what it means to be a person.

We need not tarry over Kant's concept of freedom and the difficulties it poses. It is sufficient for us to acknowledge that, for modern

---

9. This determination of freedom by the moral law gives proper meaning to Kant's seemingly paradoxical statement that "the moral law is, in fact, a law of causality through freedom" (*CPrR* 49, Ak 5:47). The fact of obligation forces us to become either righteous or not. In that way, morality forces personal identity (freedom) to be substantive (an actual moral agent) rather than formal (a possible moral agent). Thus, the moral law "causes" us to become the kind of people we must "through freedom" choose to be. We can see, here, the short jump from Kant to Hegel. Pure practical reason, for Kant, has a causative function. It fixes identity by forcing us to determine our wills one way or the other. In this way, unlike speculative thought, practical reason "becomes, in the field of experience, an efficient cause through ideas" (*CPrR* 49, Ak 5:48). What *ought* to be (the moral law) gives substantial form to what *is* (our wills). Hegel drops Kant's humanistic assumption that the freedom of each person is the site of transition from *ought* to *is*, but Kant's notion that ideas are causative in their power to give birth to being through becoming remains. What *ought to be*, for Hegel, *is*, and history as a whole functions as the forum for the effectual force of the idea to exert its power in becoming. Although space limits analysis of the development of modern thought, my suggestion is that Kant's inability to show how moral change is consistent with we-matter-most humanism motivates Hegel's shift from personal freedom to universal history as the explanation for the transformative dynamism of modernity.

humanism, change is a palpable necessity. Kant consistently describes
our condition as one driven by the harsh demand of obligation: "We
stand under the discipline of reason. . . . Duty and obligation are the
only names we must give to our relation to the moral law" (*CPrR* 85,
Ak 5:82). The moral law does not confirm who we are; it urges us to
change, and this can give the impression that morality overrides and
oppresses our identities as persons. However, Kant defines our identities as vested in the dynamic power of freedom rather than in a fixed
substance. Thus defined, personal identity is not acted upon by obligation as a lump of clay is shaped by a potter. Animated by moral
purpose, capable of transforming who we are by choosing to adopt
duty for its own sake, our identities as persons serve as the sole consequential basis for moral change. If I affirm duty for duty's sake, then
righteousness obtains. This logical relationship between personal identity and the highest good, and not Kant's specific doctrines of the
moral law, human reason, and our power to adopt duty for its own
sake, establishes the core meaning of Kant's postulate of freedom.
Thus, for our purposes, it is enough to say that, for Kant, the postulate of freedom follows the logic of we-matter-most humanism. It
establishes personal identity as necessary and sufficient for the highest good. To know and choose duty for its own sake determines identity, and that is enough.

There are, however, complications. Who we are, however determined by our freedom, is not exhausted by our will. Our lives have all
sorts of phenomenal characteristics that, however shaped by freedom
to serve righteousness, exist as enduring features. We have bodies that
produce a steady stream of desires and inclinations. We have memories and expectations. Were we to undertake to repudiate such desires,
then we would overthrow our humanity. We would enter into a project of vain overreaching and fall victim to just the moral mysticism for
which Kant expressed sympathy but rejected nonetheless. Kant does
not counsel such a cure of the soul. He is adamant that we should not
undertake to extirpate our desires, for in so doing, we assault our
humanity. The transforming drama of freedom cannot sever us from
ordinary life. The full sweep of our lives needs to be carried across the
change from living wrongly to living righteously. No triage of the soul
is permitted, no ascetical overleaping. We must pursue the ideal of duty
for its own sake with the confidence that such an aspiration does not
entail a repudiation of our intrinsic desires and ordinary humanity. We
must choose duty confident that it does not entail choosing to destroy

ourselves. In short, we need to remain continuous across the changes demanded by the hard taskmaster of duty, not only in the formal sense of being exactly that person who freely chooses righteousness but also as the person with quotidian needs and desires.

In order to affirm the necessity of our distinctive and altogether human lives for the highest good, Kant clarifies the goal of the moral life. For Kant, the good will is not the highest good. Since Kant envisions a moral project for embodied persons and not disembodied wills, he views the full and complete goal of the moral life as a total correspondence of all phenomenal features of our lives with the noumenal determination of our wills by the moral law—the unity of virtue and happiness. Under such conditions, our feelings, desires, and emotions perfectly reinforce and reflect our free affirmation of duty for its own sake. This correspondence of desire (happiness) and will (virtue) allows us to live in uninterrupted harmony with the moral law. Thus, the highest good entails a fully effected change within the whole person, a good will given full, sensual expression in the total form of the life of the individual. This form of life transparent to the moral law is, strictly speaking, the highest good.[10]

Put this way, Kant seems to be backsliding from the logic of we-matter-most humanism. Our desires and inclinations are conditioned by external factors. The impediments to the moral law abound. Our parents, teachers, and friends have a decisive influence on what we feel and desire. Our personalities are profoundly vulnerable to any number of other influences. A morally punctilious man may suffer from depression. A person altogether committed to the duties of good governance might find the job tedious or the burdens oppressive. Thus, when Kant turns to stem the tendency to overreach and deny our ordinary humanity by defining the highest good as more than choosing duty for its own sake, he seems to undermine the claim that our identities as persons provide the sole basis. After all, happiness depends upon how I feel about events and desires I cannot control. If that happiness is necessary for the highest good, then we cannot entertain illusions that personal identity is sufficient. It is to defeat exactly this conclusion and to preserve the sufficiency of personal identity (as

---

10. See *CPrR* 114–17, Ak 5:110–13. For a detailed explanation of the nature and role of Kant's conception of the highest good, see Stephen Engstrom, "The Concept of the Highest Good in Kant's Moral Theory," *Philosophy and Phenomenological Research* 52, no. 4 (December 1992): 742–80.

defined by freedom) for the highest good that Kant adduces the postulates of God and immortality.[11]

The Postulate of God

Kant presumes an auspicious cosmic frame of reference for moral change. "The highest good is possible in the world," Kant allows, "only on the supposition of a supreme cause of nature which has a causality corresponding to the moral intention" (*CPrR* 129–30, Ak 5:125). An omnipotent Creator has the power to set up the world in such a way that happiness is coordinate with righteousness. To the degree that the moral vision of modern humanism requires us to endorse moral change that serves, rather than subverts, human dignity, we must believe in such a Creator. This belief allows us freely to choose duty, knowing that we are not, finally, at war with ourselves. Fulfillment will follow from righteousness. We need not sacrifice any part of our ordinary humanity for the sake of the highest good, for virtue will be crowned with happiness in the ultimate scheme of things. A just God guarantees it.

Such confidence can seem like wishful thinking. The complex structures of human desires and the even more inscrutable and uncertain external conditions for their fulfillment resist analysis. Indeed, it would be impossible to identify those conditions in their full scope. For Kant, however, the confidence that moral duty is a viable and fulfilling vocation is not based on empirical observation; it depends upon a moral faith. The affirmation of the supremely consequential role of personal identity forces us to say that freedom is sufficient. The affir-

---

11. Kant explains the logic of this move to theological premises in many places. For example, in *Religion within the Boundaries of Mere Reason*, Kant states that although morality needs nothing other than its sublime truth, a truth that we know subjectively, in the inner voice of conscience, and objectively, in the potency of practical reason, we must understand how morality can be the determining ground of our everyday lives. We have a "natural need" to think of more than our transcendent destiny in the dignity of the moral law. We also wish to understand how this transcendent destiny can fulfill "all our doings and undoings taken as a whole" (*R* 34, Ak 6:5). We want to give "objective reality" to the unity of all the dispersed features of our lives, and do so under the governance of the good will. To use Kant's scholastic vocabulary, we wish to combine, in our minds, "the purposiveness [deriving] from freedom and the purposiveness of nature" (*R* 35, Ak 6:5). We wish to join the perfection of our moral nature—the moral law freely adopted—with the intrinsic dynamism of our passional nature toward satisfaction and happiness. In short, we want to see how our being righteous is an integral human vocation. As a consequence, "morality thus leads inevitably to religion" (*R* 35, Ak 6:6), for religion, according to Kant, is the human attempt to conceive of how we as human beings, and not just as rational beings, are related to the highest good.

mation of enduring continuity of personal identity requires us to believe that we can do our duty with the confidence that all the constituent features of who we are will have a role in the highest good. To link both convictions, we must believe the cosmos is divinely structured to reinforce and reward righteousness. The force of the "must believe" secures the certainty of the conclusion.[12]

The Postulate of Immortality

We do not just worry about whether or not the world, as a whole, is congenial for total human fulfillment based on moral freedom. Even if we are convinced of the existence of a divine lawgiver who establishes the conditions of existence in such a way as to allow the harmony of righteousness and happiness, we cannot help but notice that nobody seems to achieve this combination. Righteous people must make sacrifices and endure hardships. Vice is rewarded, and virtue punished. The wicked prosper, and the righteous suffer. Thus, in order to preserve the confidence that righteousness is consistent with the fulfillment of the full sweep of our desires and needs, Kant adopts the postulate of immortality. We can reasonably affirm the continuity of will and inclination, noumenal freedom and phenomenal happiness, "only under the presupposition of an infinitely enduring existence and personality of the same rational being," and "this is called the immortality of the soul" (*CPrR* 127, Ak 5:122).[13] Our identities as persons are continuous for as long as it takes for happiness to catch up with righteousness. However distant the final goal, we have the full allotment of time in which to make the pilgrimage.

---

12. Kant advances a similar argument to justify the postulate of God as moral Creator in the *Critique of Judgment* (*CJ*), par. 26: "The moral proof of the existence of God" (Ak 5:447–53). "We must assume a moral world-cause," concludes Kant, "that is an Author of the world, if we are to set before ourselves a final end in conformity with the requirements of the moral law" (translation from *Critique of Judgment* [trans. James Creed Meredith; Oxford: Clarendon, 1952], 450). For an analysis of the importance of the *Critique of Judgment* for properly interpreting Kant's religious reflection, not only on this issue but also on the controverted question of divine assistance, see Adina Davidovich, "How to Read *Religion within the Limits of Reason Alone*," *Kant-Studien* 85 (1995): 1–14. As Davidovich shows, Kant is committed to "the rational ideal of the Highest Good," which "demands that the universe be brought to a state in which virtue is realized and rewarded by happiness" (11). This rational ideal dictates Kant's doctrine of God as the moral governor who ensures that the universe is properly ordered to support a humanistic faith.

13. See Kant's meditation on the way in which "moral sentiment," when confronted by the unmerited suffering of the righteous and unworthy happiness of the wicked, endorses the idea of immortality, even if animated by skeptical doubts about a future state (*CJ* par. 26, Ak 5:451–53).

With the postulates of God and immortality, Kant is able to adopt a view of the highest good that includes happiness, but which does not undermine the requirements of we-matter-most humanism, whether viewed in terms of the supremely consequential role or enduring continuity of personal identity. God's moral intent in creation ensures that external factors are, finally, keyed to the principles of righteousness. The immortality of the soul allows us to discount our present experience of conflict between desire and will. Kant is entirely sensible of this gain. Even though the highest good requires a unity of righteousness and happiness that we cannot effect by sheer force of will, we can be confident that righteousness will, in the fullness of time, come to entail happiness. The choice in favor of righteousness will reinforce, rather than overreach, the limits of our merely human frame.

This prospective confidence protects against overreaching; our embodied existence and all the contingent conditions for our fulfillment will be met. But this same confidence does not undermine the ambition of modern humanism on behalf of the sufficiency of personal identity for the highest good. We remain supremely consequential, and Kant reinforces this faith by developing a metric of worthiness. He establishes a clear relationship between the righteousness that depends upon our freedom and the happiness that depends upon the auspicious moral order of the cosmos. As Kant puts the matter, "Morals is not really the doctrine of how to make ourselves happy, but of how we are to be *worthy* of happiness" (*CPrR* 134, Ak 5:130). Free self-determination of our identities as righteous renders us worthy of happiness, and the postulates of God and immortality secure the conditions under which our worthiness is always and inevitably rewarded. In this way, the cosmic frame of reference operates under a strict moral logic. The congenial cosmic context reinforces, rather than subverts, the sufficiency of personal identity for the highest good. Kant is clear on this point: "Happiness in exact proportion with the morality of the rational beings who are thereby rendered worthy of it, alone constitutes the supreme good of that world wherein, in accordance with the commands of a pure but practical reason, we are under obligation to place ourselves" (*CPR* A814/B842). The moral order is tailored to the measure of the righteous.

Kant's use of worthiness to link righteousness and happiness is crucial, for it signals the logic by which he hopes to affirm the demands of modern humanism. After all, since happiness is to be allocated "in exact proportion," the manner in which one acquires moral worthiness "constitutes the condition of everything else (which belongs to one's state) in the concept of the highest good" (*CPrR* 135, Ak 5:130). The postulate of freedom ensures that we can acquire such worth. Therefore, such a choice is sufficient for everything else to follow of necessity. As Kant puts the matter, "Complete fitness of intentions to the moral law is the supreme condition of the highest good" (*CPrR* 126, Ak 5:122). Casting the issue from the divine perspective, Kant observes, "To be in need of happiness and also worthy of it and yet not to partake of it could not be in accordance with the complete volition of an omnipotent rational being" (*CPrR* 114–15, Ak 5:110). God rewards righteousness necessarily.

We can see, therefore, that the postulates of God and immortality do nothing more than establish the background conditions for the humanistic logic of worthiness. God and immortality are the fixed coordinates upon which the variable of freedom functions according to the constant of worthiness. Viewed from this perspective, the only open variable is whether or not we choose righteousness.[14] The way

---

14. For the subtle way in which Kant uses God and the divine intention to create a purely moral world as a "condition" for the highest good, and at the same time preserves the functional sufficiency of freedom, see his discussion of righteousness and the highest good in relation to Epicureanism, Stoicism, and Christianity in *CPrR* 131–36, Ak 5:126–33. The existence of a moral Creator and the consequent harmony of righteousness and happiness are theoretical conditions for the possibility of a rational affirmation of Kant's humanism, but they are not practical conditions. Righteousness alone, and the consequent worthiness it entails, is sufficient. Put in the negative, Kant insists that "the greatest well doing does [us] honor only by being exercised according to worthiness" (*CPrR* 136, Ak 5:131). Kant's echo of the Christian doctrine of the Trinity reinforces this purely regulative role for God, a role that is completely constrained by moral necessity. God is the Holy Lawgiver, the Beneficent Ruler, and Just Judge (see n. 3, *CPrR* 135, Ak 5:131). In none of these modes does God act and provide a practical condition for the highest good. God is the reliable horizon for moral change, not a constituent element of the transformative process.

Interpreters can easily conflate the sense in which God is necessary as the horizon of moral hope with the actual source and cause of moral change. Philip J. Rossi suggests that Kant, unlike full-blooded humanists, does not place "human destiny under human control" ("Moral Autonomy, Divine Transcendence, and Human Destiny: Kant's Doctrine of Hope as a Philosophical Foundation for Christian Ethics," *Thomist* 46, no. 3 [July 1982]: 447). Such a claim typifies misreadings of Kant's religious convictions. It ignores the care with which Kant so consistently makes free choice of duty the sole modal function in the morally determined cosmos. For Kant, we live in a world governed by a rigorous moral order that is keyed to the logic of worthiness. In this sense, God supplies a condition for our attainment of the highest good just as gravity does for the movement of the planets. Should change occur, we can no more appeal to God than to gravity. The conditions for the alteration of planetary motion are to be found in the movement of other bodies, not in gravity as such, so also the conditions for alteration of our relation to the highest good are to be found in personal identity, and personal identity alone, and not

is open for Kant to affirm moral change without overreaching. Given the necessity of happiness united with righteousness through the concept of worthiness, Kant can acknowledge the role of happiness in the highest good in order to preserve the continuity of ordinary, worldly, and phenomenal personal identity, and he can still conclude that personal identity (as determined by freedom) is the necessary and sufficient condition for the highest good, for righteousness produces worthiness, and worthiness merits happiness. In a world created by a morally motivated deity, and given the fullness of time allocated to the immortal, what is merited necessarily becomes real.

The way in which God and immortality support Kant's affirmation of the sufficiency of freedom for the highest good is by no means a side issue. We need to recognize that the underlying logic of we-matter-most humanism is the only reason Kant ever gives for these postulates. We have, according to Kant, a moral interest in the most auspicious possible conditions for our moral vocation, and all three postulates are necessary in order to satisfy that interest (*CPrR* 147–51, Ak 5:142–46).[15] For the vocation of modern humanism and its characteristic concerns, the moral interest is clear. If we fail to affirm the core meaning of freedom—that we are sufficient for righteousness— then the desire for change becomes a covert form of crushing authoritarianism. Rousseau's worries flood back. Without the postulate of freedom, the desire for righteousness is either accepted as an internalized form of extrinsic demand or renounced as an alienating echo of social conventions. Unless our identities as persons include a potency sufficient to attain the highest good, we must either submit

---

in God or the moral order as such. Gravity ensures that large bodies will influence each other, even at great distances. The existence of God as Holy Lawgiver, Beneficent Ruler, and Just Judge guarantees that moral change within us will produce righteousness crowned with happiness. In such a cosmos, governed by a God bound to the logic of worthiness with as much necessity as the force of gravity, our freedom functions as a sufficient condition for all morally significant change. We are very much in control of our destiny, and we "depend" upon God and the moral order only in the vast, metaphysical sense in which nothing would be as it is if this particular world and its moral governance did not exist.

15. G. Felicitas Munzel provides a subtle and detailed account of the way in which Kant's moral vision governs the formulation of the postulates (see *Kant's Conception of Moral Character: The "Critical" Link of Morality, Anthropology, and Reflective Judgment* [Chicago: University of Chicago Press, 1999], 207–15). She shows that, for Kant, a rational faith arises from the need to affirm "the conditions of [the] realizability" of "an individual moral certitude" (207). My thesis is that we-matter-most humanism captures most clearly the logical form of the "moral certitude" that motivates Kant.

to nonpersonal requirements for moral change or, like Rousseau, renounce change.

The postulates of God and immortality address Hume's concerns about overreaching. Eliminate God, and the risks entailed in all projects of change, whether personal or political, are easily criticized as imprudent and futile. Unless we have confidence that the world is, finally, hospitable to righteousness, then morally motivated change is a matter of calculation, subordinated to a cool assessment of the limitations of life lived in a world that is, by all observation, hostile to the moral project. Eliminate immortality, and our desire for change leads toward wild swings of optimism and pessimism. We either deny the real impediments to moral reform, slashing and burning our way through life in the vain hope of achieving a morally integrated life here and now, or we despair of moral striving, knowing how hard it is to change social and personal habits. But the postulates of God and immortality allow Kant to avoid fanaticism and quietism and conceive of moral change in which the embodied and empirical character of our identities as human beings is affirmed and thus remains continuous. From the divine perspective, and unconstrained by a finite period of time, happiness is possible. However, it comes to those whose righteousness makes them worthy, and to them alone. Thus, we can embark on radical moral change confident that, in the long run, such change connects us to our identities as persons, both as necessary and sufficient, continuous and supremely consequential. God guarantees that the righteousness is not disjunctive; immortality removes the empirical worries that such a guarantee seems rarely, if ever, fulfilled; worthiness links that guarantee to what we do with our freedom.

With the three postulates of freedom, God, and immortality, Kant is able to establish the architecture for his moral vision. His humanism, at least at this theoretical level, does not echo the superstition or enthusiasm that he wishes to criticize. Against crushing authoritarianism and vain overreaching, he connects personal identity to the highest good by showing how we are both continuous and consequential. In this way, the impulse toward change is made consistent with the moral interests of modern humanism. Moral change seems entirely consistent with a horror of dependence and a fear of difference. However, this structure must be tested by actually telling the story of moral change, and the logical weight of the story may be too much for the structure so painstakingly erected.

Three False Views of Evil

We might be convinced that change is possible, both in terms of our fundamental identities as free and rational creatures and in the context of a divinely ordered cosmos that guarantees that the worthy shall enjoy the highest good because of their righteousness. But we are still faced with a further, and for Kant much more troubling, question. Why do we need to change in the first place? How could it ever have come about that we are morally equipped to know that we must change, but not morally determined enough to simply choose righteousness, and thus set in motion the machinery of worthiness and reward? This question is crucial, for it shifts the theoretical conditions for the possibility of morally meaningful change into the actual conditions under which we must live our lives. Therefore, the question of why we need to change is the place where Kant must begin if he is to tell his story of the soul.

Kant's explanation of why we need to change functions under the same constraints as his moral theory. It must not backslide into Rousseau's expulsion of change from the human vocation, and it must avoid Hume's strategy of reducing the heroic impulse to a gentle management of life. The desire to change must be a rational one, based on an ambition serious enough to make change fundamental to our destiny, but not so ambitious that we are helpless creatures who either desire what we cannot have and seek what we cannot find or submit in dependence to supernatural powers that promise what cannot be attained by natural means. In short, Kant's account of our actual need for change must conform to the logic of we-matter-most humanism just as closely as did his account of the possibility of change in his moral theory.

We can state the problem of change in terms of that logic. Within the moral universe of we-matter-most humanism, we are necessary and sufficient for the highest good. However, if our identities as persons are sufficient for what is best, then why is there any gap between what is and what ought to be? We *are*; therefore, what is best should obtain. To put this into Kant's distinctive vocabulary: we *know* the moral law; we *desire* righteousness; we *have* the freedom to will duty for its own sake. Therefore, the moral law should hold sway. Nothing stands in the way: we are free, and the cosmos is congenial. Even if we allow for a process by which our inner potency toward righteousness develops and comes to full expression, the dynamism is an internal dynamism. If being is becoming, then such a drama involves change, but the change entails becoming oneself rather than becoming different. Such a change is not dramatic and transformative; it is organic and developmental. As a consequence, and in spite of Kant's strenuous commitment to transformative desire, the moral life threatens to reduce to "being ourselves," either as an already achieved condition or as an ongoing project of self-expression.[16]

Kant is well aware of the centrality of this problem. If who we are is sufficient for the highest good, then some account must be given for why we need to change. Only a fool labors to ensure that the sun will rise. Thus, the question is pointed. If the highest good springs from who we are, then why must we worry ourselves so about morality? The need to answer such a question motivates the first part of *Religion within the Boundaries of Mere Reason,* "Concerning the Indwelling of the Evil Principle Alongside the Good, or Of the Radical Evil in Human Nature." There, Kant is not simply offering critical comments on a central Christian teaching, comments that can be disregarded in the analysis of his humanism of reason and freedom. Kant is not undertaking a side journey into the strange world of Augustinian theology and its pessimistic doctrine of original sin. Quite the contrary, Kant sets about to explain why change is central to the human vocation. He wishes to show why the grammatical tense of the moral law is obligatory and not predictive, why we "ought to" be righteous rather than simply "shall." He does so by stipulating that evil is the cause of the gap.[17] No

---

16. As Paul Ricoeur observes, Kant develops an account of our moral vocations in which change has a formal place. "But this dynamism," worries Ricoeur, "is fundamentally self-expressive. The externality of desire (either Aristotelian formation of desire through socialization, or Platonic elimination of desire through sensuous forms of truth) is repudiated by Kant." Rejecting the implicit Aristotelianism of Hume's philosophy of common life, Kant eliminates external springs of change. Yet, repudiating Rousseau's drive toward *apathia* and self-affirmation, Kant denies that *stasis* is the goal of life. Kant insists that human life has drama, but his humanism is left with the person alone as the inner source of change. Ricoeur's claim is that such change is purely immanent to the person and cannot reach toward genuine otherness. As Ricoeur notes, even if our inner drive is a "rational desire," this inner potency "seeks itself in the form of life which perfectly expresses it: the threefold moral law" (all quotations from *Oneself as Another* [Chicago: University of Chicago Press, 1992], 215). Ricoeur's reading of Kant's project does not recognize how seriously Kant took this problem. Kant would rather court self-contradiction than backslide into a humanism in which simply being ourselves is enough for the highest good. Indeed, as we shall see, Kant's drive toward "otherness" is so intense that he cannot provide a satisfactory account of personal continuity across moral change. Thus, Ricoeur misdiagnoses the difficulties that limit the plausability of Kant's moral vision.

17. Throughout this chapter I follow Kant's use of the term "evil" to designate purely moral phenomena. In *Religion within the Boundaries of Mere Reason,* Kant gives no attention to the question of physical evil.

other explanation of the need for moral change is possible. As such, if a reflective and self-critical humanism is to come to terms with the actual conditions for moral change, it must inquire into the nature, origin, and consequences of this evil.[18]

Kant entertains three explanations for the cause of evil. The first, let us call it the Manichean view, explains evil and the consequent gap in terms of suprahuman forces. Good and evil stem from higher powers that vie for control, and our experience of the gap is a symptom of this cosmic conflict. The second, or innate-goodness view, denies that evil exists within the human person. We are essentially good, and the gap exists because we are placed in a world not yet fully humanized. The third, or mixed view of our condition, proposes that we are somehow a combination of both good and evil. The gap and our restlessness stem from our mixed condition and our quite natural desire for a unified identity. Kant rejects all three because they contradict the logic of we-matter-most humanism.

The Manichean explanation of the gap treats evil as a cosmic force. Evil is suprapersonal; it sweeps across the stage of history and drives a wedge between a primordial golden age and the way we now live. The gap, then, is the work of the gods, the cruel destiny of history, and we are stretched across this gap with no hope of recovering integral existence by our own efforts. Our only hope rests with higher powers: gods to be propitiated, deities to be placated. Kant associates this view of the origin of evil with antiquity and exotic mythology. Hesiod's cosmogony of decline and Hindu myths of worlds created and destroyed serve as illustrations. However, any external account of the need for change fits this type. Voltaire's eloquent outcry after the Lisbon earthquake may rebel against a religious acceptance of suf-

---

18. Susan Meld Shell's study *The Embodiment of Reason: Kant on Spirit, Generation, and Community* (Chicago: University of Chicago Press, 1996) analyzes Kant's too often neglected treatments on embodiment and history. Shell makes a convincing case that Kant's thought includes reflection on the actual moral projects of socially and physiologically determined persons, what she calls "the requirements of worldly consciousness" (306). Shell's efforts are characteristic of contemporary rereadings of Kant that emphasize his interests in history, character, and emotion. However, also characteristic in this extended digression into Kant's treatment of particularity is a neglect of the problem of evil. Shell does not attend to the ways in which Kant handles the particular identity of persons as subjects that need to change because she, like so many commentators, simply takes for granted the horizon of modern humanism. Her efforts are devoted to adjusting various aspects of this horizon to post-Hegelian concerns and showing how Kant anticipates such adjustments. See also Nancy Sherman, *Making a Necessity of Virtue: Aristotle and Kant on Virtue* (New York: Cambridge University Press, 1997).

fering and death, but his view, no less than the Hindu view of worlds created and destroyed, presupposes that what matters most is beyond our control. Either the suffering and death of the inhabitants of Lisbon was evil, in the strict sense of depriving those unfortunate souls of the conditions for the highest good, or it was not. If it was, then Voltaire implicitly rejects the humanistic proposition that we matter most for what is best. Cruel nature matters more.

Whereas ancient cosmogonies exhibit a pessimistic fatalism about the origin of evil and the possibilities of righteousness, Kant identifies a "more recent" view, an innate-goodness view that cultivates an "opposite heroic opinion . . . that the world steadfastly (though hardly noticeably) forges ahead in the very opposite direction, namely from bad to better" (*R* 45, Ak 6:19). Here, the drive toward the triumph of the highest good stems from neither oracles nor revelations. Instead, this "heroic opinion" insists that, contrary to outward appearances, we are innately good. We might be surrounded by natural, social, and even personal causes of evil, but deep down inside, we are good and have a natural propensity toward what is best. With an innate pre-disposition toward goodness, then, the optimist reads the travails and disasters of history as temporary setbacks. Our innate goodness, the "seed of goodness," the "natural foundation of goodness," guides us toward what is best. Evil does not have the final word. We will close the gap between how we presently live and how we ought to live because, finally, some part of us, the highest, best part, already resides on the other side of the gap. This inner potency toward goodness draws all the rest of our lives toward the highest good. As Kant writes, summarizing the innate-goodness view with a quote from Seneca that also serves as the epigraph for Rousseau's *Émile*, "We are sick with curable diseases, and if we wish to be cured, nature comes to our aid, for we are born to health" (*R* 46, Ak 6:20).[19]

---

19. The quotation is from Seneca's *De ira* 2.13.1. Although Kant hints that Rousseau holds an optimistic view, Rousseau did not, in fact, believe in progress. He saw history as a fall from original purity, and although that fall was inevitable, even necessary in order for human beings to enter into a civilized state, Rousseau held out no clear or systematic hope for the future. As I have argued, Rousseau does not endorse morally meaningful change. He was an optimist of *being*, not *becoming*. For a sympathetic treatment of Rousseau's theodicy and the eighteenth-century context, see Ernest Cassirer, *The Question of Jean-Jacques Rousseau*, 71–82. Cassirer perceptively notes that "Rousseau's solution of the theodicy problem consisted in his removing the burden of responsibility from God and putting it on society" (77). God's work is perfect; the refinements and mannered artificiality of society corrupt. As we shall see, Kant also shifts theodicy earthwards; however, unlike Rousseau, Kant puts responsibility on each of us, not on society as an abstraction.

For Kant, neither the ancient pessimist nor the modern optimist persuades. He rejects both with little argument, insinuating that the Manichean view is too fabulous to be worthy of analysis and simply observing that the innate-goodness view is contrary to all observation. In spite of Kant's quick dismissal, we do well to consider how both his humanism and commitment to change make both views impossible, for many readers of Kant have nodded with approval as he dismissed fatalistic pessimism but have been very surprised by his rejection of the "heroic opinion."[20] How can Kant reject the innate-goodness view? After all, if we matter most for the highest good, then surely we must contain the kernel of the highest good within our breasts. Just this inference seems inevitable, given Kant's eloquent panegyrics to the moral law that lie ever within our hearts. Moreover, without the innate-goodness view, do we not backslide into some version of the Manichean view, complete with revelations and oracles, sacrifices and petitions? Either the gods hold the key to the highest good, or we do. If we do, as we-matter-most humanism requires, then surely the innate-goodness view is correct. Kant, however, treats both the Manichean and innate-goodness views as impossible. Neither provides the personal interpretation of evil necessary for a humanistic understanding of our moral destiny. Both treat the moral drama as external to personal identity.

The Manichean view submerges humanity in a whirlpool of evil that is fundamentally extrinsic to the human person. The result is a repressive determination of our destiny. Our fate, for either good or evil, is shaped from without. This view of our condition is at odds with the logic of we-matter-most humanism. Victims of higher powers

---

In *Kant's Ethical Thought* (Cambridge: Cambridge University Press, 1999), Allen Wood argues that Kant advances an explanation of evil that parallels Rousseau's. For Kant, according to Wood, "ambition is the root of all evil" (290). If I am correct in my analysis of the logic of Kant's view in comparison to Rousseau's, then such a convergence is impossible, and Wood is attracted in this direction because he confuses Kant's many observations about the forms that evil takes in human life with its explanation and source. Here, Kant often follows Rousseau's brilliant insights into moral pathology, even as he diverges from Rousseau in his account of evil and its relation to personal identity.

20. See Emil Fackenheim, "Kant and Radical Evil," in *The God Within: Kant, Schelling, and Historicity* (ed. John Burbidge; Toronto: University of Toronto Press, 1996), 21. Goethe's response was especially bitter. In a letter to Johann Herder, quoted by Fackenheim, Goethe wrote, "Kant required a long lifetime to purify his philosophical mantle of many impurities and prejudices. And now he has wantonly tainted it with the shameful stain of radical evil, in order that Christians too might be attracted to kiss its hem."

(although in *Religion within the Boundaries of Mere Reason* Kant mentions only divine powers, such forces may be natural or supernatural), we cannot be sufficient for the highest good. Ancient or modern, this turn away from the human point of view and toward some greater perspective turns evil into a by-product of deeper and more significant forces. We do not hope for a good will; rather, we hope for the triumph of our gods over those of another. Or, like Voltaire, we rebel against the fact that our relation to the highest good is vulnerable to cruel misfortune. For the modern materialist, we hope for nothing at all and resign ourselves to the way things are. Whether we turn with redoubled energy to reading the oracles, shake our fists at a god, or smile with irony upon moral striving convinced that our ideas of good and evil are natural or social, we can have no humanistic objections to crushing authoritarianism or vain overreaching. Our diminishments and excesses are either epiphenomena of an agon of the gods—or they are just part of the mute world into which we are thrown.

Kant is clearly more sympathetic to the "heroic opinion" of the proponents of innate goodness. No danger of either priestcraft or moral despair exists here. Nonetheless, he rejects the "heroic opinion" outright. A celebration of innate goodness is inconsistent with a humanism committed to moral change for exactly the same reason that the Manichean view is inconsistent. To be sure, the optimist sees humanity rising above, rather than drowning beneath, the currents of evil, but an innate determination also depersonalizes our moral destiny. Instead of making moral change the consequence of who we are, as individuals, the "heroic opinion" treats change as an inevitable process. For some optimists, our humanity is good, and our common human nature impels us forward, drawing us across the gap between the evil we presently experience and the good for which we are born. Others embed our identities in the historical process and, reading the tea leaves of the past, predict a happy outcome. In both cases, being human is enough; the innate disposition toward goodness works its magic against evil and closes the gap. But in that process, no matter how glorious the outcome, you and I matter only in a generic sense. The suprahuman gods are replaced by "human nature," but the upshot is the same. Good and evil are not personal; the power that drives moral change rests in something greater than the features of our lives that identify us as distinct and unique persons. We do not matter most as unique individuals; we matter only as placeholders for an innate propensity toward goodness.[21]

Kant's deepest reasons for rejecting the Manichean and innate-goodness views, then, amount to the same principle: moral predicates must be personal predicates, or to use his language, moral predicates must be imputable. This notion is central to my overall assessment of Kant's cure of the soul, and we have already seen it in action, implicitly, with the concept of worthiness that links virtue and happiness. So we do well to be as precise as possible. According to Kant, something is imputable if and only if it is "adopted through the free power of choice" or is caused by "a freely acting being" or has "originated from freedom."[22] We need not enter into the details of Kant's moral theory and anthropology, especially the enigmatic status of freedom as a power or act that can serve as an origin, cause, or determination. These difficulties, real though they are in Kant's system, are not central. More decisive is the formal point. Moral terms are imputable if and only if the person alone is a sufficient explanation for their predication. An act or personal quality is morally praiseworthy or blameworthy only if "the human being alone is its author" (*R* 47, Ak 6:22).

Kant wraps himself in enigmatic tautologies when he describes the dynamics of freedom. Having restricted concepts of time, cause, and substance to the phenomenal realm constructed by our perception and thought, Kant tests the limits of language when he tries to explain how a noumenal act of freedom (if the very notion of "act" is intelligible without concepts of time and causality) can determine the maxims and character that constitute the actual persons we experience in

---

21. The reason why Kant rejects the innate-goodness view clearly separates him from the Stoic interpretation of our moral destiny. For Kant, Stoic theory rightly views morality as based on reason and freedom: "They could not have laid down a better or nobler principle for a foundation" (*R* 77, Ak 6:58). Their error, however, rested in explaining the gap. For Stoic theory, reason needs to triumph over inclination. However, for Kant, the Stoic conception of the gap and our destiny across the gap mislocates evil. Unlike the Stoics, Kant refuses to adopt a strategic dualism in order to preserve a zone of innate goodness within the identity of the person. For Kant, "considered in themselves natural inclinations are good, i.e., not reprehensible, and to want to extirpate them would not only be futile but harmful and blameworthy as well" (*R* 78, Ak 6:58). Indeed, a Stoic project of superseding human embodiment and passion would, for Kant, be a classic case of vain overreaching and, as such, is contrary to the logic of we-matter-most humanism. Who we are—all of who we are—is necessary for what is best, and this includes our inclinations as well as our reason. Our goal as moral beings, for Kant, should be to redeem ourselves rather than our reason.

22. Kant's use of the concept of imputation abounds in *Religion within the Boundaries of Mere Reason*. These examples come from *R* 50, Ak 6:25; *R* 58, Ak 6:35; *R* 60, Ak 6:38.

the world. These tangled phrases and formulations need not distract. As we have seen, the important affirmation involves the logic of we-matter-most humanism. As individuals, we must be necessary and sufficient for the highest good, and how Kant explicates that logical connection with anthropological categories is a matter of indifference. It is enough, for Kant, to say that I or you are good because of who we are as individual persons. This close connection between who we are and moral predicates must be true; otherwise, we-matter-most humanism is false. Moral faith cannot bear the thought that this humanism is false; therefore, the connection obtains.

Just such a vision of the highest good and its relationship to personal identity constrains what Kant can say about the nature of evil and the cause of the gap. If moral predicates are imputable, then evil can only be a moral predicate if you and I are sufficient explanations. For Kant, then, using the vocabulary of his moral anthropology, "evil can only attach to the moral faculty of choice. Nothing is . . . morally (i.e., imputably) evil but that which is our own deed" (R 54–55, Ak 6:31). Again, we must beware trying to peer too deeply into words such as "moral faculty of choice" or "our own deed." They are placeholders for whatever makes an individual different from everybody else, placeholders for whatever gives an individual identity as a distinct person. So for Kant, the essential principle is clear. The relationship of moral predicates to personal identity makes any external or generic explanation of good and evil impossible. Good and evil are personal predicates, imputable states of affairs, and therefore, actual persons, and not "human nature," are the only proper subjects of moral predicates. We can only say that a person is good or evil because of his or her identity, because of who he or she is.

While the imputable status of moral predicates requires Kant to reject the Manichean and innate-goodness views of the status of good and evil, Kant's rejection of the mixed view requires a further specification of the relationship between moral terms and personal identity. Precisely because good and evil are imputable, experience guides us to say that people are partly good and partly evil. People do some things that are good and other things that are evil, so we should impute to them both and, therefore, assume a mixed moral status. Although Kant observes that "experience seems to confirm this middle position between the two extremes" of complete goodness and evil, he rejects the mixed view as well (R 47, Ak 6:22). Again, his reasoning depends, not on the cogency of his moral anthropology, but upon the logic of we-matter-most humanism. This logic requires him to treat moral predicates as determinative and disjunctive, as well as personal and imputable.

For Kant, our moral predicates are determinative in the sense that they constitute our personal identities. In his vocabulary, the "freedom of the power of choice"—that strange noumenal act that makes us who we are—"cannot be determined to action through any incentive except so far as the human being has incorporated it into his maxim" (*R* 49, Ak 6:23–24). Here, Kant envisions an anthropology in which some deep power of self-determination gives direction and shape—a "propensity," to use his term—to the complex structure of intentions and attitudes that establishes our distinctive stance in the world. Of course, Kant allows that we might analyze the complex structure of a person's character and choices in mixed terms, but the decision either for or against the moral law is fundamental, and our overall stance with respect to the world can be only good or evil. Our "disposition as regards the moral law," writes Kant, "is never indifferent"; it is either good or bad (*R* 49, Ak 6:24). We are either working towards conformity to the moral law, or we are not. There is no third (mixed) possibility. Again, we can tear out our hair trying to parse Kant's anthropology—the nesting relationships of the power of choice, incentives, and maxims; the layers of inclination and propensity that he deploys to describe the structure of character—but to do so only distracts. His central claim is that morality is the most important thing, and therefore, moral predicates are determinative of personal identity.

Like "imputable," "determinative" is a concept central to my overall analysis, so precision is necessary. A description of a person is determinative, for Kant, if and only if that description is a necessary condition for identifying that person. That is, no personal identity exists such that the person can be identified first in a nonmoral way and then assigned moral predicates. This must be the case, for morality is an overriding feature of life. For modern humanism, criticizing crushing authoritarianism and vain overreaching must trump all other considerations. We cannot say that the despot's sharp sword is necessary for social order, and therefore is justified. We cannot say that fanaticism leavens society with useful utopian ideals or that quietism is a necessary opiate of the masses. We cannot because moral change must be fundamental and indispensable. No compromises are possible. The need for moral change must go to the core of our destinies as persons. Good and evil, then, must be determinative in the deepest possible sense, and for this reason, the mixed view is impossible.

I hope these observations are sufficient to show that Kant's approach to moral terms flows from the logic of modern humanism. As we-matter-most humanism requires, Kant must presuppose that the highest good follows from personal identity, which leads him to say that moral states of affairs are both imputable and determinative. Since we are necessary and sufficient for what is best, the presence or absence of the highest good is only explicable by something imputable to us, that is to say, only explicable because of our identities as persons. To say otherwise entails backsliding into some form of crushing authoritarianism, for to allow that we are not sufficient creates a logical possibility that something else is necessary, and the defenders of dogma rush in with their arguments about the supernatural revelation and the human need for divine guidance. Furthermore, because we are necessary for what is best, the presence or absence of the highest good must stem from our identities as persons; otherwise, some fundamental part of who we are need not be necessary, and this opens the door to vain overreaching. If the highest good does not require our full participation, then it is just a family argument about what part of the soul must be excised and left behind. Within the logic of we-matter-most humanism, then, good and evil are bonded to personal identity. In the end, how Kant explicates this bond is unimportant. His confusing moral anthropology has value only to the extent that it shows how the bond functions logically. And as I have argued, that bond functions according to the underlying entailments of we-matter-most humanism, and these entailments, not the plausibility of Kant's moral anthropology, govern his approach to evil and the need for change.[23]

---

23. Kant signals the primacy of humanistic logic over anthropological cogency when he distinguishes between the empirical, observable character of the moral life and its intelligible character. "Experience," Kant notes, "can never expose the root of evil" (*R* 61, Ak 6:39). Indeed, the very categories of freedom are noumenal, that is to say, consequences of how we must think about the world and our place in it, and not the result of observation. Therefore, we must not undertake to reflect about the nature of good and evil and the human relation to morality in terms of a picture of human life that, somehow, maps onto our experience. Instead, for Kant, our reflections must take place "in the representation of reason" (*R* 62, Ak 6:39). We can either conceive of the "representation of reason" as an occult realm of speculative fancy, or we can treat Kant's remarks as straightforward observations that our moral theories are entailments of fundamental moral prejudices. I have chosen the latter approach. "Freedom" is noumenal in the strict sense of being entailed in our basic moral beliefs. Because we matter most for the highest good, something fundamental to who we are must be necessary and sufficient such that the highest good is imputable and determinative. "Freedom" is Kant's word for that "something fundamental." Nothing besides the conviction that we matter most makes the notion of freedom either more plausible or intelligible for Kant.

Kant's Radical-Evil View

The same logic that guides Kant's rejection of the Manichean, innate-goodness, and mixed views also shapes his own radical-evil view. If something fundamental about who we are is necessary and sufficient for the highest good, then the highest good obtains because of who we are. But even a child knows that the highest good does not obtain. We experience the gap between how we live and how we ought to live. Only someone bewitched by Rousseau's therapy of moral exculpation could imagine that, contrary to our first, second, and third impressions, what is best really does obtain, and evil is merely a shadow play of false consciousness. Therefore, we must conclude that we are not necessary and sufficient for what is best. We are, to use Kant's vocabulary, radically evil.[24]

If we insist on proceeding anthropologically, then the only way to preserve moral change as a rational goal for human life in the face of evil seems to be a retreat from the logic of we-matter-most humanism. For example, we can return to the mixed view. The gap is real, we might allow, but not determinative of who we are. Our moral aspirations are only part of our complex human lives, aspirations that must be balanced with other (nonmoral) dimensions. This way is

---

24. My reading of *Religion within the Boundaries of Mere Reason* is opposed to that offered by Gordon Michalson in *Fallen Freedom: Kant on Radical Evil and Moral Regeneration* (Cambridge: Cambridge University Press, 1990). Michalson observes that Kant's account of moral evil and the possibility of moral change is beset by a number of vacillations or "wobbles." The most important are (1) humanity as innately evil and the ultimate source of goodness, (2) evil as innate and the result of freedom, (3) moral change as obligatory but evil as inextirpable, and (4) moral change as purely human yet requiring, perhaps, some divine assistance (8). Michalson is right to avoid calling these contradictions. Kant makes distinctions adequate to avoid contradiction in each case. Nonetheless, the conjunctions are strange. Michalson explains them as a consequence of Kant's dividing his loyalties between modern Enlightenment and premodern Christian cultures. "Kant's problems," Michalson writes, "are the problems of a thinker who is straddling worlds but who cannot possibly possess the historical perspective to assay the terrain causing his uncomfortable posture" (5). By my reading, nothing could be further from the truth. Kant's strange conjunctions of claims stem from the logic of his humanism.

In *Kant's Conception of Moral Character*, Munzel amasses textual evidence to show that the problem of evil within human character arises "from within Kant's thought" rather than from "a theological doctrine imported from outside" (134). She argues that Kant's moral theory and anthropology positively require him to adopt the doctrine of radical evil outlined in book 1 of *Religion within the Boundaries of Mere Reason*. In what follows I seek to advance the same argument, but my approach is different. Munzel undertakes a close reading of the often changing nuances of Kant's distinctive vocabulary and theory. I use the heuristic device of we-matter-most humanism and its logical requirements in order to show the intrinsic necessity of radical evil in Kant's moral vision.

open, but morality loses its overriding importance, and the consequences for the modern prejudices against authority and overreaching are significant. If we are a great deal more than our moral characters, and if our lives are far more complex and diverse than the moral dimension, then given the intrinsically complex nature of human life, our objections to crushing authoritarianism are purely relative to an overall balancing of concerns, moral and otherwise. Perhaps individuality needs to be restrained, even repressed, in order to maintain social stability and provide people with an adequate sense of belonging. Perhaps human life cannot flourish without adequate opportunities to indulge in fanatical beliefs and irrational behavior. Perhaps, contra Hume, we would be better off with the leaven of enthusiasm and the submissive, monkish virtues of superstition. So, if we rebel against Kant's radical-evil view and take Hume's approach, then we should at least be clear that the zealous modern prejudices against crushing authoritarianism and vain overreaching lose their unequivocal and overriding status.

This retreat from moral rigorism and the high drama of moral change is not necessary. To be sure, in Kant's account of radical evil, we are bonded to good and evil such that these moral notions are necessarily imputable and determinative. But this is a statement about personal identity, not the powers and potencies that persons might possess by virtue of being free and rational creatures. Kant intends nothing more than an explication of the relation between personal identity and moral predicates when he makes confusing use of general notions such as "innate" or "by nature." For example, he says that when we apply predicates of good or evil to persons, we should say "of one of these characters . . . that it is *innate* in him" (*R* 47, Ak 6:21). Or again, Kant says, in a programmatic declaration, "*The human being is* (by nature) *either morally good or morally evil*" (*R* 47, Ak 6:22). His use of "innate" and "by nature" sounds like a return to the innate-goodness (or evil) view. But such a return is impossible, on Kant's own terms. Kant insists that "we shall always be satisfied that nature is not to blame for it (if the character is evil), nor does it deserve praise (if it is good), but that the human being alone is its author" (*R* 47, Ak 6:21).

If we remain with Kant's vocabulary of freedom and nature, then these formulations can seem hopelessly contradictory: good and evil are grounded in the exercise of freedom, *and* good and evil are innate, or consequences of our natures. However, Kant is not using "innate" or "by nature" as descriptions of human anthropology; he is using them as terms within the logic of we-matter-most humanism and its commitments to the relation between personal identity and the highest good. When Kant uses the term "innate," he denotes a feature of our identity that is determinative. Except for something innate, you or I would not be the individual persons we are (see *R* 55, Ak 6:32). When Kant speaks of a universal propensity toward evil or says that we are evil by nature, he intends to signify an observation that all persons of the class "human beings" fail, in fact, to be the kinds of people necessary and sufficient for the highest good (see *R* 56, Ak 6:32). Thus, for Kant, if you and I are evil, then we are so innately—that is to say, in a way determinative of and imputable to our identities as persons. Empirical observation shows that all persons are evil, and therefore, he says that we are evil "by nature." In other words, persons are evil with the same reliable certainty as the rising and setting of the sun. In both cases, the problem of evil, however deep and ubiquitous, is a purely personal problem. It has to do with who we are, as individuals.

I hope that I have persuaded readers that understanding Kant's account of evil and our need for change does not depend upon his often shifting moral anthropology—or an unconscious loyalty to the piety of his childhood. When observation of persons combines with the logic of we-matter-most humanism, the radical-evil view necessarily follows. Imputable and determinative evil clings to our personal identity. Within Kant's system it has nowhere else to go.[25] Because we matter most for the highest good, either we, as individuals, are the necessary and sufficient explanation for evil, or evil does not exist as a moral phenomenon. To acknowledge moral evil, therefore, necessarily implicates us in it. Because moral predicates are imputable, we cannot shift moral blame outwards and away from ourselves. Because

---

25. With tortured complexity Michalson traces the shifting nuances and terminology of Kant's philosophical anthropology, following a long line of distinguished commentators who seek clues to Kant's doctrine of radical evil in the distinctions between *Wille* and *Willkür* or *Anlage* and *Hang*, or "evil by nature" and "evil by necessity." Michalson's judgment is that Kant's definition of moral evil "consists of a series of delicate balancing acts" in which "balancing shades into self-contradiction" (*Fallen Freedom*, 47). Kant's position is neither complex nor delicate. If evil is moral, then it must be the form of our freedom. Evil must be determinative of and imputable to who we are as persons. Kant does not try to balance his shifting characterizations of that determinative and imputable status. Instead, he simply arranges prevailing anthropological categories on an ad hoc basis in order to express and reinforce the inexorable logic of we-matter-most humanism as it encounters the reality of evil and the necessity of change.

moral predicates are determinative, no part of ourselves is free from evil. The logic of we-matter-most humanism draws moral predicates into a close relationship with personal identity; therefore, if there is a *moral* basis for our need for change, then we must be the very source of that need. We are the problem that moral change seeks to solve.[26]

Kant's radical-evil view may strike readers as fatal to the project of modern humanism, for it seems to submerge the person in a whirlpool of innate evil, a propensity that determines who we are. However, Kant's fearless embrace of radical evil, far from fatal to the transformative vision of modern humanism, is a necessary condition for explaining why the moral prejudices against crushing authoritarianism and vain overreaching are legitimate, for only the radical-evil view can explain the overriding need for moral change. As a purely personal problem, evil requires a purely personal solution. We need to change because we are not who we ought to be. For just this reason, and no other, the moral prejudices against crushing authoritarianism and vain overreaching, prejudices that motivate intense efforts to transform inherited forms of law, social structures, and religious beliefs, are justified as genuinely humanistic projects. The world must be reshaped to serve *our* problem. Thus, far from a pious anomaly, Kant's doctrine of radical evil is the necessary basis for a story of moral change told according to the logic of we-matter-most humanism. Only if evil is imputable and determinative can we affirm the reality of evil, the necessity of change, and the deepest commitments of modern humanism to the central role of personal identity.[27]

---

26. Here, Fackenheim offers a helpful assessment of the constraints under which Kant operates: "Kant's shift to radical evil is made for a strictly philosophical reason; and this reason is, strangely enough, the need to give a full and adequate justification of moral freedom" (*The God Within*, 21). My goal has been to explicate, in terms of the larger constraints of we-matter-most humanism, why Kant must give an adequate justification of moral freedom and how, in that justification, "moral freedom" is best understood as a series of logical commitments regarding the relationship between morality and personal identity.

27. Kant draws the same conclusion at the end of "Conjectural Beginning of Human History," his meditation on the origins of human culture. Kant concludes that the only conceptually consistent account of the origin and significance of evil requires us to assign sole responsibility to each and every person. Summing up his account, he writes:

An exposition of [man's] history such as the above . . . teaches him that he must not blame the evils which oppress him on Providence, nor attribute his own offense to an original sin committed by his first parents. (For free actions can in no respects be hereditary.) Such an exposition teaches man that, under like circumstances, he would act exactly like his first parents, that is, abuse reason in the very first use of reason, the advice

Now that Kant has explained why we need to change, the plot thickens, and the central dramatic enigma emerges. First, how can we have a consequential role? How can we, as evil, serve as a basis for the highest good? In short, how can we, not simply as free and rational creatures but as actual persons who have, by virtue of our very identities as persons, caused evil, also provide its remedy in a turn to righteousness? Familiar to Western culture, these questions are properly Augustinian. The problem defines the theological preoccupations of Western Christianity; indeed, the controversies of Pelagianism, Arminianism, Synergism, and in the modern period the humanist concern about crushing authoritarianism are all formulated against the background of the central Augustinian question: What has the power of righteousness? All presuppose the Augustinian principle that only pure righteousness has power over evil. The debates center on deciding who possesses this supremely consequential power—human persons or something else.

Our participation involves more than potency, more than consequential influence. As we have seen, connection to the highest good also requires continuity, which leads to the second half of the dramatic enigma of change. This is the Athanasian dimension of the problem of change, and it has to do with continuity between who we are as the source of evil and who we will become as participants in righteousness. Given the width of the gap, how can we see ourselves as the same? How can we conceive of change as anything other than annihilation? These questions are less familiar. Western culture does not tend to formulate worries about the future under the guidance of Athanasius's most famous principle: That which is not assumed is not redeemed. Our eagerness for change tends to overwhelm the need to show that the future, somehow, "assumes" or "accounts for" the past and present. However, as I have attempted to show so far, the drama of humanistic change is deeply, and rightly, committed to personal con-

----

of nature to the contrary notwithstanding. Hence he must recognize what they have done as his own act, and thus blame only himself for the evils which spring from the abuse of reason. (*Kant on History* [ed. Lewis White Beck; New York: Macmillan, 1985], 68, Ak 8:123).

The same message is embedded in Kant's famous formulation of the true meaning of enlightenment: it "is man's release from his self-incurred tutelage" (3, Ak 8:35). Our need for moral change is entirely self-caused. For Kant, this self-blame does not debilitate and demoralize. Because such a view of evil reinforces the logic of we-matter-most humanism, it is "useful for man, and conducive to his instruction and improvement" (68, Ak 8:123). Only a doctrine of radical evil can support a story of moral change in which the person is supremely consequential, both as cause of the need and source of the deliverance.

tinuity. Something like Athanasius's principle stands behind the humanistic concern about vain overreaching, and it cannot be neglected.

To see how Kant resolves the dramatic enigma of our participation in the highest good, both in terms of Augustinian concerns about potency and the Athanasian emphasis on continuity, we must turn to his story of the soul. A humanistic revision of the standard Augustinian plot of sin and repentance, this story focuses, as does Augustine, on the question of potency. The difference, of course, is that Kant reverses the ascription of effective power. He permits no recourse to divine grace in our turn to righteousness. Even though we are in bondage to sin, we retain the power of pure righteousness that can redeem. The turn from evil to good must come entirely from within. In freedom, we can embrace duty for its own sake, and by the relentless mechanisms of worthiness, the highest good will obtain. Only by telling the Augustinian story in this way can Kant remain true to the antiauthoritarian prejudices that animate modern humanism.

Unfortunately for Kant, and by extension for the ambitious critical agenda of modern humanism, Kant cannot support self-wrought personal change and at the same time affirm the humanistic criticisms of vain overreaching. The Athanasian concern about continuity necessarily emerges, and however successful Kant may be in imputing potency for change to human persons, he cannot show how moral change "assumes" that which it "redeems." I hope to show that this does not stem from an omission on Kant's part. It does not result from the fact that he gives too much attention to the question of potency and not enough to that of continuity. Rather, I will argue that, in affirming the supremely consequential role of personal identity for the highest good, Kant cannot maintain continuity. He cannot affirm that we are sufficient for the highest good in the sense that it follows from our freedom and at the same time affirm that we are necessary in the sense of remaining continuous persons across the changes wrought by freedom. The logic of modern humanism drives him into the quicksand of contradiction. But I am jumping ahead of myself. We need to let Kant tell his humanistic story of the soul.

–Chapter 5–

THE NEED FOR ATONEMENT

No one chooses to possess the whole world if he has first to become someone else.

—ARISTOTLE, *NICHOMACHEAN ETHICS*

Few commentators take Kant's radical-evil view seriously. Because Kant's moral philosophy is so full of encomiums to the sublime beauty and commanding power of the moral law, readers find it difficult to imagine that Kant could really believe that human beings are innately evil, and as a result, sympathetic readers slide into exculpation. Kant, we imagine, accommodated his moral philosophy to Christian theology and seemed to affirm the doctrine of original sin in order to evade the repressive Prussian censors.[1] This hypothesis may save Kant from the radical-evil view—but at the cost of his intellectual integrity and

---

1. The death of Frederick the Great in 1786 led to changes in the religious and educational policies of the Prussian state in which Kant worked. In 1788, Frederick's successor, Frederick William II, appointed new administrators for the church and education. The new administration issued a strict censorship edict that imposed silence on any who might challenge the ecclesiastical doctrine of the Prussian church. The atmosphere of repression led Kant's admirers to assume that the delay in publication of the *Metaphysics of Morals* in 1791 stemmed from official interference. A former student wrote Kant, "People around here are saying . . . Woltersdorf, the new ecclesiastical authority, has managed to get the King to forbid you to write any more" (letter from Kiesewetter to Kant, 14 June 1791, Ak 11:173, quoted from *The Conflict of the Faculties* [trans. Mary J. Gregor; New York: Abaris, 1979], xi). Kant's struggle to secure publication of *Religion within the Boundaries of Mere Reason* testifies to the plausibility of worries about repressive censorship. Kant managed to gain approval for publication by manipulating a clause in Prussian law that allowed the publication of any academic book approved by a German university faculty. An imprimatur from the philosophy faculty at the University of Jena allowed Kant to publish *Religion within the Boundaries of Mere Reason* in 1793.

courage. However, we need not speculate about Kant's fear of censorship and assume dissimulation. Instead, we can put Kant in his "historical context." Child of pietism and product of a religious age, Kant could not help, we might say, harboring premodern thoughts about innate human evil, thoughts that worked their way into his philosophical theology.[2] Or we might separate Kant's works and treat *Religion within the Boundaries of Mere Reason* as a philosophical exercise in cultural criticism, not at all necessary for understanding the logic of his moral thought, and very likely less disciplined and careful.[3] In this way, the radical-evil view can be isolated from the core of Kant's humanism and downplayed as an altogether excusable failure to fully apply his own best insights. He should have criticized Christian doctrine for its lack of confidence in the human person, but perhaps Kant felt that he needed to make some concessions to the Christian worldview in order to ensure that his readers would remain open to proper instruction on more important matters.

However unsupported textually and impossible logically, the prevailing rejection of Kant's radical-evil view is not unintelligent. Commentators are often so blind to the necessity of the radical-evil view because they are so sensible of the difficulty it creates. Kant himself clearly articulates this problem. "This evil is *radical*," he affirms, "since it corrupts the ground of all maxims" (*R* 59, Ak 6:37). The affirmation of innate evil leads to an inference familiar to centuries of Christian theologians and very much on the mind of any reader who has grasped the logic of the radical-evil view. Because evil determines our identities, "it is also not to be *extirpated* through human forces, for this could only happen through good maxims—something that

2. This is Michalson's interpretive assumption: "The theory of radical evil is finally symptomatic of the fact that Kant has not yet thrown off the habits of mind produced by Christian culture" (*Fallen Freedom*, 9).

3. Ernst Cassirer's assessment is typical. For him, the decade that saw the publication of *Religion within the Boundaries of Mere Reason* was characterized by Kant's turn from fundamental systematic concerns to the application of his philosophical insights to current events and practical problems. "The critical philosopher," observes Cassirer of this period, "who had just completed the whole of his theoretical edifice, turns journalist," and he does so "in order to take up in concert [with the Berlin school of enlightenment philosophy] the fight against political and intellectual reaction in Prussia" (*Kant's Life and Thought* [trans. James Haden; New Haven: Yale University Press, 1981], 367). Given this judgment, Cassirer treats Kant's *Religion within the Boundaries of Mere Reason* as an epiphenomenal work that is "not on a par with the writing on the foundation of his system, with the *Critique of Pure Reason* or of *Practical Reason*, with the *Foundations of the Metaphysics of Morals*, or the *Critique of Judgment*" (381).

cannot take place if the subjective supreme ground of all maxims is presupposed to be corrupted" (*R* 59, Ak 6:37). Kant formulates this difficulty again and again in *Religion within the Boundaries of Mere Reason*. "If humankind is corrupt by nature," he asks, "how can a human being believe that on his own, try hard as he will, he can make a 'new man' of himself" (*R* 124, Ak 6:117)? In short, if evil is innate, then either (1) we become good as a consequence of external intervention, or (2) we simply remain evil.

The traditional Christian approach adopts solution 1 to the problem of evil. Christ dies for us; therefore, we are saved. But any recourse to external explanations of moral progress entails a renunciation of the logic of we-matter-most humanism. If Christ is necessary, then we are not sufficient. For this reason, Kant consistently argues against the Christian solution to the problem of our radical evil. But this seems to force Kant to affirm solution 2 and the conclusion that we are inevitably evil. However, inevitable evil is the death of moral aspiration and contradicts the moral faith of we-matter-most humanism even more deeply than the Christian doctrine of salvation through Christ. Therefore, even though evil is imputable and determinative, Kant insists upon a third possibility: "It must be possible to *overcome* this evil" (*R* 59, Ak 6:37). We must be able to become good, and this change must be self-wrought. The power for change must rest within us. This third possibility, however difficult to explicate, attracts Kant's unwavering commitment. And it must be so, for otherwise modern humanism fails.

In view of this fundamental commitment, Kant embarks upon an anthropodicy. Whereas classical theism must square evil with the presumptive power and goodness of God, modern humanism must coordinate an affirmation of the sufficient power of personal identity for the highest good with the reality of evil. This anthropodicy follows the same logic that produced the radical-evil view. First, how can our identities, determined by evil, give rise to new identities, now determined by goodness rather than evil? We-matter-most humanism requires Kant to answer this question by simply reversing the Augustinian solution. We are a sufficient explanation for change; therefore, the goodness we seek can be imputed to us. The logic of we-matter-most humanism and its opposition to crushing authoritarianism require this affirmation, and I call it the "personal-potency requirement." Kant is well aware of this requirement and devotes a great deal of effort to showing how we might reasonably believe that we possess such potency for moral change. The first section of this chapter, "Personal Potency and the Horror of Dependence," charts these efforts.

A second question motivating Kant's anthropodicy is Athanasian, and it is equally important, although less obvious at first glance. How can we become new persons, reborn from evil to goodness, without becoming different persons entirely? We must say that in becoming morally different we remain morally continuous to a degree sufficient to ensure that we are the self-same subjects who were evil but are now good. Again, the logic of we-matter-most humanism and its rejection of vain overreaching require such an affirmation, and I call this the "personal-continuity requirement." Kant is less clear about this requirement, but it emerges again and again in *Religion within the Boundaries of Mere Reason,* coming into clearest focus when he discusses the moral need for atonement. The second section of this chapter, "Personal Continuity and the Fear of Difference," focuses on this aspect of Kant's anthropodicy.

The personal-potency and personal-continuity requirements pose severe difficulties, certainly difficulties deep enough to tempt a reader to think Kant's embrace of the radical-evil view is ill considered and the consequent requirements of a humanistic anthropodicy are impossible to satisfy.[4] The possibility of moral rebirth faces a seemingly insuperable problem. A thing cannot change itself, at least not in the fundamental sense of becoming a different thing, for such a possibility would lead to the absurdity that something is what it is and not

---

4. Kant recognizes a natural tendency to treat the problem of evil so that such difficulties are avoided. Because all of us feel the power of impulse and inclination, as well as the distorting influences of custom and social convention, we are tempted to describe the conflict between good and evil as a struggle of the "real me" against something fundamentally external to our identities. My reason wars against my inclinations; my innate goodness struggles against stifling institutions. Kant treats these redescriptions of moral conflict in anthropological or sociological terms as various forms of Stoicism, and he rejects them as mislocations of the conflict between good and evil. Kant uses the cosmic pictures of Christian doctrine to express his point. Moral good differs from moral evil "not as heaven from *earth,* but as heaven from *hell*" (*R* 79, Ak 6:60). The conflict, then, is not between ourselves and something else, a way of thinking about good and evil that gives rise to theodicy problems (how could the world be set up in such an inauspicious way?). Instead, the conflict is within our identities as moral beings. Our destinies depend upon the outcome of a conflict between two antithetical principles, both of which only exist as imputable to and determinative of personal identity—(1) the principle of duty for its own sake and (2) any other mode of life. Therefore, the problem of evil is purely personal. Evil does not make the world or God inexplicable; instead, for Kant, evil throws into doubt our role as the fulcrum from evil to good and, as such, requires an anthropodicy.

what it is because of itself. Continuity poses a problem as well. The chasm of difference created by the moral revolution necessary to transform our hearts seems to annihilate, rather than reform, our identities. How can a good being have anything to do, morally, with an evil being? Critical thought, however, is a heroic endeavor, and Kant is not deterred by these difficulties. He knows that his moral faith must provide the suitable conditions for narrating a life of moral change, and he is confident that he can tell a genuinely humanistic story of the soul. But contradiction corrupts the narrative. The Athanasian concerns about personal continuity cannot be satisfied under the logical constraints of we-matter-most humanism. The third and final section of the chapter, "The Failure of We-Matter-Most Humanism," offers a meditation on the consequences of this failure for modern humanism.

Personal Potency and the Horror of Dependence

For Kant, the personal-potency requirement is obvious and stems from the same logical foundation as we-matter-most humanism's rejection of authoritarianism in all forms. Obligatory dogma and required patterns of life entail implicit repudiations of our sufficiency. No matter how benevolent the power, no matter how attractive the outcome, any account of moral change that requires us to depend upon an external force contradicts we-matter-most humanism. Even though we are evil—and are so fundamentally and because of who we are—we must become good because of who we are; otherwise, no matter how positive the change, it cannot be imputed and therefore is not a properly moral change. As Kant reports with an urgency born of his awareness that modern humanism turns on the drama of anthropodicy, the evil man "must be able to *hope* that, by the exertion of *his own* power, he will attain to the road that leads [to righteousness]." And this hope must be maintained, "for he ought to become a good human being yet cannot be judged *morally* good except on the basis of what can be imputed to him as done by him" (*R* 71, Ak 6:51). The horror of dependence rebels against all but an imputable destiny and therefore requires self-wrought moral transformation.

On this point, Kant is unequivocal and simply declares that moral change must be possible. This aspect of the problem of evil is solved by the sheer certainty that we are supremely consequential for the highest good. Kant reiterates the requirement of personal potency: "The human being must make or have made *himself* into whatever he is or should become in a moral sense, good or evil. Both must be the effect of his free power of choice, for otherwise they could not be imputed to him and, consequently, he could be neither *morally* good nor evil" (*R* 65, Ak 6:44). Moral predicates are the deepest facts about who we are, and for that reason, they are determinative of personal identity. Yet, for Kant, the human creature is unique in the capacity to alter identity. At the most fundamental level, we are free; we are our power of becoming.

This presumption of a personal potency toward change is not immediately obvious. "How it is possible," acknowledges Kant, "that a naturally evil human being should make himself into a good human being surpasses every concept of ours. For how can an evil tree bear good fruit?" (*R* 66, Ak 6:44–45). We seem condemned to be evil, for an evil tree cannot bear good fruit. But what seems absurd regarding trees need not be absurd regarding persons. After all, as Kant observes, the moral identity of persons "cannot be mediated through insight into the causal determination of the freedom of a human being, *i.e.,* into the causes that make a human being become good or bad: in other words, it cannot be resolved theoretically, for this question totally surpasses the speculative capacity of our reason" (*R* 124, Ak 6:117–18).[5] Therefore, we have no reason to object to the affirmation that we really can change from evil to good.

Kant insists upon the possibility of self-wrought moral change for the same reasons that he advances the postulates of God, freedom, and immortality. The fundamental conditions of moral existence are only accessible in a critical analysis of what is entailed in the indis-

---

5. The vocabulary that Kant uses to describe our moral transformation invites the theoretical inquiry he rejects. He often describes our change of heart as a "decision," a "choice," or as something "done" (*R* 68, 65, 71; Ak 6:48, 44, 51). These terms suggest an identifiable psychic event or act that is the underlying key to our identities. Such a reading is, however, impossible. Deeds, choices, and actions are good or evil because of who we are—they must be; otherwise, they are not imputable. They cannot be the cause or basis for the moral determination of our identities. In spite of his constant recourse to causal images and hypothetical (in the strict sense of that term) psychic events, Kant is as committed to avoiding any theoretical gap between who we are and our moral status. The inscrutable "ground" of our heart simply *is* who we are, and precisely because that identity matters most, it must be the cause, not the effect, of the specific features of our lives such as choices and deeds. The value of translating Kant's formulations into specific rules for the relationship between morality and personal identity is that the confusion resulting from his use of the language of causality and discrete mental events can be avoided. For Kant's discussion of the special use of the concept of cause with respect to freedom and the moral law, see his "Of the Right of Pure Reason to an Extension of Its Practical Use Which Is Not Possible to It in Its Speculative Use" (*CPR* 52–59, Ak 5:50–58).

putable certainty of our moral vocations. We know what is actual and possible by considering what is morally necessary. This holds true for our status as persons and our ability to change. We are moral beings, and as such, even though determined by evil, we remain compelled by duty. Even if we assess our current condition as innately evil (an assessment itself compelled by the logic of we-matter-most humanism), "the command that we *ought* to become better human beings still resounds in our souls; consequently we must also be capable of it" (*R* 66, Ak 6:45). We must have a potency sufficient to effect real moral change, not because of any property we can identify within our experience of ourselves and not because of any analogy to the properties of beings, as such. Rather, we must affirm our power to change because a humanistic faith requires us to affirm that we are sufficient for the highest good. Thus, in spite of the apparent implausibility of saying that we have the power to make ourselves righteous, we simply must affirm our personal potency; otherwise, we contradict the certain (our sense of the inner dignity and supremacy of our moral vocations) by the merely probable (what we can know about ourselves and the world through observation and analysis).[6]

We need to be as clear as possible about the force of this *must;* otherwise, we misread Kant's explanations of the possibility of moral change. Kant's argument is simple and is summarized in a single affirmation: "Duty commands nothing but what we can do" (*R* 68, Ak 6:47). Either we can change ourselves, morally, or we cannot. If we cannot, then either the moral project is futile, or our moral change depends upon an external force or potency that is supervenient. Neither is consistent with the moral project of modern humanism, and therefore we must be able to change ourselves.

To deny the possibility of moral change makes moral aspiration futile. It makes moral criticism into an empty protest and leads to the

---

6. As Kant insists, "The objective reality of a pure will or of a pure practical reason (they being the same) is given in the moral law a priori, as it were by a fact" (*CPrR* 57, Ak 5:55). Moral experience provides that which empirical observation cannot: the overwhelming certainty of sheer givenness. See, as well, the constant rhetoric of "stability and objective reality," of truths "now confirmed by fact" that can "be clearly seen as real" found in the preface to the *Critique of Practical Reason* (3–14, Ak 5:3–14). However much we might privilege the natural sciences and their practices of empirical observation, Kant leaves no doubt that he regards the force of our moral sensibilities as yielding far greater epistemic compulsion. We can entertain many different conceptions about the ways of the world, but, for Kant, we can think only one way about how we ought to live in the world.

conclusion that evil must simply be accepted. Our moral sense would simply be a source of fruitless anxiety, a cursed impulse to do what cannot be done, and a pointless cause of guilt and needless self-sacrifice. Kant never entertains this possibility, for it utterly defeats the transformative project of modern humanism. Surely we cannot say that moral change is impossible and that we seek righteousness in vain.

The second possibility—the notion that moral change is possible but depends upon a supervenient, extrapersonal power—is also repugnant to Kant. Crushing authoritarianism and vain overreaching diminish human dignity precisely because they drive a wedge between who we are and the highest good. Religious dogma and supernatural faith propose a higher power and greater goal as necessary and, in so doing, clear the way for legitimating the very diminishments of human dignity against which modern humanism protests. Therefore, Kant rigorously applies the logical requirements of we-matter-most humanism. Whatever might be entailed in affirming our present identities as morally evil, Kant will not pay the price of dependence in order to secure a righteous future. Our hope is neither moral nor ours unless we seek an imputable righteousness. If righteousness depends upon any external power, then it cannot be imputed, which is inconsistent with the requirement of personal potency. Therefore, no matter how determinative our evil, we must believe that we are able to effect a moral revolution of our identities. No other conclusion is consistent with the moral faith of modern humanism.

The *possibility* of a self-caused change in identity follows from the logic of we-matter-most humanism. It must be affirmed in order to do justice to the ambitions of modern humanism. However, the *plausibility* of such a change is an entirely different question. Here, Kant's anthropodicy, as developed in *Religion within the Boundaries of Mere Reason,* is not primarily a matter of charting entailments. Instead, Kant works hard to show how self-wrought change is consistent with some of our deepest intuitions about the impediments to change and the limits of human potency. First, Kant helps us grasp the conceptual intelligibility of the change in our identities. If moral predicates are basic to who we are, so basic, indeed, that we must say that evil is innate, then how can the power for change come from who we are? To answer this question, Kant gives a precise account of the determinative, but not exhaustive, status of moral predicates. Just as importantly, the ordinary facts of our lives speak against Kant's affirmation of the personal-potency requirement, which leads to the second point of inquiry. The imperatives of duty may be categorical, but their actual psychological force is slender. Indeed, the fact that we are evil testifies to the psychological weakness of duty alone. To counteract this weakness, Kant speculates about how the psychological force of duty is enhanced by our moral imaginations. Finally, even if we concede the possibility of moral revolution, we necessarily view moral change as more than a matter of the heart. The highest good is for persons, not rational wills, and therefore, our character and behavior must change as well. This takes time and effort. To address this concern, Kant uses the metric of worthiness to explain the possibility of divine assistance in the overall project of bringing our lives into full conformity with our inner commitment to righteousness.

Evil as Determinative but Not Exhaustive

In Kant's terminology, we are not so much wicked as perverse. The human heart is not diabolical. One does not "incorporate evil *qua* evil for incentive into one's maxim" (*R* 60, Ak 6:37). Instead, our hearts are bent by any number of deformations that render our maxims impure. This perverse heart retains a propensity toward goodness. Continuing to compel us in our ongoing sense of duty, the moral law is the seed of inner transformation. We need, then, to be careful in our understanding of the relationship between personal identity and moral predicates. Moral evil is abroad and does determine our identities. However, though determinative, evil is not exhaustive, and as a consequence, the springs of rectitude remain vital within us.

Kant's restriction of the scope of innate evil does not entail backsliding to the mixed view. We *are* evil in the fundamental sense of not being who we are were we not evil. In this precise sense, evil determines our identities. Nonetheless, if we see how the failure to adopt the moral law for its own sake, by rendering our maxims impure, determines our identity as evil, we can recognize that this form of personal identity is not inconsistent with an ongoing personal potency for moral change. A righteous destiny is not impossible because "the restoration of the original predisposition to good in us is not therefore the acquisition of a lost incentive for the good, since we were never able to lose the incentive that consists in the respect for the moral law" (*R* 67, Ak 6:46). As persons, we are innately evil in the specific sense Kant intends—evil is imputable and determinative—but as human beings, we retain, by nature, a potency toward goodness.

Righteousness is not, then, a blind hope. The highest good entails restoring our impulse toward goodness to its proper seat as the pure incentive for our maxims, and this impulse, although it presently does not determine our personal identity, is a resident possibility, already part of our inheritance as human beings.

Archetypes and Symbolic Stimulation

The naked assertion that "ought implies can" may follow from the logical requirements of we-matter-most humanism, but as a statement about human motivation, it is unpersuasive. One is hard-pressed to imagine that a proposition such as "Choose maxims which might serve as legislation for the Kingdom of Ends" communicates sufficient psychological force to lead an actual human will to conform to such a grand commandment.[7] Kant is sensible of this limitation, and he clarifies the specific way in which duty takes on motivational force. We do not function as moral philosophers, enumerating, in our heads, the proper form of the universal moral law. Instead, our moral imaginations form a picture of the righteous life.[8] As Kant reports, "Human beings cannot form for themselves any concept of the degree and strength of a force like that of a moral disposition except by representing it surrounded by obstacles and yet—in the midst of the greatest possible temptations—victorious" (*R* 80, Ak 6:61). We imagine a life of rectitude, and this imaginative construction, both stimulated by actual examples of righteous people and guided by our moral sense, takes a determinate shape already imprinted on our imaginations as an archetype (*Urbild*).[9] In so doing, the punctilious urgency of duty

7. See Lewis White Beck's observations about the psychic impotence of the moral law in *A Commentary on Kant's Critique of Practical Reason* (Chicago: University of Chicago Press, 1960), 221.

8. See Kant's general discussion of moral education based upon the "biographies of ancient and modern times with the purpose of having examples at hand" (*CPrR* 158, Ak 5:154). The vivid presentation of moral principles through their exemplification in life helps to vivify the moral imagination. In biographies, the highest good does "not remain objective laws of morality which we merely admire and esteem in relation to mankind in general. Rather we see the idea of them in relation to man as an individual" (*CPrR* 161, Ak 5:157).

9. The Wood and di Giovanni translation I have been following translates *Urbild* as "prototype" rather than "archetype." With the word *Urbild*, Kant clearly intends to denote a fundamental and ideal picture of the righteous life, and the English word "prototype" fails to capture the proper sense of Kant's use. The prototype of an invention is a first try, often imperfect. The archetype is the idea the inventor has in mind and toward which a succession of prototypes aspires with greater and greater accuracy. Since Kant is clear that the idea of moral perfection

takes on a fleshly form as the animating principle of a human life, and thus the moral law becomes a fully shaped existential aspiration.

Kant describes the potency of this archetype as a *"practical faith in the Son of God"* (*R* 80, Ak 6:62). Our moral desire for change seeks a concrete, humanly enacted goal, and to the extent that we conceive of an ideal life, we are able to give our moral desire a realistic picture of fulfillment. At this point, however, we need to be absolutely clear about Kant's continued commitment to the personal-potency requirement. In no sense do we depend upon the actual existence of a person who lives a perfectly righteous life. The possibility of moral change stems from a moral faith in the logic of we-matter-most humanism, and that faith "can never be understood by reason nor verified by examples from experience" (*R* 81, Ak 6:62). That is to say, no reasons we can give, theoretical or experimental, are more certain than the proposition that we are sufficient for the highest good. Therefore, for Kant, "there is no need of any example from experience to make the idea of a human being morally pleasing to God an archetype for us; it is present, as such, already in our reason" (*R* 81, Ak 6:62). Whatever force the archetype—or the actual persons who attract our moral admiration as embodying the moral ideal—might apply to our present evil disposition, the leverage is entirely within our distinctiveness as rational creatures. The potency of the "Son of God" is within the ambit of our personal identities; it is part of our inheritance as human beings, an inheritance contravened but not extinguished by our determination as evil. Thus, the symbolic potency of any ideally realized life of righteousness is a properly personal potency, and we rightly impute to ourselves the change stimulated by such symbolic representations of moral righteousness.[10]

---

always already exists in our reason and cannot be adequately represented in outward experience, "archetype" more adequately expresses Kant's use of *Urbild* than does "prototype." Indeed, a clear exposition of Kant's Christology could exploit the difference between prototype and archetype to good effect. We possess, in our reason, an archetype of moral perfection, and actual historical persons such as Jesus of Nazareth are prototypes, sensuous representations that allow us to see the moral perfection "in history," stimulating us to tinker and improve upon them in our moral imaginations. In view of these considerations, I will translate *Urbild* as archetype throughout.

10. See Kant's humanistic revision of the prologue to the Gospel of John (*R* 79–80, Ak 6:60–62). "The human being" takes the place of the divine Word as the only-begotten Son by whom all things were made. The sufficiency of who we are for the highest good guides Kant to assert that the human person is the logos of all things. This revision simply restates Kant's conviction, surveyed in chapter 4, that the order of the cosmos is structured around the moral vocation of human beings.

Kant vigorously enforces the personal-potency requirement throughout his discussion of the role of religion in our drive toward moral change. At their best, religious traditions preserve the vivid products of the moral imagination. We might well acknowledge that Christianity has preserved an especially powerful portrayal of a life of pure righteousness. Jesus, we might say, is a man whose teaching is so edifying and action so transparent to the moral law and whose motivations are proven so pure in suffering and death, that his image is remarkably, even supremely, potent in awakening the idea of moral goodness within us.[11] Kant does not wish to eliminate this potentially helpful stimulus from our moral imaginations; quite the contrary, he has every hope of buttressing its moral potency. However, Kant's affirmation of the symbolic value of Christianity never slips into the mode of dependence. If our moral change is to be imputable, we alone must be a sufficient explanation for its occurrence. Nothing else can be necessary. Thus, however much Kant wishes to give sensual form to the ideal of moral rectitude, he insists that this fullness resides within our potency as moral creatures.[12] The levers of change are necessarily within; Kant always respects the personal-potency requirement.[13]

---

11. When discussing the role of exemplary persons, Kant places an especial emphasis on the role of suffering. Kant remarks that we see the purity of people's motivations in situations of pain and sacrifice "because it is in suffering that they most notably show themselves" (*CPrR* 160, Ak 5:156). The clarifying importance of suffering is sealed in a self-sacrificing death (*CPrR* 162, Ak 5:158).

12. In the *Groundwork of the Metaphysics of Morals,* Kant is very clear that exemplars of moral virtue must be properly engaged to avoid dependence: "Imitation has no place in moral matters, and examples serve only for encouragement, that is, they put the feasibility of what the law commands beyond doubt and they present graphically what is more generally expressed by the practical rule. But they can never justify our setting aside their true original inherent to reason and our guiding ourselves by examples" (Ak 4:403. I draw this quote from Munzel's *Kant's Conception of Moral Character,* 289). No matter how we conceive of the archetype, no matter how complex our hermeneutics, no matter how profound our theology of the symbol, no matter how we parse our participation in Jesus' life, for Kant, the logic of modern humanism is clear. Jesus' role must reduce to an external and dispensable stimulus.

13. We can see, then, how the personal-potency requirement leads to projection theories of religion that further tighten the relationship between the human person and the symbolic power of religious forms. Since the power of the archetype resides within, it is natural to conclude that its origin and source also rest within the human psyche, externalized by a process of representation and objectification. For a classical account, see Ludwig Feuerbach's *The Essence of Christianity.* Feuerbach offers a helpful illustration not only of the consequences of Kant's personal-potency requirement but also of Kant's failure to conform to the personal-continuity requirement. Feuerbach completes the humanistic reduction of the supernatural to innate human powers, but he renounces the fundamental humanistic commitment to personal identity as sufficient for the highest good, adopting instead a collective and corporate entity that he calls "species being," which bears the proper redemptive power of change. If my assessment of Kant

Worthiness and Divine Assistance

When I restore my antique automobile, I begin with the engine, then move on to the transmission, passing on to body work. In a gradual manner I renew the vehicle to its original splendor. Restoring the heart is quite different. For Kant, our maxims are either formed by the incentive of rectitude or not—we either are determined by evil or not—there is no question of degrees. Nonetheless, the idea that we can become morally good in the blink of an eye contravenes our experience. Moral change seems an arduous process, not an instantaneous revolution. To help buttress the plausibility of his claim on behalf of personal potency for moral change, Kant distinguishes between a change in personal identity and a change in character, belief, and behavior. Empirical conformity to the moral law admits of infinite gradations. "Virtue in this sense," observes Kant, "is acquired little by little, and to some it means a long habituation (in the observance of the law) in virtue of which a human being, through gradual reformation of conduct and consolidation of his maxims, passes from a propensity to vice to its opposite" (*R* 67, Ak 6:47). But we should not confuse the process by which our lives become integrated in conformity to our moral identities with the underlying necessity for change in our moral identities. That change "cannot be effected through gradual reform but must rather be effected through a revolution in the disposition of the human being" (*R* 68, Ak 6:47). A change of heart is an act of freedom, a moment of rebirth and new creation.

Once Kant distinguishes between the revolution necessary in our change in identity and the long process that might be required for outward changes in behavior, he has the conceptual means to accommodate our sense that the moral project, as a whole, cannot be carried forward entirely out of the resources of the individual person. External factors help and hinder our efforts to change. Kant has no interest in denying this fact about human life. Nonetheless, Kant exploits the distinction between change in moral identity and change in moral behavior in order to distinguish between our moral worthiness and our moral fulfillment. If we change ourselves by adopting the moral law as the basis for our maxims, then we have changed our identities. We

---

in the next section is correct, then Feuerbach moves in this direction because of the inability of we-matter-most humanism to give a noncontradictory account of the continuity of personal identity—the endurance of the very source of moral change. "Species being" is elastic enough to undergo change. One can celebrate and serve "humanity" while overseeing executions and training a vanguard.

are no longer determined by evil; instead, we are determined by good, and in that fundamental sense, we are worthy of being called good persons rather than bad. Furthermore, if we are worthy by virtue of self-wrought moral revolution within our hearts, then, argues Kant, external assistance in the gradual process of moral reform conforms to the personal-potency requirement. The worthiness of the person secures the rewards. God can intervene and assist us in bringing the heterogeneity of our desires, intentions, and behavior into full conformity with our inner determination toward the good, for in so doing, supernatural assistance does nothing more than accelerate a process that, given the postulates of God and immortality, will occur in any event. To the worthy person, then, any assistance is "deserved," and therefore the consequences of assistance are imputable.[14]

Kant shrouds this moral change that leads to worthiness and deserts in epistemic uncertainty; we cannot ever get underneath our psychic lives and the layers of self-deception in order to see who we are, in this fundamental sense. So, strictly speaking, we can never know whether we are worthy and, therefore, deserve supernatural assistance. But Kant is not constructing a moral theory out of what can be deduced experimentally, or even what can be proven theoretically. Instead, he is ordering our relationship to the world and its claims upon us according to the logic of we-matter-most humanism. This logic produced the personal-potency requirement in the first place. Therefore, when ordering our relationship to traditional religion and its beliefs about the possibility of divine assistance, Kant has a double interest. First, he is aware of our sense of how daunting the project of moral change seems. We have a long way to go in order to live up to the purity of moral obligation, and for this reason, Kant thinks a religious belief in divine

---

14. Here, my analysis diverges, in part, from John E. Hare's account of Kant's appeals to divine assistance. Hare offers a lucid exposition of the problem of the moral gap and Kant's commitment to closing the gap in such a way that we matter most for the highest good. However, in explaining Kant's anthropodicy, Hare manifests typically Augustinian preoccupations by running together the personal-potency requirement and the personal-continuity requirement. As a result, Hare takes Kant's failure to satisfy the personal-continuity requirement in his account of atonement as a general failure to explain the possibility of self-wrought moral change. By dividing the anthropodicy problem as I have done, we can see that Kant does provide a self-consistent account of our potency for moral change, and in so doing, he may legitimately appeal to divine assistance in any case where the human person is worthy. Such appeals may have no plausible basis, but they are consistent with the logic of we-matter-most humanism. As we shall see, Hare is quite right in arguing that Kant's account of atonement fails, but that incoherence turns on the personal-continuity requirement, not the question of potency for change and the possible role of divine assistance. See Hare's *The Moral Gap: Kantian Ethics, Human Limits, and God's Assistance*, 60–68.

assistance is beneficial. The more realistic the goal, the more likely we are to strive toward it. However, Kant's second interest rests in clarifying the limits of this assistance. We are supremely consequential for the highest good only if we are a sufficient reason for its achievement, and as a consequence, external assistance must follow from who we are. External assistance must be an imputable consequence of our moral identities. The notion of worthiness secures this logical relationship here, as it does throughout Kant's different discussions of the ways in which righteousness comes to full expression in human life. Because a person with a transformed moral identity is worthy, external assistance is deserved; the plus of assistance follows from who the changed person *is*, morally speaking.[15]

---

15. The same logic of worth and deserts guides Kant's treatment of the suprapersonal influence of history. Not only may we hope for divine assistance in overcoming the constellation of impediments distinctive to our personal situations; we may also have some confidence in the benevolent movements of providence. In the history of religions, for instance, the representations of the moral imagination have become more and more adequately aligned with the necessities of duty. Thus, Kant is able to narrate a version of biblical history in which the representations of goodness move from the external incentives of Jewish law to the goodness of Jesus (see *R* 94–98, Ak 6:78–84). Kant adopts the same progressive optimism for the development of human society in general. We may rightfully anticipate an evolution in public life toward greater and greater conformity to the highest good. In both cases, these auspicious developments do not undermine the personal-potency requirement. Kant is clear: "The profit which will accrue to the human race as it works its way forward will not be an ever increasing quality of *morality* in its attitudes." After all, our moral standing, our worthiness, depends entirely upon our free disposition toward the moral law. "Instead," Kant continues, "the legality of [prevailing social] attitudes will produce an increasing number of actions governed by duty, whatever the particular motive behind these actions may be." In no sense does a better society make people righteous. The individual person is the sole and sufficient basis for the purity of intentions that defines righteousness; external factors can never be relevant. "In other words, the profit will result from man's good deeds as they grow ever more numerous and successful, i.e., from the external phenomena of man's moral nature" (all quotations from *The Contest of the Faculties*, par. 9, in *Kant's Political Writings* [ed. Hans Reiss; Cambridge: Cambridge University Press, 1970], 187–88). Like Kant's account of divine assistance of the worthy individual, his accounts of general providence take pains to distinguish between the moral identity of the individual, which depends entirely upon that person, and the auspicious conditions for manifesting that moral identity in outward action.

Kant's positive assessment of historical progress leads Michalson to conclude that "the mood" of Kant's treatment of history is quite different from the dark pessimism found in *Religion within the Boundaries of Mere Reason*. For Michalson, the earlier writings construct a "rationalizing teleology" that presupposes the humanizing conventions of social life. By Michalson's reading, the doctrine of radical evil in book 1 of *Religion* repudiates this earlier optimism, as "late in life" Kant takes "seriously some of the more sinister implications of his own theory of freedom," which, in turn, leads to "episodes of philosophical flatfootedness" as the residual optimism clashes with the growing pessimism (*Fallen Freedom*, 27). However, if we read Kant's account of human worthiness and divine assistance appropriately, and apply the same analysis to his optimistic assessment of the general providence, then his view of historical progress is entirely consistent with his insistence that good and evil must be imputed of individual persons.

This form of dependence—assistance based upon inner worthiness—is entirely compatible with the requirement of personal potency. We need not believe in such assistance, but properly conceived, such assistance is not inconsistent with we-matter-most humanism. We seek a life of integrated righteousness in which the social, as well as the personal, constitute the highest good, and if our aspirations are to be realistic and effectively motivated, we must believe that such a life is possible. This necessity led Kant to postulate the existence of a God who sets up the world as an essentially congenial stage upon which to act out our moral dramas, as well as the postulate of immortality, which removes all temporal barriers to our hope for moral progress. The special interventions of grace and the general aids of providence serve the same purpose and according to the same logic of worthiness. They contribute to our need for reassurance that righteousness will find its way toward full expression. As long as these external aids follow from worthiness, this hope supports, rather than undermines, the effectiveness of modern humanism.[16]

I am not interested in exploiting the difficulties Kant faces in making plausible his account of our potency for change. Because critical thought tries to see things as they are, not as they seem, it always courts the strange and counterintuitive, and Kant's thought is no exception. Instead, my goal has been simple: to show that, however underdetermined by our ordinary sense of human powers and capac-

---

16. Munzel tracks the same strategy in Kant's attempts to parse the relationship between moral identity and the process of moral self-realization in his treatment of pedagogy (*Kant's Conception of Moral Character*, 254–333). As Munzel explains, "Ultimate responsibility does lie with the individual; the essential act of the revolution of conduct of thought is just the virtue that cannot be taught. In connection with the fact that character is a matter of the subjectively practical realization of freedom, the conclusion resolves the apparent contradiction between Kant's pedagogical and moral orders" (260). Munzel's goal is to show that Kant's moral philosophy, and by extension the larger project of modern humanism, need not endorse a formal libertarianism in order to avoid paternalism and other authoritarian threats. "The provision and fostering of external conditions and ultimate individual responsibility," argues Munzel, "do not contradict one another" (261). My analysis concurs. However, Munzel, like so many interpreters of Kant and defenders of the ambitions of modernity, is bewitched by the questions of dependence and freedom. The Augustinian problems dominate. She does not attend to the Athanasian problems of disjunction and continuity. These problems are very much a part of the pedagogical environment. Consider the widely noted discontinuity reported by those who have "converted" from traditional upbringings to critical intellectual inquiry, the inability of the "modern theologian" to converse with his or her grandparents about central matters of faith, the sociologists' Olympian perspective in comparison to those who feel the immediacy of cultural demands. I shall argue in the next section that Kant faces contradictions in articulating the conditions for continuity and that these contradictions typify the failures of modernity.

ities, Kant's account of the possibility of self-wrought moral change follows the logic of we-matter-most humanism and does so without contradiction. We can say that our situation is fraught with evil. Oppression abounds. Dogmatism is rife. Superstition predominates. Guided by the logic of we-matter-most humanism, we can even say that all this evil stems from persons. We are not victims of anything but ourselves. Yet, at the same time, we can say, without contradiction, that we matter most as the sufficient source of the highest good. We have the potency to make all the difference necessary to reform and renew personal and public life. These affirmations provide the basis for telling a coherent story of the soul engaged in the drama of moral change, and for this reason, Kant has gone halfway toward articulating a successful humanistic anthropodicy. The urgency of the horror of dependence, the zealous desire to overturn traditional hierarchies and authorities, is consistent with a confidence that we retain an effective power for moral change. Thus, at least on the question of personal potency, Kant can construct a picture of human destiny that is as plausible as the humanistic faith that inspires us to affirm the sufficiency of human beings in the first place.

Personal Continuity and the Fear of Difference

Without doubt, in *Religion within the Boundaries of Mere Reason*, Kant is primarily concerned with the personal-potency requirement. He worries about the subordination of human initiative and responsibility to higher powers, and as a result, a great deal of his analysis involves establishing the sufficiency of human potency toward righteousness. Nonetheless, Kant is aware of the personal-continuity requirement. After stating his solution to the problem of self-wrought change in book 2 of *Religion within the Boundaries of Mere Reason*, Kant allows that a humanistic anthropodicy still faces great difficulties. No matter how much potency we concede to the person, and no matter how we allocate the role of divine assistance through the metrics of worthiness so that the person remains the sufficient explanation for the highest good, Kant allows that a person who has changed from evil to good *"nevertheless started from evil,"* and this point of departure creates a moral disjunction (*R* 88, Ak 6:72). The problem, here, rests in continuity. Kant sees that the story of our souls must explain how an evil person is connected to the good person he or she seeks to become.

The story is difficult to tell because Kant does not shy away from the strongly disjunctive consequences of moral change. Thus, for Kant's humanism, the problem of evil takes on a new form. If we have to change, then how can Kant say that our identities as persons are necessary for the highest good? Indeed, as we seek the highest good, we must, as evil, *seek not to be* in order for righteousness to obtain. Where is the place for continuity in this kind of change?

The ways in which the personal-continuity requirement shapes this aspect of the problem of evil, both for Kant and the humanistic faith he represents, are crucial for my overall argument. So, before moving to Kant's proposed anthropodicy, we need to be clear about the constraints imposed by the logic of we-matter-most humanism. A humanistic account of moral change must acknowledge the determinative and disjunctive status of moral predicates. About this Kant is utterly clear, as his rejections of the intrinsic-goodness and mixed-identity solutions to the problem of evil testify. Thus, (1) evil is determinative, and as such, if we are to be called evil, then we are who we are if and only if we are so described. The good is also determinative, and if we can change and be called good, then we are who we are if and only if we are so described. Furthermore, (2) good and evil are disjunctive as well as determinative. Therefore, if we are evil, then we cannot be good, and if we are good, then we cannot be evil. The combination of (1) and (2) produces a dramatic conclusion about moral change. It is a fundamental change in personal identity. If I start out evil, and Kant insists that I do, then becoming good entails becoming someone I am not. The logic of we-matter-most humanism allows no other outcome, and as a consequence, Kant must work overtime to show how the humanistic faith that creates the disjunction also provides the basis for bridging the gap and ensuring personal continuity.

Kant identifies the Christian doctrine of atonement as the locus for reflection about continuity. Closely related to the notion of worthiness, the machinery of debt and punishment that characterizes a great deal of Christian reflection on the saving significance of Jesus' death provides Kant with the conceptual resources to explain the nature of the disjunction created by moral change. The legal-moral language clarifies the consequences and constraints of moral character. The choices we make and the life we lead constitute the material form of our freedom, our identity as moral persons. Insofar as we matter at all for the highest good, our embrace of evil matters as well. As we have seen, because our identities are consequential, evil is imputable.

However this imputation is not simply verbal, as if the consequences of evil were exhausted in the very ascription of the word to persons. Rather, evil carries a burden of material liability. Following mainstream Protestant doctrines of atonement, Kant conceptualizes this material liability in terms of debt. Using the Pauline language of the old man of sin and the new man of righteousness, Kant explains that the old man incurs a debt. It is an imputable moral status that stems from the identity of the person as evil.

The notion of debt is attractive to Kant not simply because it has a central role in certain streams of Protestant piety; more importantly, the notion of debt requiring payment signals the material liability of evil, just as worthiness secures the material rewards of righteousness. In this way, a moral logic establishes the strict conditions under which our identities as moral persons function as supremely consequential, as the open variable in a morally governed cosmos. Debt ensures that suffering and debility are distributed in "exact proportion" to the evil that is necessarily imputed to individual persons. The gears of the moral universe turn on our freedom. Of course, Kant is no more able to provide empirical evidence that the consequences of debt follow than he was able to show that worthiness is rewarded. Such confidence stems from "pure practical reason." That is to say, we must believe that our lives have consequences, and those consequences must be determined by our identities as moral agents.

An important difference exists, however, between Kant's use of the words "debt" and "worthiness." He consistently employed "worthiness" to talk about the connection between present identity (a righteous persons who lacks the happiness necessary for the highest good) and the future. In this way, "worthiness" serves to explicate the prospective consequences of a change that has already occurred. It answers the question "How is my present identity going to be the sufficient basis for all the morally meaningful aspects of my future life?" by reassuring us that whatever influences and assistance we might need to achieve an integrated life will all stem from the fundamental fact of who we are. In this way, as we have seen, the concept of worthiness reinforces the personal-potency requirement by organizing the full realization of righteousness according to a moral logic. In contrast, Kant uses "debt" to give logical clarity to the retrospective dimension of change, and this retrospection involves the fundamentally different problem of continuity across change. "Debt" speaks of the enduring consequences, and "debt payment" entails establishing a morally significant connection between present identity (as one now righteous) and past identity (as one once determined by evil). As the bridge between who we were and who we have now become, "debt" is a morally disciplined connection between two different identities, one determined by evil and the other by righteousness. For this reason, "debt" functions in Kant's analysis as a disciplined moral calculus for meeting the personal-continuity requirement. It answers the question "How am I connected to the person I once was and now so deeply regret?" With the notion of imputable debt and payment, the logical difficulties raised by this question can be properly formulated.

To begin, as long as we are evil, we cannot pay the debt incurred by our evil identities. Because evil is determinative and disjunctive, an evil person simply is evil, and even though all human beings retain the possibility of righteousness (evil is determinative, not exhaustive), there is no imputable element of goodness with which to balance out the accounts. To say that an evil man cannot pay the debts of his evil is hardly surprising, but precisely because Kant affirms our personal potency for change, we seem to possess the power to become righteous. Therefore, Kant leaves open the possibility that the new man, born with the intrinsic potency for righteousness that all of us possess, might pay the debt of the old man. The transaction seems simple. Yesterday I incurred a debt; today I pay off the balance.

Yet, what seems so simple in the world of finance turns out to be impossible in the world of moral transactions. As Kant observes, a man who changes from evil to good endures as a continuous embodied being: "*Physically* ([i.e.] considered in his empirical character as a sensible being) he still is the same human being" (*R* 90, Ak 6:74). However, the same might be said of a person after he suffers a massive brain injury or even death. Bodily continuity is by no means a sufficient basis for personal continuity. We may need a body in order to be a person, but in no sense are our bodies the basis or sufficient condition for personal continuity. Of this Kant is well aware. What is important, for Kant, is that after a man changes from evil to good, "he is *morally* another being" (*R* 90, Ak 6:74). Since, for Kant, moral predicates are intrinsic to personal identity—as we have seen, we-matter-most humanism necessarily defines moral predicates as determinative —moral change entails personal change. Within the logic of we-matter-most humanism, a morally changed person is quite simply another person. Therefore, the new man is a different person from the old man. The man who owed the debt yesterday is not the same man as the one who has the righteousness to pay today.

The difference in moral identity makes all the difference. Moral debt, unlike financial debt, is imputable. The old man owes the debt, and only he can pay it. Here, Kant is true to the logic of his humanism. Our moral standing is necessarily constituted by our own identities. Only the worthy are rewarded and only because of their worthiness. The same holds true for those who incur the debt of radical evil. They and only they must bear the consequences of who they are. As such, a moral debt "cannot be erased by somebody else" (*R* 89, Ak 6:72). This intensifies the problem of personal continuity. The new man, whatever surplus of merit he might enjoy, cannot pay the debt of the old man because moral change creates a disjunction of persons and because moral debt, unlike financial debt, is a moral predicate, is therefore imputable, and cannot be transferred. In theological language, the new man cannot *atone* for the old man. No morally significant relationship seems to exist between the person I presently am and the person I seek to become.

Kant expresses the same difficulty of establishing continuity across moral change when he uses the closely related concepts of punishment and satisfaction. As we have seen, Kant's postulate of divine existence serves to support the affirmation that the world is set up to bring about the triumph of righteousness and the unity of virtue and happiness. As such, not only will the righteous prosper, but the evil person, and the forms of life that sustain evil, will fail. The notion of divine punishment gives dramatic form to this failure. The old man, as evil, is liable to punishment; his way of living will lead to frustration and defeat. This punishment, like debt, is a moral predicate and is imputable. The upshot is the same strict assignment of liability. Here, Kant gives the issue clear expression. As determined by evil, the old man deserves punishment: "*After* his conversion, however, since he now leads a new life and has become a 'new man,' the punishment cannot be considered appropriate to his new quality (of thus being a human being well-pleasing to God)" (*R* 89, Ak 6:73). The old man, and only the old man, should endure punishment. Only the old man can be held morally accountable for the consequences of his identity as an evil person. Thus, the new man, as a morally different person, cannot offer satisfaction; he cannot rightfully endure punishment for the old man. The evil person deserves punishment, and that punishment cannot be suffered by another without violating the intimate bond between moral predicates and personal identity.

We should be clear, then, that Kant's use of the concepts of debt and punishment are not "legalistic" in any narrow sense. "Debt" and "payment," "punishment" and "satisfaction," express the humanistic conviction that our lives are consequential. They are abstractions that help bring to the fore our existential anxieties about the disjunctive dangers of moral change, worries that who we now are (as those seeking moral change) may have no role in a hoped-for reign of righteousness. Just these concerns are at stake when Kant adopts the divine perspective in order to use the concept of ubiquitous and imputable punishment to reinforce the idea of the enduring consequences of personal identity. Supreme Justice, he explains, dictates that "no one deserving punishment can go unpunished" (*R* 90, Ak 6:73). We should beware reading this as a speculation regarding what God needs. Kant has no interest in this relation between God and particular persons, except as governed by an overriding moral logic. As he reports, "we understand nothing of such intangible relations of the human being to the highest being" (*R* 89, Ak 6:72). Rather, Supreme Justice signifies the logical requirements of we-matter-most humanism. God sets up the world so that we matter most for the highest good, as both supremely consequential and necessarily continuous. We will be punished (or rewarded) because of who we are, and for no other reason—God has no choice in the matter. These consequences of debt (or worthiness) will endure forever—the demands of Supreme Justice are deathless.[17]

We live in an age that shrinks from the necessity of punishment and regards retribution with horror. For this reason we can too easily miss

---

17. In his analysis of Kant in "Christian Atonement and Kantian Justification," *Faith and Philosophy* 3, no. 4 (October 1986), Philip L. Quinn reads Kant's use of the divine perspective too literally. In his detailed treatment of Kant's doctrine of atonement, Quinn focuses on the need for consistency in divine justice as such. This leads Quinn in the same direction as so many other interpreters. He interprets the problems of atonement as further variations on the theme of worthiness and divine assistance and assumes that the deepest difficulty, for Kant, is finding a way to identify the source of sufficient surplus merit to pay the debts of sin. This creates the consequent need for God "to supplement one's efforts" (455). The upshot of the supplement is a view, which Quinn ascribes to Kant, that "requires the cooperation of freedom and grace" (455). My goal is to translate the question of divine justice into Kant's more logically fundamental humanism (as Kant does so often in his moral philosophy). This shifts attention away from the classical Augustinian preoccupation with the relationship of divine and human potency, a preoccupation easily grasped with concepts of divine justice and human merit, and focuses on the Athanasian problem of our relation to our future. This self-relation and the requirement of continuity are the basis of Kant's concern about atonement, and it is the central problem facing the humanism that Kant advocates.

the real role of the seemingly compulsive concern that Kant has for debt and satisfaction. Kant is no more committed to a picture of life as governed by the logic of pitiless debt collection than classical Christian doctrines of atonement are invested in a picture of God as a bloodthirsty cosmic accountant. Both wish to understand the nature of our hope and the logic of redemptive change. For Kant, this means that debt should be understood as the means to conceptualize the positive acts and conditions that give life substantial form as a unified whole.[18] Under conditions of personal change from evil to righteousness, to pay off the debt entails "accounting for" or "atoning for" the kind of person one once was. Debt discharged is like worthiness rewarded. Debt discharged integrates the full sweep of a person's life under a moral logic and establishes the continuous role of all aspects of our identities as persons across moral change, which is the essence of the personal-continuity requirement. Meeting this requirement is one important role of the doctrine of atonement within Christian theology; it is the only role for the doctrine of atonement in Kant's anthropodicy.[19] And this role is central, for Kant must formulate an account of atonement that meets the personal-continuity requirement; otherwise,

---

18. Compare this with Anselm's use of honor and satisfaction in his classical account of atonement in *Cur Deus Homo*. Anselm, unlike Kant, takes the divine perspective seriously for its own sake, and his treatise is far more aptly described as a theodicy rather than an anthropodicy. See 1.13 and the discussion of the need for satisfaction that ends with a typical formulation of the theodicy problem: "Either the honor that was taken away must be repaid or punishment must follow. Otherwise, God will be either unjust to himself or powerless to accomplish either." In spite of this difference, Anselm's approach clearly resembles Kant's. Both are concerned to identify and explicate the ordered means by which change occurs such that the dramatic difference between sin and redemption does not create a disordered and fragmented disjunction. In this sense, Anselm represents a theocentric version of the humanistic worry about personal continuity, keyed to the need for divine continuity rather than human continuity. Nonetheless, like Kant, Anselm uses the logic of debt and satisfaction to achieve clarity about the conditions for that continuity.

19. In his introduction to the Wood and di Giovanni translation of *Religion within the Boundaries of Mere Reason and Other Writings*, Robert Merrihew Adams offers a helpful explanation of the underlying concern about personal continuity that animates all of Kant's discussions of debt, punishment, and atonement. Kant, as Adams accurately reports, formulates the issue as "How can I be well-pleasing in the eyes of the moral judge?" The gaze of the moral judge, however, serves to bring out the deeper, existential question of our participation in righteousness. As Adams expresses the question, "How can I, as a morally serious person, affirm my own life?" (*R* xvii). To atone entails seeing oneself, across the full range of one's life, as able to participate in the highest good. Adams concludes, as do I, that Kant's depiction of atonement is the weak point in his overall account of moral change (see *R* xxiv—xxv). My goal is to formulate this weakness as a logical contradiction and trace its consequences for the moral project of modern humanism.

he fails to do justice to the moral vision of modern humanism that affirms the supreme dignity of each and every person, not only as dynamic sources of potency for change but also as finite entities with distinctive histories and commitments. After all, persons cannot be intrinsically valuable if they are not even connected to the righteousness that they seek.

The challenges posed by Kant's own humanistic commitments are evident. Insofar as he affirms the personal-potency requirement, he emphasizes dynamism and disjunction, and this widens the gap over which continuity must be established. Furthermore, the imputable status of debt and punishment, itself a necessary commitment to meet the personal-potency requirement, prevents any other person from providing the conditions for continuity. Debt, like any other consequence of our moral identities, "is not a *transmissible* liability which can be made over to somebody else . . . but the *most personal* of all liabilities, namely the debt of sins which only the culprit, not the innocent, can bear, however magnanimous the innocent might be in wanting to take the debt upon himself for the other" (*R* 89, Ak 6:72). In other words, as the new man is born in the revolution of freedom, no one can atone for the debt of the old man. So it seems that the debt can never be paid.

In order to avoid the disjunctive consequences of his own way of thinking about personal identity and its relation to the highest good, Kant provides an anatomy of moral change. He defines the "concept of moral conversion" (*R* 90, Ak 6:73), emphasizing the precise moment of transformation. With this concept, Kant intimates that, in the decision to change, we know that we shall have to bear the consequences of our old way of life, consequences full of pain and suffering. At the very least, we shall have to bear the burden of regret, at worst, the very real effects of past choices and deeds. Kant allows that after the change in identity entailed in moral conversion, strictly speaking, such sufferings "are still fitting *punishment* for someone else" (*R* 90, Ak 6:74). The old man should suffer, not the new man. But the new man, physically continuous with the old man, does suffer and in so doing pays the debt of the old man. Therefore, employing a role that Christian theology gives to Jesus, a "vicarious substitute"—the new man born in the decision to choose duty for its own sake—stands in the place of the old man and pays the debt or endures the punishment. In this way, the new man assumes what ought to be endured by the old man. The righteous person I seek to become pays the debt of the sinful person I presently am.[20]

The development of this view of atonement is complex, reflecting Kant's attempts to turn away from direct contradictions of his own humanism. First, as Kant explicates the cogency of the idea of vicarious substitution, he admits that any treatment of the suffering of the new man as, somehow, counting on behalf of the old man must be an imputation of moral consequences outside the logic of justice. The new man suffers and thus builds up a surplus of merit, but the old man benefits from this surplus, and his debt is paid. This transaction, familiar to Christian theologians, does not follow from the relation of moral predicates to personal identity that Kant establishes as the logic of we-matter-most humanism. It does not function according to the metrics of debt and worthiness. Not liable, the new man suffers; not worthy, the old man receives the benefit. Nonetheless, Kant insists that a transfer of moral significance does take place across the divide between the old man and new man. It must be so in order to meet the personal-continuity requirement.

Here, his argument backslides in two directions. First, Kant presumes the background of physical continuity between old man and new man, which creates the illusion of an underlying "person" who is the subject of both debt and payment. Bodily continuity is no doubt a crucial feature of moral change; after all, bodily continuity definitely connects the two moral identities of the old and new man. However, this continuity is "empirical" in nature and has no relevance to the moral logic of the cosmos. For this reason, Kant has no basis on which to affirm this incontestable physical connection as morally significant. He has already rejected bodily continuity as sufficient for personal continuity, insisting that moral change is real personal change. This disjunction, and not bodily continuity, must be the sole background against which to reflect upon the nature of moral debt and the possibilities of its payment.[21]

---

20. For a clear account of the central role of a "vicarious substitute" in Kant's approach to atonement, see Karl-Heinz Menke, *Stellvertretung: Schuesselbegriff christlichen Lebens und theologishe Grundkategorie* (Freiburg: Johannes, 1991), 94–98.

21. Philip L. Quinn interprets Kant's account of atonement as structured by a distinction "between the physical identities of persons and the moral identities of persons" ("Saving Faith from Kant's Remarkable Antinomy," *Faith and Philosophy* 7, no. 4 [October 1990]: 424). By Quinn's reading, this distinction allows Kant to affirm both continuity (physical) and change (moral). I hope that I have persuaded the reader that Kant makes the distinction between physical and

Kant never makes his reliance upon bodily continuity explicit. Instead, he backslides in a second direction by appealing to divine agency. What another might do or endure can become our own, he allows, if "imputed to us *by grace*" (*R* 91, Ak 6:75). Although the new man is morally different from the old man, by the agency of God, that which must be imputed to the new man (the merits of his suffering) is, somehow, redirected toward and imputed to the old man (as payment of his debt). A relation is established, and this relation secures continuity across the disjunction of moral identity. But the price is high. The relation is not moral, at least not under the constraints of we-matter-most humanism. Earlier, when Kant considered whether we might rightly hope for divine assistance, he affirmed the possibility of a morally regulated form of divine assistance. Such divine intervention only occurs *because of* the identity of the persons as righteous. The personal-potency requirement dictated that only the worthy may rightly receive aid. Now, the situation is very different. The suffering of the new man is counted on behalf of the old man *in spite of* the identity of the morally distinct persons on both sides of the disjunction. By an act of God, uncompelled by worthiness (indeed, contrary to worthiness), what ought to be imputed to one is imputed to another. The old man who ought to suffer does not; the new man who ought not suffer does. This contradicts the personal-potency requirement and its stipulation that moral rewards and punishments must be assigned by strict assessments of worthiness and debt.[22] Clearly, then,

---

moral to highlight the irrelevance of the former for the drama of personal change. Kant cannot presume a background of physical continuity without contradicting his own humanism. Moral predicates are determinative, and as such, moral change is personal change, regardless of physical continuity. Physical continuity may be necessary for personal continuity, but it cannot be sufficient.

22. Kant's forthright use of the language of divine punishment that overrides moral limits signals his inability to translate the Christian doctrine of atonement into an effective element of a humanistic anthropodicy. He defines punishment, for example, as "the effect on the subject of God's displeasure" and treats satisfaction as required by Supreme Justice whether it can be provided or not (*R* 89, Ak 6:73). The divine perspective creates the illusion of fungible punishment and satisfaction: anyone will do as the object of divine wrath. This projection of special "moral" needs upon God is fundamentally at odds with Kant's usual use of the divine perspective. Throughout his moral theology, Kant projects our moral needs upon the divine, making God the caretaker for the overall cosmic process that guarantees the fulfillment of our moral hope. Here, Kant seems to recognize that we have a contradicting moral need to believe that God operates outside the context of strict moral compulsion according to the logic of we-matter-most humanism. He may be right about the need, but if so, then he cannot be right about the nature of morality. Most specifically, as I wish to highlight, he cannot be right about the relationship between personal identity and the highest good.

the "concept of moral conversion" does not provide Kant with a way to articulate a humanistic doctrine of atonement.

Later in *Religion within the Boundaries of Mere Reason,* when Kant entertains once again the question of atonement and the problem of personal continuity, he repudiates the standard Christian view and in so doing brings to light the failure of his own solution. "It is totally inconceivable," he writes, "how a rational human being who knows himself to deserve punishment could seriously believe that he only has to believe the news of a satisfaction having been rendered to him [by another]" (*R* 123, Ak 6:116). Morally significant dimensions of life must be properly imputed, and if punishment is deserved, then it must be endured by the person who is the source of the transgression, and by no other. "No thoughtful person can bring himself to [a] faith" in the moral efficacy of payment or satisfaction by another, insists Kant (*R* 123, Ak 6:117). One can hardly imagine a more thorough denunciation of the notion of a vicarious substitute. Yet, this is precisely the role that Kant assigns the new man in his own account of atonement. Whether Christ or the new man, whether inhabiting the same body or not, it does not matter who the vicarious substitute is. If anyone other than the old man suffers, then the relation of moral predicates to personal identity (imputable and determinative) is overturned. No matter how Kant tries to finesse the concept of moral conversion, the logic of we-matter-most humanism produces a clear contradiction. The personal-continuity requirement leads to the conviction that we need to be atoned for by a vicarious substitute. But such a vicarious substitute is ruled out by the personal-potency requirement since all worthiness and debt stem from the moral identity of the person. Thus, Kant cannot affirm that we are both supremely consequential for the highest good and, at the same time, continuous across the change necessary to attain the highest good.

In the end, Kant tries to force his way out of this difficulty by the same tactic that secures the fulfillment of the personal-potency requirement: deduction from the overwhelming certainty of the humanistic faith. Without atonement, moral change, however possible by virtue of an assumed potency within each person, is fraught with a moral disorder. Without the integrating logic of debt, the moral change we seek becomes a "new moment" that bears no morally meaningful relationship to our present condition. Without continuity, our hope reduces to a functional erasure of the past in which

moral change involves (1) extraordinary and extramoral divine intervention, (2) a therapy of forgetfulness, or (3) the harsh demand that
we take a scalpel to our souls. None of these alternatives satisfies the
logic of we-matter-most humanism, which teaches that because of
who we are, not in spite of who we are, the highest good obtains.
Neither grace nor forgetfulness nor self-mutilation is a humanistic
cure of the soul.

Kant sees this constraint, and although he articulates the difficulty
in terms of absolution from guilt and payment of debt, the deeper
insight is not far from the surface. He allows that an inability to
express the continuity of persons across moral change "might be disadvantageous to reason in many respects, most of all morally" (*R* 92,
Ak 6:76). It would be very strange indeed for the modern humanist
to decry supernatural faith and bemoan the otherworldly ideals of
holiness while, at the same time, finding himself or herself unable to
explain how the seemingly worldly aspiration toward righteousness
is fundamentally connected to our current lives. As a consequence,
Kant insists that we *must* believe that we are continuous moral beings
across morally disjunctive change, connected through the logic of debt
and payment, even though he cannot provide a cogent account of that
connection. We simply must accept the idea of vicarious substitution,
the idea that another person is necessary for our relationship to the
highest good, for "we cannot *make* the removal of sin *comprehensible
in any other way*" (*R* 124, Ak 6:118). Who I become (the new man)
must be the sufficient explanation for the fate of who I am (the old
man). "Ought" implies "can," and that settles the matter. The power
of becoming, the utter imperative of moral change, the relentless zeal
of modern criticisms of hierarchy and authority, superstition and
fanaticism—these potent forces will, somehow, cover the wound of
disjunctive moral change.

At first glance Kant's trust in the project of becoming different
seems to succeed. Just as the personal-potency requirement was met
with the self-consistent claim that we enjoy the power to become different in spite of our radical evil, so, it seems, Kant meets the personal-
continuity requirement with a self-consistent assertion that we are
connected across moral change. He seems to succeed by appealing to
the practical necessity of a humanistic faith as a way of "cutting the
knot (by means of a practical maxim) instead of disentangling it (theoretically)" (*R* 125, Ak 6:119). I must believe that I will be the kind
of person who can properly account for the full sweep of my life; I

must believe that the transformative forces of modern humanism will, in the end, redeem life rather than break life in two. This belief, however, is more than implausible; it entails a contradiction.

Consider one final time the problem of atonement. Moral predicates are determinative of personal identity. Therefore, when I change from evil to good, I become different. Moral predicates are also imputable. Therefore, any moral feature of who I am—debt or punishment—must be imputed to who I am, just as any moral feature of who I become—merit or surplus—should be imputed to who I become. In view of these necessary constraints, which Kant so ardently insists upon when describing our personal potency for change, he faces contradiction. His account of atonement requires the affirmation of one of three propositions. If the merit or surplus of who I become (the new man) is imputed to who I presently am (the old man)—and Kant insists that this is the only way in which we can fulfill the personal-continuity requirement—then (1) I do not change morally, (2) moral predicates are not determinative, or (3) moral predicates are not imputable. None of these propositions is consistent with the logic of we-matter-most humanism. Yet no other alternative is available to Kant for meeting the personal-continuity requirement.

In view of this dilemma, only two outcomes of Kant's analysis of atonement and his efforts to meet the personal-continuity requirement are possible. Either he contradicts the logic of we-matter-most humanism by admitting one of the three propositions, or he allows that atonement is not possible. His own most developed approach based upon the "concept" of moral conversion (which he advances only to retract) involves the vicarious substitution of the new man for the old man. Such a solution entails one of the three propositions above, all of which imply a rejection of modern humanism. To avoid this outcome, Kant can abandon the effort to provide a humanistic account of atonement. Such a concession entails admitting that the personal-continuity requirement cannot be met and that modern humanism cannot provide a cogent account of moral change in which we genuinely participate. Here, then, is the difficulty Kant faces. Adopting a proposition that contradicts we-matter-most humanism makes any forthright form of modern humanism a misologistic faith. Admitting that one cannot account for the continuity that we-matter-most humanism requires makes modern humanism unable to meet a requirement that it insists must be met. Both alternatives suggest rather strongly that, in spite of the best efforts of one of its greatest proponents, modern humanism is a form of life that is either articulately self-contradictory or inarticulate and unable to provide an intelligible account of its own moral vision. Neither outcome commends modern humanism.

The Failure of We-Matter-Most Humanism

Modernity and its preoccupations tend to emphasize the danger of crushing authoritarianism. However, domination is not the only way to wreak havoc on the lives of others, or oneself. Fanatical moral and political projects are just as destructive of persons as authoritarian systems. Indeed, as Hume saw so clearly, the essence of escapist deception rests in an all-too-human heroic impulse: the desire to begin afresh, to count ourselves and our present needs and desires as fundamentally corrupt and nugatory. An overreaching moral or religious agenda turns this escapist desire into a violent and consuming passion: "I must renounce my sexual desires; I must repudiate my ambitions and achievements." The personal-continuity requirement expresses the humanistic aspiration to block this violence against ourselves: "I matter most, not some imaginary perfect person." Real people with needs, desires, and personal histories, not angels or New Men who are free from bourgeois ideology, are necessary for the highest good. However great might be our interest in moral change, we should not want to annihilate ourselves in order to clear space in the world for someone else.

In view of the indispensable role of personal continuity in the humanistic vision, we cannot disregard the problem of atonement, whether formulated as Kant does with the concepts of debt and punishment or in some less rigorous way. Like so many critics of authoritarianism and patrons of freedom, Kant may well think that securing dynamism and endorsing change is enough. Nonetheless, Kant is not insensible of the importance of telling a story of the soul in which the present is connected to the future. Atonement, he observes, is the greatest difficulty, "which makes doubtful the possibility of realizing in us the idea of a humanity well-pleasing to God" (R 84, Ak 6:66). This difficulty does not stem from the illusions of theology and speculative philosophy, and it is certainly not the result of an abstract and divine need for "justice." Rather, the difficulty emerges out of the basic health of our moral intuitions. Unless we are connected to that which we seek, then our hopes and ambitions destroy and debilitate. Without personal continuity, we can hardly matter most for the highest good. Indeed, we cannot matter at all, for change ensures that we are not. Thus, failure to meet the personal-continuity requirement entails the failure of the humanistic anthropodicy as a whole. Atonement is no side issue for humanists.

Of course, Kant's own failure to satisfy the personal-continuity requirement in his account of atonement does not necessarily mean that modern humanism cannot answer such questions in a different, more subtle way. Perhaps the strict logical formulations of we-matter-most humanism are too limiting. Perhaps other approaches exist for affirming modern humanism's commitment to the supremely consequential and continuous role of personal identity for the highest good. Perhaps there are some more insightful and finally self-consistent ways to explain moral change that allow humanism to grapple successfully with the relationship between our lives and the righteousness we seek on the basis of our identities as persons. Nonetheless, Kant's incoherent account of atonement should warn us that a humanistic faith may very well fail as a way of thinking and living. The horror of dependence and fear of difference that run through modern life as an electric current may fail to produce a humane cure of the soul. The great modern confidence in the transformative power of the human person may block any coherent account of the continuity of personal identity across change.

Demonstrating this larger failure would require a history of modern humanism and a survey of the many forms of postmodern life that have emerged to negotiate the disjunctions and discontinuities that erupt in a society committed to change without atonement. Nonetheless, we can easily see evidence of the failure. Ralph Waldo Emerson issues exhortations that epitomize the moral vision that I have attempted to analyze as we-matter-most humanism: "Imitation is suicide"; "Trust thyself"; "Whoso would be a man, must be a nonconformist."[23] We are to trust in our inner integrity. We are to assert our individuality, always with the confidence that this will bring us to the highest good. "God will not have his work manifest," promises Emerson, "by cowards." "To believe your own thought, to believe that what is true for you in your private heart is true for all men," he preaches, "that is genius." Be yourself; be yourself; a thousand times we hear, be yourself. Throw off the cobwebs of inherited dogma and

---

23. All quotations in this and the next paragraph are from Emerson's essay "Self-Reliance," in *Essays: First and Second Series* (New York: Houghton Mifflin, 1929), 45–57.

live as though you are sufficient for the highest good. Only then will life be radiant with dignity, manifesting the luminous depths of humanity. You and I should turn away from submission and live as men and women who matter most simply by virtue of our identities as persons. The personal-potency requirement is very much a part of the rhetoric of our culture.

Emerson was a great propagandist for modern humanism, but he did not trade in lies and deceptions. Even as he crafts the antiauthoritarian slogans of modern humanism, he points out the price we must pay, and that price is paid in the currency of personal continuity. As Cain slew Abel, the horror of dependence and the personal-potency requirement turn against the fear of difference and the personal-continuity requirement. We should be like infants, says Emerson, for "infancy conforms to nobody; all conform to it." We should be like young boys, cultivating their aristocracy of spirit that "would disdain as much as a lord to do or say aught to conciliate." Social life is a curse, and rebellion is necessary, for "society everywhere is in conspiracy against the manhood of every one of its members." Morality becomes a pawn in the struggle for independence. "No law can be sacred to me," writes Emerson, "but that of my nature. Good and evil are but names very readily transferable to that or this; the only right is what is after my constitution; the only wrong what is against it." Should evil be our vocation, then so be it. "If I am the Devil's child," Emerson announces, "I will live then from the Devil." We should never live against ourselves, even if this requires the inarticulate isolation of infancy, the impulsive episodes of adolescence, even a rejection of the very terms and concepts of moral self-description.

As Emerson's rhetoric soars, the travails and disjunctions of our world, saturated in the horror of dependence, come into view. The chasm that separates Kant's old man from the new man is all too real. Like children, today we destroy in a tantrum what tomorrow we wish we still had. Like adolescents, we rebel against authority and then wring our hands with regret as our own children roll their eyes at our feeble attempts to help them "clarify the consequences of their behavior" with the impoverished moral vocabulary of a "liberated conscience." In utter confusion about the status of morality, we compulsively add the qualifying phrase "for me" or "I feel" before iterating any statement with the word "ought." Or we default to surrogate moral language: "I do not think lying will be an effective way to relate to others; cheating is not a healthy decision." We try to exercise influence and offer guidance, but always at a steep discount so that neither we nor our children will feel the bondage of obligation.

Ever the prophet, Emerson anticipates our situation: "The wisdom of the wise man consists herein; that he does not judge [others]; he lets them judge themselves and merely reads and records their own verdict."[24] Under the constant pressure of reform and "humanization," our culture becomes thinner and thinner. Not only do we step back from the impulse to judge; we lose interest in reading and recording the verdicts of others. Instead, we turn our faces toward the future and try to navigate to a safe shore. To be sure, we do not use Kant's notions of debt and worthiness to express our sense that our lives are fundamentally disintegrated. Instead, we dine in ethnic restaurants in suburban strip malls, complaining that contemporary culture is boring and banal. At each turn, the connective tissue of traditional culture is severed, and we scramble for alternative methods for keeping life glued together. We seek other ways of telling the stories of our souls, but always guard against anything that might smell of authority.

Not only must we cut ourselves off from the constraints of adulthood, of society, and of morality, but we must sacrifice even the constraints of continuous personal identity. Here, the clear-sighted Emerson sees how continuity corrupts the pure logic of affirming our personal potency. Our supremely consequential identities require us to renounce any desire or need for continuous identity. "Valor consists in the power of self-recovery," he writes of the blows of fate, "so that man cannot have his flank turned, cannot be outgeneralled, but put himself where you will, he stands."[25] The personal-potency requirement must be met. But Emerson is aware of the endless flux of modernity, and he harbors no illusions of joining Rousseau in the project of simply being oneself. To be is to become; to be oneself involves freeing oneself to become different. The cost is continuity, and it must be paid. A man can affirm the supremely consequential role of his identity only "by preferring truth to his past apprehension of truth, and his alert acceptance of it from whatever quarter; the intrepid conviction that his laws, his relations to society, his Christianity, his world, may at any time be superseded

---

24. Emerson, "The Over-Soul," *Essays: First and Second Series,* 286.
25. Emerson, "Circles," *Essays: First and Second Series,* 309.

and decease."[26] Our thoughts and actions create bonds as imprisoning as any imposed by society, and these too must be thrown aside. "Why drag about this corpse of your memory," asks Emerson, "lest you contradict somewhat you have stated in this or that public place?" Why, indeed, ought we to let *our own selves* stand in the way of independence and freedom? "Bring the past into the thousand-eyed present," Emerson urges, "and live ever in a new day."[27] The present alone redeems, and it need not answer the demands of past and future.

Since we live in time, not in the Eternal Now, we should not be surprised that Emerson slides toward an anti-humanism of pure power. For Emerson, a larger, greater unity transcends the merely personal. "Persons," he writes, "are supplementary to the primary teaching of the soul."[28] As Emerson observes, the deepest and most permanent cure of the soul involves "accepting the tide of being."[29] Emerson's oracular Platonism maintains a strongly spiritualist tone, but one could just as well say that persons are supplementary to History or *Volk* or Democracy or Utility. Emerson, like most humanists, softens the threat of this absorptive unity by calling it a "higher self-possession" in which the purified soul recognizes that all persons are one in the truth that does not admit of "property" and the selfish claims of the individual.[30] Perhaps, but if so, then that which we seek is not imputable, and the logic of we-matter-most humanism must be tossed aside. History cannot provide continuity unless we renounce our power to effect the highest good. One cannot affirm the personal-potency requirement and, at the same time, meet the demands of the personal-continuity requirement.

In the end, as I hope my close reading of Kant's failed account of atonement shows, Emerson's pious gestures toward the unifying power of the soul are empty. To the extent that modern humanism endures, it requires an implicit neglect of the Athanasian concern about continuity. We should not worry about remaining consistent persons; we should not concern ourselves with atonement. After all, as says Emerson in one of his most famous lines, "A foolish consis-

---

26. Emerson, "Circles," *Essays: First and Second Series*, 309.
27. Emerson, "Self-Reliance," *Essays: First and Second Series*, 57.
28. Emerson, "The Over-Soul," *Essays: First and Second Series*, 277.
29. Emerson, "The Over-Soul," *Essays: First and Second Series*, 284.
30. Emerson, "The Over-Soul," *Essays: First and Second Series*, 277–78.

tency is the hobgoblin of little minds."[31] His point has nothing to do with a misology that rejects the logical principle of noncontradiction. His focus falls on modern humanism's cure of the soul. We need not make sense out of our lives; we should not even want to make sense out of our lives, for to do so would lash us to our past. Instead, should we change our minds, we must say today that which contradicts our most dearly held beliefs of yesterday. "Greatness appeals to the future," Emerson reports.[32] The greatest of men must have the courage to live in dislocation; they must be able to endure discontinuity. For if we are to live as though we are sufficient for the highest good, then we must give up the "corpse of memory" and simply live! As Nietzsche teaches, forgetfulness, the strength to dismiss the continuity requirement, is the gift that the powerful give to themselves.

The critical tropes that express the horror of dependence, tropes we surveyed in the first chapter—the affirmation of diversity over singularity, the future over the past, formal criteria over material—are all methods for disposing of the corpse of memory, whether personal or collective. The upshot has been anger and tears rather than joy and celebration. The power of memory overshadows life, and for the ardent humanist, the tools of criticism must be sharpened with an ever greater fury. Patriarchal indoctrination must be extirpated root and branch, and the very memory of traditional family structures effaced. The liturgical inheritance of classical Christianity, saturated with the language of the Father, who sent his only begotten Son, must be purged and cleansed of this memory. The vast array of sexual taboos that structure and discipline the violent cauldron of human desire must be swept away. No Spanish Inquisitor ever burned with such fervor. The critical spirit of modernity outstrips its predecessors in violence and vigilance.

But I must stop. I cannot begin to assemble an adequate account of the many material failures of modern humanism—the tyrannical demand to "accept everybody," the Agent Orange of critique spread over traditional forms of life, the sharp whips and coarse hair shirts of authenticity. However, if we see the true nature of Kant's failure to provide an account of atonement, then we can gain some insight into the failure of humanistic culture. In exhausted modern forms, in the

31. Emerson, "Self-Reliance," *Essays: First and Second Series*, 57.
32. Emerson, "Self-Reliance," *Essays: First and Second Series*, 59.

intensities and perversities of messianic postmodernism, or in the
efforts of many to find a humane way to stitch together some sem-
blance of a life well lived, the various forms of modern humanism cannot do the basic work of establishing the conditions for continuous
personal identity. They cannot give an explanation of how we endure
across morally meaningful change. These epiphenomena of modern
humanism cannot explain how men and women can devote all their
efforts to ushering in a genuinely human, rational, and free way of
life in which *they*—not some projected, ghostly, and eviscerated form
of themselves—can participate. No account is given that explains how
we are both consequential for and continuous in moral change.

However inevitable, however championed by prophets such as
Emerson and celebrated by the many patrons of "difference," this failure is a bad fate. Unable to describe the conditions for continuous personal identity through change, modernity easily slides in two directions.
First, it tends to suppress the reality of change, backsliding into the
two positions articulated by Rousseau and Hume. With Rousseau, a
great deal of what passes for humanism simply insists that being who
one is constitutes the highest good. Such a conviction drains all moral
urgency out of the conviction that we matter most for the highest good.
We *are,* and all that remains is to join the chorus of affirmation.
However pure in theory, the results are not always pleasant to behold
in practice. My self-affirmation might conflict with yours, and as
Emerson recognized with dim hesitation, and Nietzsche with brilliant
and aggressive clarity, such conflict transcends moral categories. The
clash of self-affirmation is a conflict of power; it is a conflict of the
intensity of my being against the intensity of yours, and this conflict
is beyond good and evil. Fortunately, Hume's retreat from change
offers an alternative. A careful management of change deflates the
degree and intensity of transformations. After two centuries of humanistic rhetoric, this is now much easier. One needs none of Hume's
rhetorical genius to sound "conservative" when advocating change.[33]

---

33. Martha Nussbaum's contributions to public debates are paradigmatic. In *Cultivating Humanity: A Classical Defense of Reform in Liberal Education,* she advances the argument that animating prejudices of modern humanism are age-old conventions, veritable pillars of the great Western tradition of education. She allows that her proposals for higher education do entail important changes. The examined life, the step back to a world perspective, empathetic identifi-cation with others: if fully implemented, these educational values will require pedagogical, cur-ricular, and institutional changes, which inevitably bring "pain and turmoil" (7). Nonetheless, Nussbaum argues, in Humean fashion, that the changes are not disjunctive or disruptive. They

We can call Hume's mitigated humanism an exercise in "bricolage." But what is easier rhetorically is no more satisfactory today than it was in Hume's time. Morally meaningful change becomes incoherent. We cannot serve "ordinary life" by urging fundamental changes in human behavior. The upshot is a complacency born of prudence, and in our day, the imperatives of transformation, both social and personal, are redefined in terms of therapeutic adjustment and economic necessity.

Unwilling to enter into Dionysian celebrations of being, unsatisfied with Hume's careful and modest adjustments, modernity often escapes from Kant's contradictions by throwing over the constraints of we-matter-most humanism, as Emerson's gestures toward the "tide of being" anticipate. The source of potency and the conditions for continuity rest in a suprahuman entity. Programs for dramatic change urge us to forget ourselves, forget the particular constraints imposed by the determinate details of our lives. Here, a grim determination prevails. The wheels of change must grind forward. Progress is necessary, inevitable. Should we fear for the intelligibility of our lives, fear that we shall never see ourselves as full participants in the highest good, we must put our trust in History, or in Scientific Method, or in the Democratic Process. These forces and powers shall provide a suprapersonal continuity. We may need to break an egg, but the omelet of the Triumph of the Proletariat shall justify all sacrifice. We may be required to abstract from personal concerns and moral categories, but the Objectivity of Reason, the Empire of the Facts, shall reign. We might have our heads severed from our shoulders, but the Will of the People shall be all in all.

If this counts as humanism, of any sort, then the word has lost its meaning. Kant's logical failures are vastly preferable to the cruel consistency of faith in Progress, for we genuinely and rightly want that which Kant, in particular, and modern humanism, in general, cannot provide: a view of the highest good in which we are consequential and continuous. We seek independence, yet we want to be bonded

---

are nothing more than simple extensions of traditional principles of education, part of "a long history in the western philosophical tradition." Such change only brings "pain and turmoil" to those who fail to understand the inherited traditions. To test Nussbaum's claim, take a glance at her picture of a freethinking Socrates. Only one hundred years of Whiggish readings of the Platonic dialogues could give plausibility to her conscription of Socrates to the cause of socializing students to be good, obedient members of the culture of modern humanism.

together into meaningful forms of human solidarity. From political theory to popular wisdom, we try to square the circle. We want an account of political power both expressive of our wills and repressive of our willfulness. We want space to "be ourselves," and at the same time, we want romance to be more than negotiation. We hunger for the bonds of mutual responsibility, but we want clear limits so that we do not fall into the abyss of self-sacrifice. We want others to accept us as we are, yet we hope that our friends will help us change and become better. We do not want freedom to collide with solidarity. We do not want the difference between your individuality and mine to corrupt or undermine our shared humanity. We want room and scope for our individuality so that our best selves might shine forth. We want a discipline that brings us to ourselves. We want redemption from crushing authoritarianism that is not a vain and finally violent form of overreaching. We want moral changes that redeem us rather than destroy us.

In view of these needs, to the extent that our humanist culture avoids either Nietzschean violence or the many suprahuman higher powers paraded before us as saviors, we are frozen between the contradictory impulses of personal potency and continuity. Indeed, the equipoise of contradiction is the essence of the postmodern condition. As it struggles to remain humane, postmodern theory and reality offers neither freedom nor solidarity, neither self-affirmation nor self-discipline. At its best, postmodernity offers an irony that secures a carefully managed balance, a limited freedom and a thin solidarity, a moderated self-acceptance and a mitigated self-discipline. For most, however, modernity is recycled, though now in highly conventional forms. The Rousseauians are Humeans, and the Humeans are Rousseauian.[34] The antiauthoritarian impulse to "be yourself" is now common wisdom, and the imperatives of authenticity are as oppressively conventional as were the traditional commandments of Christian morality. Being an "individual" (Rousseau) is a fixed and obligatory role for any who would seek full integration into common life (Hume). Lawrence Kohlberg's account of "normal" moral development is but one illustration. The failure to secure continuity across

---

34. Notice the conservative logic of Charles Taylor's efforts to balance authenticity and solidarity in *The Ethics of Authenticity*. He wishes to hold together that which modern humanism both insists upon and drives into antagonistic contradiction.

change finds similar domestication. Economics, sociology, and modern historical study have made the disjunctive changes of modernity into veritable laws of the human soul. Adolescent rebellion is treated as inevitable, even desirable. A great deal of our culture, whether economic, psychological, or educational, is devoted to finding strategies for survival. We must educate ourselves to endure a lifetime of wrenching economic change. We must undertake multicultural therapy in order to prepare for a career of closing deals regardless of moral and social conflicts and contradictions.

At best we muddle through, knowing intuitively, if not conceptually, that the two requirements are rivals, not partners, in a universe constructed according to the logic of we-matter-most humanism. Postmodern irony is a survival mechanism, not a hard-won achievement. We neither strenuously insist upon respect for the supreme consequentiality of personal identity nor demand a clear and full affirmation of the conditions for personal continuity as we seek moral change. But neither the muddling nor the rivalry need be so. Christianity, unlike modern humanism, does offer an account of atonement. As such, it holds out the hope that we might actually be able to adopt a cogent and articulate account of moral change. We might discover a rationally defensible cure of the soul in which we are genuinely consequential and continuous. Surely that would be no immoderate gain, both for the plausibility of our moral prejudices and for the health of our minds.

–Chapter 6–

Atonement and the Christian Cure of the Soul

God bids us to do what we cannot, that we may know what we ought to seek from him.

—Augustine, *On Grace and Free Will*

The First Letter of John articulates the basic parameters of the Christian view of change. Saturated with sharp antitheses between darkness and light, sin and righteousness, children of the devil and children of God, death and life, the drama of human life moves across a wide gap. One can hardly imagine an account of human destiny that would require greater change. In this transformation, the author of 1 John is singular in his description of the dynamic power that is necessary and sufficient: it is love. Not generic and diffuse, this love is not a sentiment or general principle. The power necessary to move from darkness to light, from sin to righteousness, is God's love, and this love comes to us in Jesus of Nazareth. As 1 John teaches, "God's love was revealed among us in this way: God sent his only Son into the world so that we might live through him" (4:9). Jesus Christ is the power of salvation, so much so, in fact, that his very name, like the unspoken name of the God of Israel, has power (3:23). In view of such power, we certainly cannot matter most for the highest good. His potency, not ours, makes change possible.

Even this abbreviated evocation shows that Christian teaching collides with the conviction that we matter most for the highest good. No matter how we conceive of Jesus' role "for us," the contrast between Christianity and modern humanism on the question of the potency necessary and sufficient for change is patent. Even if my heuristic formulation of the logic of we-matter-most humanism fails to capture the subtle and diverse claims that constitute the tradition of modern humanism, a collision on the Augustinian question of the source of redemptive power is inevitable. Christianity teaches that Jesus is the power of new life. Little that Christians say or do makes much sense without this basic affirmation. Indeed, this affirmation is so fundamental to the Christian view of human destiny that I do not see how it can be defended, either doctrinally or apologetically, without undertaking an extensive reiteration of just those things that Christians say and do.[1] Even that reiteration would simply show that a conviction that Jesus is supremely consequential for human destiny is so deeply embedded that it cannot be removed without falsifying vast stretches of Christian language and practice. I cannot prove that Jesus has the power to save, any more than Kant can prove that we have a personal potency for moral transformation. Within the Christian frame of reference, such a confidence is more certain than anything one might say on its behalf, and one cannot prove premises from conclusions.[2] Thus, I simply assume, as the Augustinian tradition so fervently affirms, that Jesus is the sole and sufficient source of redemptive change.

To say that Jesus is the power of salvation is not enough. Kant's rigorous analysis allowed me to formulate the personal-potency and personal-continuity requirements. As I have shown, the way in which Kant addresses these requirements founders on the problem of atone-

---

1. For an account of the fundamental status of the affirmation that Jesus matters most, see George Lindbeck's discussion of the regulative role of Nicene and Chalcedonian creedal affirmations in *The Nature of Doctrine* (Philadelphia: Westminster, 1984), 92–96. Lindbeck identifies a principle of "Christological maximalism" that is expressed in the ecumenical creeds and operative in the apostolic witness. This principle expresses what I intend by the phrase "Jesus matters most." For Lindbeck, such an affirmation "follows from the central Christian conviction that Jesus Christ is the highest possible clue (though an often dim and ambiguous one to creaturely and sinful eyes) within the space-time world of human experience to God, i.e., to what is of maximal importance" (94).

2. Bruce D. Marshall offers a detailed and sustained argument showing why Christian theology must ascribe epistemic primacy to fundamental Christian beliefs or, instead, court absurd assumptions about the nature of meaning and criteria for truth. See *Trinity and Truth*, 17–140. Marshall's approach presupposes more developed beliefs about the Trinitarian identity of God. I restrict myself to straightforward Christian beliefs about the role of Jesus in redemptive change. These beliefs entail Trinitarian claims, but I will not explicate them and their connection to the conviction that Jesus matters most for the highest good. Instead, I will focus on the connection between convictions about Jesus and personal identity.

ment. As I have attempted to suggest, this inability to establish continuity is not peripheral to the project of modern humanism. Identifying the power sufficient to effect personal change is fundamental to the humanistic cure of the soul, but absent a coherent account of personal continuity, this commitment to personal change is indistinguishable from self-destruction, self-abandonment, and self-sacrifice. Only a cogent account of continuous identity can secure a confidence that change serves who we are, fulfilling and protecting our distinctive identities as persons, rather than assaulting and rending the delicate fabric of our lives. However, the logic of we-matter-most humanism blocks a cogent account. Either we can satisfy the requirement of personal continuity by violating the constraints of we-matter-most humanism, or we can remain true to those constraints by renouncing the need for personal continuity. In neither case do the basic commitments of modern humanism admit of self-consistent explication. Premises cannot be proven by conclusions, but bizarre and self-contradictory conclusions do cast doubt on the soundness of the enabling premises.

Although modern humanism cannot fulfill the continuity requirement, the requirement and the logical pressure it generates mark an important common commitment with Christianity. They share an Athanasian concern that we have some way of understanding our connection to the changes we seek. Who we currently are must be "at-one" with who we seek to become; otherwise, our hope is self-destructive rather than redemptive. In view of this agreement about the importance of personal continuity, the relevant difference between Christianity and modern humanism rests in the cogency of their respective accounts of atonement. Here, my thesis is simple. Where modern humanism fails through self-contradiction, Christianity succeeds. Christianity avoids contradiction because of the premise that Jesus is "for us" as incorporative power. This premise allows for an account of substitutionary atonement in which the actions of Jesus are imputable to and determinative of persons.

Because Christianity succeeds, it can offer something that modern humanism cannot. Christianity can propose a cure of the soul in which we might seek change with some confidence that we are both consequential and continuous. We can matter in the redemptive love of God in Christ because we can see the cogency of saying that the power of Christ is "for us" as the potency for change and the basis of continuity. Thus, Christianity can provide a self-consistent basis for the essence of humanism: the hope for morally meaningful change in which human persons are fulfilled rather than sacrificed, integrated rather than disjoined.

In what follows, I will offer an account of the Christian hope in the saving power of Jesus, both in terms of the potency ascribed to Jesus and the continuity he makes possible. I intend this account to be ecumenical and conventional. Given the contested state of atonement theory within the Christian tradition, I will not offer a developed theory of atonement. I have my own ideas about how to proceed in formulating a full account of atonement, but providing the scriptural, patristic, philosophical, and pastoral premises for such an account, defending them, and showing their entailments would require inordinate time. Moreover, such a theory extends beyond the purpose of this inquiry. My goal is to assess the Christian view of personal change and to do so in comparison to modern humanism, not to make dogmatic proposals of my own. As a result, my purpose will be to show, in outline, the role of atonement in the Christian cure of the soul.

Although I wish to restrict myself to "mere Christianity" in this chapter, the analysis will be novel insofar as I use the analytical precision gained from the close readings of Rousseau, Hume, and especially Kant to highlight the ways in which Christian belief connects personal identity to the highest good through the saving power of Jesus. The upshot will be formulations of Christian teaching that may strike readers as atypical. One rarely finds explicit discussions of change and continuity in classical Christian theories of atonement. Nonetheless, I do not think this focus on personal identity alters the standard Christian view, and that is certainly not my intent. Instead, this use of modern humanism will, I hope, provide fresh insight into the way in which Christianity has always understood the relationship between personal identity and the highest good. Whatever novel formulations might emerge, I hope that they serve no other purpose but to offer greater clarity about just what is entailed in the standard view that Jesus saves.

To take advantage of the benefits of comparative analysis, I will proceed according to the same sequence as my consideration of Kant. In the first section, I develop the greatest point of convergence between Christianity and the logic of we-matter-most humanism. Both agree that we must be the source of the need for change; otherwise, that change fails to turn on personal identity. For Christianity, this conviction is expressed in the doctrine of sin. However one conceives of the saving power of Jesus, that power is manifested and exercised because of who we are. We need his potency for righteousness because we are captive to the power of sin. In this sense, we are clearly consequential for the drama of change. The second section addresses the collision of Christianity and modern humanism over the question of the relationship between personal identity and the potency for change. Christianity teaches that Jesus is the supremely consequential person for all; modern humanism insists that each of us, as individuals, is sufficient for ourselves. This fundamental conflict of faith admits of no direct resolution; however, I can make some observations about the subtle rational advantages of saying that Jesus saves. The third section tackles the question of personal continuity across the change wrought by Jesus' saving power. Unlike modern humanism, Christianity advances an account of personal identity that actually makes sense on its own terms. This obvious rational advantage motivates the fourth and final section, in which I consider the proper shape of a Christian humanism that embraces change in which we can matter as both consequential and continuous persons.

The Need for Change

Christianity is full of antagonism toward the way things are, fraught with the urgent need for change. The Gospels tell stories of Jesus against a background of transgression and defilement, faithlessness and blindness. Again and again, the redemptive power of Jesus stands in sharp contrast to prevailing powers of destruction. Wealth enslaves; hypocrisy prevails. False prophets devour; bad trees bear bad fruit. The holy temple in Jerusalem is desecrated; religious authorities are corrupt. As Jesus goes to his death, this background of evil assumes a direct role in his fate. Abandoned by his disciples, denied by Peter, betrayed by Judas, and arrested by those responsible for corporate worship, he is brought before a judge who refuses to take responsibility for justice. He is denounced by the children of Israel, scourged by the Gentile soldiers, mocked by a thief crucified by his side. Whatever Jesus represents, whoever he might be, the foundational stories of Christianity clearly present him as a man over and against the world. Following him will require swimming against the current because basic patterns of human life flow away from, rather than towards, righteousness and innocence.

How did the extraordinarily inauspicious context for Jesus' life come about? What caused the current of life to flow toward hypocrisy, violence, and death? How did things become so grim, so fraught with evil? Why must change be so disjunctive, an about-face rather than a straightforward intensification and fulfillment of what already obtains? Just as Kant's theory of radical evil grows out of a need to explain the urgent and revolutionary critical prejudices of modern humanism, the Christian doctrine of sin sets out to answer questions about the sharp edge of the Christian juxtaposition of Jesus' righteousness with the world's captivity to demonic powers. Although the constraining premises are very different, the broad outlines of the Christian account of sin are very similar to Kant's conclusions.

To begin, the Christian understanding of sin, like Kant's, is governed by the logic of what matters most. Kant's primitive commitment to the animating prejudices of modern humanism, and the logical constraints they entail, determines his judgments about evil and its relationship to us. The principle that we are necessary and sufficient for the highest good forces the self-consistent humanist either to deny the reality of evil or make it a consequence of personal identity. So also is the Christian teaching on sin governed by a fundamental faith that Jesus is the power of God unto salvation. The fate of his righteousness governs Christian reflection on the nature of evil and its status as a personal reality. In both cases, then, the power for change determines the shape, gravity, and scope of the need for change and establishes the setting for the drama of the soul. The solution to the narrative tension—the potency necessary and sufficient for the highest good—dictates the particular characterization of the problem. As a consequence, the deepest reason for adopting either Kant's humanistic or the Christian theological view of moral evil rests in their positive vision. For modern humanism, who we are in relation to the highest good constrains what can be said about evil. For Christian teaching, who Jesus is in relation to the highest good governs.[3]

---

3. For an extended argument against an independent doctrine of sin, see Karl Barth, *Church Dogmatics*, vol. 4, *The Doctrine of Reconciliation*, pt. 1 (trans. Geoffrey W. Bromiley; Edinburgh: T. & T. Clark, 1956), par. 60.1, pp. 358–413. "Only when we know Jesus Christ," writes Barth, "do we really know that man is the man of sin, and what sin is, and what it means for man" (389). The Christian faith in Jesus as the sole and sufficient power for saving change shapes a properly Christian understanding of the need for change.

Not only does Christian teaching parallel Kant in method; the material conclusions about the role of evil in human destiny are similar. The Christian tradition teaches that human beings are universally evil. To be human is to sin. Yet, this evil is personal and not a consequence of human nature. We are not fated, by nature, to sin. Further, like Kant, Christianity affirms that evil is determinative of the identity of each person. To become a good person requires "new birth." Finally, like Kant, the Christian doctrine insists that this evil is imputable. It has to do with who we are as persons, and as a result, merits punishment. Thus, both Kant and Christianity affirm sin as universal, unnatural, determinative, and imputable.

Universal

Paul is clear: "All have sinned" (Rom 3:23). This declaration sums up the first three chapters of the Letter to the Romans, in which Paul outlines the Christian genealogy of morals. In some primordial past, human beings turned away from the radiance of the living God. As a consequence, our minds have become darkened, and our passions have become disordered. We are filled "with every kind of wickedness, evil, covetousness, malice." "Full of envy, murder, strife, deceit, craftiness," continues Paul, we "are gossips, slanderers, God-haters, insolent, haughty, boastful, inventors of evil, rebellious toward parents, foolish, faithless, heartless, ruthless" (1:29–31). This ubiquitous sin characterizes all human life. The holiness of the law revealed on Mount Sinai does not save; it only heightens the contrast between how we actually live and how we ought to live. The ignorance of the Greeks is no excuse, for even though the law was not revealed to them, it is written on their hearts, and their consciences bear witness against them (2:15). Thus, Paul concludes that "all, both Jews and Greeks, are under the power of sin" (3:9).

To a great extent, Paul's depiction of all humanity as under the power of sin has seemed incontestable, and for the same reason Kant thought that common sense confirms radical evil as ubiquitous. For Kant, the universal propensity toward evil is simply a fact for all to see. Only an ideologue, intoxicated by a theoretical commitment to the inherent goodness of all persons, could ignore the evidence. People do nasty things to each other, and if they are inherently good, they do a very good job disguising it. To be sure, a graduate degree in education is usually sufficient to overcome the evidence, but such optimism stems from confusing the ability of children to learn arithmetic with their ability to live righteously. Nonetheless, Kant's analysis does not depend upon empirical observation. He recognizes that the intensity of the humanistic desire to transform prevailing beliefs and practices requires a sober assessment of our dire need for change. If people really are already good, and society or some other external force causes evil, then personal identity is not necessary and sufficient for the highest good, and the logic of we-matter-most humanism is denied at the outset. The only way to acknowledge the reality of evil and affirm that we matter most involves ascribing the problem to us. Thus, Kant's account reinforces common sense. Evil rests in the hearts of everyone.

Like Kant's, Paul's thinking conforms to a logic that reinforces, rather than depends upon, our ordinary observations of life. Unlike Kant, he has theological, not humanistic, reasons for affirming the universality of sin. In his Letter to the Romans, Paul wants to convince his readers that the saving power of Jesus applies to both Jews and Gentiles. Everyone needs to have faith in Jesus; none are able to live in righteousness without him. The reasons why Paul insists upon the universality of Jesus are complex. However, we can understand Paul's conviction by grasping the prophetic background. Paul envisions a consummation of God's redemptive work through a coordinated pilgrimage of Israel and all the nations toward the perfection of covenant faithfulness and worship. Isaiah has prophesied that the word of the Lord shall go forth, drawing all to him. "Assemble yourselves and come together, / draw near, you survivors of the nations," says the Lord in Isaiah's prophecy (Isa 45:20). "Turn to me and be saved, / all the ends of the earth" (45:22). From this body of prophecy, Paul draws resources for his own argument to the Romans. Against those who would divide God's saving power in two—one covenant for the Jew, another for the Gentile—Paul cites Isaiah: "As I live, says the Lord, every knee shall bow to me, / and every tongue shall give praise to God" (Rom 14:11; Isa 45:23). Jesus is the power of the word of the Lord for all. Paul's affirmation of Jesus' universality leads the apostle to insist upon a universal need for change. "Christ died for the ungodly," proclaims Paul (Rom 5:6), and all are ungodly. Thus, no matter how one describes human sinfulness—as a fundamental choice against God, as disordered passions, as egotistical self-love, as a heteronomous will—all persons properly fall under that description. The universal Savior brings to light a universal need for change. Jesus matters most for everyone; the transforming invitation "Come unto me" is addressed to all.[4]

Unnatural

Although universal, sin is not a consequence of being human; it is not a natural feature of our humanity. Here, the Genesis story of the fall looms large. The possibility of evil intrudes upon the scene from the outside. The serpent is a crafty beast, and in a compressed scene, sin and shame enter into the story. Exegetes have exercised themselves on the question of how Genesis 3 explains the origin of sin. Is the serpent to blame? Was the delightful aspect of the fruit of the tree of the knowledge of good and evil the underlying cause? Was Adam's negligence the origin of sin? Did his failure to prevent Eve from falling to temptation reveal a self-involved egoism that was unwilling to risk intervention? In the end, these speculations are necessarily open-ended and inconclusive. However, an underlying constant in the Genesis story remains. Not an essential feature of created life, sin is a historical contingency and has to do with the way we actually live rather than with the created conditions of finitude, embodiment, and social life.

At first glance, the New Testament seems to contradict the notion that sin is contingent. For example, in the Letter to the Ephesians, Paul affirms and reinforces the ubiquity of sin. Outside the saving power of Christ, we read, "all of us once lived among [the disobedient] in the passions of our flesh, following the desires of flesh and senses, and we were by nature children of wrath, like everyone else" (Eph 2:3). A picture immediately suggests itself. Sin is the consequence of fleshly existence, the result of the intrinsically corruptive economy of natural desires and passions. This picture is reinforced again and again by a standard Pauline contrast between the spiritual law of righteousness and the fleshly or carnal law of sin and death (see Rom 7). In spite of these potently suggestive passages, the Christian tradition has insisted,

---

4. Wolfhart Pannenberg identifies further support for the universal scope of sin. The ubiquity of our need for change blocks "the moralism that either seeks evil in others or by inward aggression produces self-destructive guilt feelings" (*Systematic Theology* [trans. Geoffrey W. Bromiley; Grand Rapids: Eerdmans, 1994], 2:238). By erasing bright lines that might separate evildoers from the righteous, Christian teaching about the universality of sin preserves human solidarity and checks tendencies toward hypocrisy. Whether this reason for underlining the universality of sin plays any role in Paul's approach is unlikely. Pannenberg admits that "this antimoralism function of the doctrine [of sin] has often been underrated" (238).

as has Kant, that sin is "natural" or "innate" only in the sense that it is universal. Christian teaching has denied that sin is natural in the strict sense of the term. Sin is not part of human nature, in itself, and as a consequence, sin is universal but unnatural. Thus, the Lutheran *Formula of Concord* (1577) affirms that a difference exists "between the nature, which even since the fall is and remains a creature of God, and original sin; and that this difference is as great as the difference between the work of God, and that of Satan."[5]

The reasons why Christianity insists that sin is unnatural are many, and none parallel Kant's reason. For Kant, evil must not be intrinsic to our constitution as finite creatures; otherwise, we cannot believe that we have the power to change ourselves from evil to good. The personal-potency requirement blocks any understanding of "innate evil" that translates empirical ubiquity into a metaphysical or essential quality of our humanity such that becoming righteous would entail the absurd power of self-creation rather than the ability of self-determination. In contrast, Christian teaching resists a naturalistic understanding of sin for distinctively theological reasons. First, the horizon of the first chapters of Genesis constrains what might be said about natural existence. God creates all things and calls them good; therefore, no matter how universal might be sin, a belief in God's creative power and benevolence prohibits Christian theologians from saying that human beings are naturally sinful.[6] Second, developed christological doctrine teaches that the Son of God took on human nature yet remained without sin. This claim is inconsistent with the proposition that human nature is intrinsically sinful. Third, if human beings are by nature sinful, then they can change from evil to good only through destruction and re-creation in a new, disembodied form. Yet, as Job proclaims in a protest of faith,

> "I know that my Redeemer lives,
>   and that at the last he will stand upon the earth;
> and after my skin has been thus destroyed,
>   then in my flesh I shall see God" (Job 19:25–26).[7]

---

5. *Formula of Concord*, Epitome, art. 1.

6. See Augustine's treatment of Adam's sin and its relation to his created nature in *City of God* 14.11.

7. See Panayiotis Nellas, *Deification in Christ: The Nature of the Human Person* (trans. Norman Russell; Crestwood, N.Y.: St. Vladimir's Seminary Press, 1987), for a discussion of the role of the "garments of skin" in patristic thought. Nellas shows how the Fathers draw on Genesis 3:21 to explain the distinction between the integrity of bodily life and the corruption of the actual state of human existence. "That which empirical observation calls 'human nature'

The creedal affirmation of bodily resurrection reiterates Job's confident expectation of bodily continuity through redemption. This confidence requires a rejection of the idea that sin is natural.

For Kant, and for Christian doctrine, the upshot of defining moral evil as unnatural is the same. The mood is not pessimistic. Change is possible for us. For Kant, the emphasis falls on preserving the possibility of free choice of duty for its own sake. We retain the potency toward righteousness and can reasonably hope for self-wrought change. For Christian teaching, the focus shifts toward the conditions for continuity. Jesus alone possesses the potency for change, but since sin is unnatural, we retain a natural integrity that allows us to hope for a change wrought by God's power in Jesus Christ that will save and not destroy. God need not wipe the slate clean and start all over again. To be sure, the natural integrity of the human person only ensures a generic continuity, a subsisting embodied creature, and not a continuous personal identity. Nonetheless, bodily continuity, or at least the continued possibility of embodiment, remains as a necessary condition for personal continuity.[8] We cannot be the self-same persons if we cannot possess a body, for without a body, we would be something other than human. In view of the unnaturalness of sin, Christian teaching preserves, then, the possibility that God can act upon us in such a way that we endure as continuous persons.

Determinative

Like Kant, Christianity does not treat human evil as a peripheral defect, an unfortunate but subsidiary feature of human life. Sin determines our identities in the sense that a propensity toward evil is a necessary condition for identifying who we are. To not have this propensity does not

---

is," summarizes Nellas, "in biblical and patristic teaching a later nature, a state which came about after the fall, and not the original, and therefore true, human nature" (45). This distinction allows patristic thought to advance in a profoundly transformative vision of salvation as purification and *theosis* without opening up a chasm of disjunction between created existence and participation in the triune life of God.

8. I make the distinction between continued embodiment and the continued possibility of embodiment in order to accommodate Derek Parfit's probing thought experiments about the relationship between bodily continuity and continuous personal identity. His imaginative descriptions of a teletransporter that permits instantaneous reembodiment elsewhere offer helpful clarification for the Christian belief in the bodily resurrection of the dead. The constraints upon conceivable forms of personal continuity may have more to do with the possibility of having any body at all rather than one's present body. See *Reasons and Persons* (Oxford: Clarendon, 1984), 282–87.

entail being something other than human—the unnatural state of sin blocks this—but it does entail being a different person. If someone were to point to you or me and say, "That person is without sin," then we would say, "Sorry, I am afraid you must be thinking of someone else." This commitment to the determinative status of sin rules out a mixed view, just as it did for Kant. As Paul explains, you "are slaves of the one whom you obey, either of sin, which leads to death, or of obedience, which leads to righteousness" (Rom 6:16). Our identities as persons fall one way or the other. There can be no mixed identity, no equipoise between sin and righteousness. Sinners are "slaves to impurity and to greater and greater iniquity," while the obedient are "slaves to righteousness for sanctification" (6:19). The propensity toward evil, then, shapes who we are at the most fundamental level of personal identity. We would not be ourselves—we would not be the individual persons we are, with distinct memories, choices, and habits—were we not slaves of impurity.

This formal commitment to the determinative status of sinfulness motivates the ascription of total depravity to each person. Enslavement to iniquity is, writes Philipp Melanchthon in an extended diatribe against any softening of the doctrine of original sin, an "active hereditary contagion," an "innate impurity within the heart"; we are so constituted that "evil desires are innate in us," and "by nature we are born in sin."[9] At each point, Melanchthon insists on the most intimate possible status for the propensity toward evil, employing concepts such as "innate," "hereditary," and "by nature." The Augustinian tradition of speculation about original sin often seeks to identify a mechanism for the transmission of innate or hereditary sin, such that evil taints each person from the outset. These speculations can appear to backslide from a commitment to the claim that sin is contrary to nature. However, as Kant understood, the preoccupations with hereditary original sin, and the means of its transmission, stem from a conviction that the propensity toward evil is determinate of personal identity, but not a general consequence of human nature. Melanchthon is well aware that "God's creatures, and nature itself, cannot be intrinsically bad." Yet, he warns that this true statement "must not be employed to underrate the sin of original

---

9. Quotations taken from Philipp Melanchthon's *Apology to the Augsburg Confession* in *The Christian Book of Concord, or Symbolical Books of the Evangelical Lutheran Church* (Newmarket, Va.: Solomon Henkel, 1851), 58–61.

depravity."[10] We are so determined by the propensity toward evil that one can say, as does Kant, that sin is woven into the fabric of our identities to such an extent that it becomes functionally "innate" and "natural," even if not essentially so. Though unnatural, sin is as intimate to who we are as the unique features of our genetic code.

In order to avoid the appearance of contradicting the unnaturalness of sin, speculation often emphasizes the foundational role of choice in our slavery to sin. Paul suggests that what we obey, either sin or righteousness, fundamentally determines us. His suggestion can encourage us to think of human evil as grounded in a primordial choice, a primitive disobedience; indeed, a dominant train of speculation in the Christian tradition interprets the story of the fall in Genesis according to this suggestion. Adam and Eve disobey the divine commandment, and their transgression casts the die for all humanity. In the ever lengthening shadow of this primordial disobedience, we are born slaves to impurity, caught in the whirlwind of iniquity. This interpretation of the fall is not, however, obligatory. One need not think of choice as the fundamental determinative ground of personal identity, and one need not conceive of the origins of sin in a primordial act of disobedience. Other theories of human sinfulness specify an inherited weakness, a corruption of natural powers, even a pervasive atmosphere of debilitating social influence. The specific accounts of how sin comes to shape our identities, persuasive or unpersuasive on their own terms, fruitful or unfruitful within a larger theological framework, are not crucial. The determinative status of our propensity toward evil is, however, decisive. Whatever constitutes personal identity, a propensity toward evil must be fundamental.[11]

---

10. Melanchthon, *Apology to the Augsburg Confession*, 65. See also the *Formula of Concord*, Epitome, art. 1, neg. 13. The *Formula* allows that a philosophical distinction between substance and accident requires one to say that the propensity toward evil is an accident, not a substance, since only God can create substances and all that God creates is good. Nonetheless, the *Formula* warns that "common persons" fail to grasp the distinction and are inclined, therefore, to think "accidental properties" are not decisive and thus are misled by the description of the propensity toward evil as an accident adhering to the human substance. One is justified, then, in using words such as "by nature" and "innate" in popular expositions of the doctrine of total depravity in order to drive home the determinative status of the propensity toward evil.

11. When explaining the relation between sin and personal identity, Pannenberg articulates what might be called the "anti-Pelagian test" for diverse efforts to avoid Augustinian speculations about hereditary transmission: "We can uphold the element of truth in the Augustinian position as opposed to the Pelagian only if we recognize in sin a basic state of the natural constitution of the perverted life in the individual. Only thus do individuals have to identify themselves with sin as

The upshot of this commitment to a determinative role for the propensity toward evil is twofold. First, it establishes the degree of change necessary for the highest good. Paul consistently depicts the transformation of redemption in the stark terms of death and rebirth. Since the propensity toward evil is determinative, change must be dramatic; it requires a new identity as a person. A new man must replace the old man; otherwise, the determining element of sinfulness remains. In this way, a determinative propensity toward evil raises the stakes of change. It widens the gap between who we are and the highest good. For Christian teaching, the width of the gap is directly proportional to the importance of Jesus.[12] Because Jesus' importance is decisive, the gap must be wide. Indeed, because Jesus has a role greater than that which we can imagine, the gap between being one person and being another entails a change greater than we can imagine bridging.

Second, a commitment to determinative sinfulness clarifies the difficulty of change. As Kant recognized, to say that the propensity is innate seems to contradict a humanistic commitment to the personal-potency requirement. Determined by evil, we seem to lack a power for goodness. Kant insists that we possess this potency nonetheless: evil is determinative, but not exhaustive. Christianity makes no such claim on our behalf. We have no power sufficient to effect a change in our identities. We are, to use the language of the Letter to the Ephesians, "dead through our trespasses" (Eph 2:5), and death does not possess the power of life. The power for life must come from God. We are not competent, says Paul, "to claim anything as coming from us; our competence is from God" (2 Cor 3:5). The Spirit, not a potency resident within the human person determined by evil, gives life (2 Cor 3:6). As a result, a conviction

---

part of themselves, since their own existence in the body is a basic form of the self that identifies them as individuals" (*Systematic Theology*, 2:257). Pannenberg's decision to use the concept of "natural constitution" as the way to bind personal identity to sin need not persuade. Instead, the formal point is decisive: sin must be determinative such that a person cannot be identified without being identified as sinful.

12. R. W. Dale provides a helpful gloss on this aspect of Paul's approach to the problem of sin. "Whatever uncertainty there may be about the precise meaning of particular sentences and particular clauses," writes Dale of Rom 5, "it indicates very clearly that Paul believed that the Son of Adam had brought vast evils on the human race just as the righteousness of Christ has brought infinite blessing." See his *Christian Doctrine: A Series of Discourses* (London: Hodder & Stoughton, 1894), 214–15.

that we are determined by sinfulness intensifies a dependence upon Jesus as the power of change.[13]

Imputable

We justly suffer the consequences of our transgressions only if they are imputable. Moreover, a quality or act may be imputed of a person as a moral quality or act, deserving praise or blame, only if the quality or act emerges out of the identity of the person. As we have seen, Kant treats debt and worthiness as questions of imputation across change—the latter in the change from evil to righteousness, the former in the ascent toward the highest good in which virtue is rewarded with happiness. These are not strictly legal or narrowly moral questions. Instead, imputation has to do with our ability to conceive of the continuity of our lives. A punishment fits a crime because we can see how the agent of transgression is the same person as the subject of punishment. Rewards are rightly given and received only if the recipient is self-identical with the person who acted honorably. Christian doctrine approaches sin in the same way. For Paul, those who sin "deserve to die" (Rom 1:32). God is not a whimsical, petty judge. The clear vision of holiness sees into the hearts of men (John 2:25) and recognizes that evil emerges out of our distinctive identities as persons. When the Son of Man comes in glory, the Father "will repay everyone for what has been done" (Matt 16:27). We rightly merit punishment for our sinfulness because the sin emerges out of who we are.

---

13. In his *Apology*, Melanchthon resists any depreciation of original sin, in part because a doctrine of total depravity clarifies the futility of self-wrought change and Christ's indispensable role: "As it is impossible, then, to overcome this subtle and powerful spirit, Satan, without the aide of Christ; so, by our own strength, we cannot exempt ourselves from this imprisonment" (66). Although Friedrich Schleiermacher rejects any Augustinian theory of hereditary sin and relies on a general, communally mediated pattern of consciousness as an explanation for the transmission of original sin, the consequent view of sin and redemption parallels Melanchthon exactly. Summarizing his account of original sin, Schleiermacher writes, "The sinfulness that is present in an individual prior to any action of his own, and has its ground outside its own being, is in every case a complete incapacity for good, which can be removed only by the influence of Redemption" (H. R. MacIntosh and T. S. Stewart, trans., *The Christian Faith* [Edinburgh: T. & T. Clark, 1928], par. 70). In both cases, an absolute incapacity for the good clarifies the need for an absolute dependence on Jesus Christ. This follows from a treatment of sin as determinative of personal identity, whatever anthropology one might use and regardless of the explanation of how sin is transmitted.

For Kant, the conditions for imputation are strictly individual. If "good" and "evil" are personal predicates rather than general descriptions of the human condition, then we must be the necessary and sufficient explanation for the imputation of good and evil. That is, you or I, as distinctive persons, must be the authors of our sinfulness. Kant gives no single, consistent anthropological account of precisely how we cause our own sinfulness, but this is of no moment. The logic of we-matter-most humanism requires moral predicates to be imputable, and for Kant, the overriding logic of this humanism, not the particular details of moral psychology, settles the question. Christianity proceeds in a similar fashion, although from different premises. Christianity reasons from the principle of divine justice in the following way: Justice requires that we may be held responsible for moral acts and qualities if and only if they are imputable. Scripture and conscience reveal that God holds us responsible for our sinfulness. God is perfectly just; therefore, our sinfulness must be imputable.

A great deal of debate in the history of Christian teaching on original sin rests in divergent ways of rendering this syllogism more perspicuous. How, exactly, does sin enter into the human condition through Adam such that sin might be properly imputed to us? Two trends of thought dominate. The first describes the conditions under which all human beings, as persons, are present in Adam's original fall, which leads to a theory of "immediate imputation" in which the unique identity of each person is, somehow, present in the first sin. The second trend of thought divides the question of sin into two elements: one involving the propensity to sin, which is in some way passed on from generation to generation but is not, itself, an imputable transgression, and the other involving actual sin, which follows inevitably from the inherited propensity and is imputable and liable to punishment. Classified as a theory of "mediate imputation," this second trend more nearly follows Kant's account.[14]

The doctrine of immediate imputation begins with the many Pauline descriptions of human destiny that depend upon a notion of commu-

---

14. For a clear account of the distinction between immediate and mediate theories of imputation and their relation to prevailing streams of Western Christian theology, see Charles Hodge, *Systematic Theology* (New York: Scribner, Armstrong, 1872), 2:192–214. For a further account of intra-Protestant debates about the relations between hereditary defect, actual sin, and imputable punishment, see also Julius Mueller, *The Christian Doctrine of Sin* (trans. William Urwick; Edinburgh: T. & T. Clark, 1885), 2:329–34.

nal headship and corporate representation. In a crucial passage in Romans, Paul draws a comparison between the way in which sin comes into the world through one man, Adam, and the way in which redemption comes into the world through one man, Jesus. "Many died through the one man's trespass," says Paul, and even more surely has "the grace of God and the free gift in the grace of the one man, Jesus Christ, abounded for the many" (Rom 5:15). Paul reinforces this notion of life and death bound up with the fate of a single man in 1 Corinthians, drawing attention to the same parallel. Death comes through Adam, while life comes through Jesus. "Since death came through a human being," Paul writes, "the resurrection of the dead has also come through a human being; for as all die in Adam, so all will be made alive in Christ" (1 Cor 15: 21–22). Theories of immediate imputation try to develop these Pauline patterns of thought with theories of corporate representation. Some theologians conceive of this representation in a physical, realistic fashion. Adam is the father of the human race. Our lives are contained in his, *in potentia,* and his fall is as much our fall, as the life breathed into him is our life. The notion of representation can also take on a legal, covenant form. We are "with Adam," just as we are represented by legal deputies and elected officials, and are "with them" as persons rightfully bound by their decisions. Their actions have judicial standing as actions of all those whom they represent. So, just as the elected sovereign expresses the will of the people, so also does Adam's disobedience express our collective disobedience.

To a large extent, the mediate theory of imputation emerges out of the difficulty of making immediate imputation plausible. Life passed on is one thing, but transgression is another. In what sense can my inherited transgression be imputed? Further, how can we bear responsibility for a representative we did not, in fact, elect? To resolve these questions, theologians argue that Adam's transgression introduces disorder into our inherited condition. We suffer from a propensity toward sin by virtue of our common condition. However, in itself this propensity is not imputable, since it comes from an inherited corruption, not our identities as particular persons. As such, it does not merit punishment. Nonetheless, this propensity is so powerful that none can avoid committing actual sins, and these sins are, indeed, imputable. They deserve punishment. In this way, proponents of mediate imputation affirm the universality of sin, while at the same time conforming more closely to prevailing intuitions about the conditions for a just imputation of moral qualities and acts.

How a theological program explains the imputation of sin has important systematic consequences. It shapes, and is shaped by, an explanation of redemptive change and the consequent imputation of righteousness. Nonetheless, I have no interest in resolving the debate between the various streams of explanation. To a great degree, that debate turns on the background assumptions we hold about the rightful imputation of actions to persons. A culture that makes strong claims on behalf of the corporate identity easily accommodates theories of immediate imputation. Modern individualism and the consequent desire, exemplified in Kant, to restrict reward and merit to discrete persons and their own actions requires a default to some form of mediate imputation. However, we should beware easy distinctions. Rarely does considered analysis of actual moral practice admit of purely corporate or individual approaches. Even our highly individualistic culture socializes us to feel a national pride, and our system of representative government, although based upon an ideology of individual choice in voting, is unintelligible without a degree of corporate identity.

Parsing these issues and supporting a particular account of how a universal, unnatural, and determinative state of sin is properly imputed to all persons is beyond the scope of this inquiry. I wish only to show a common Christian logic throughout.[15] All that is necessary, then, is to affirm the imputability of our need for change.[16] Christianity teaches

---

15. Hodge's analysis highlights this common logic, addressing specifically the ambiguities in Augustine's reflections on the nature and origin of sin:

> It is a matter of minor importance how [Augustine] understood the nature of the union between Adam and his posterity; whether he held the representative, or the realistic theory; or whether he ultimately sided for Traducianism or against Creationism, or for the latter as against the former. On these points his language is confused and undecided. It is enough that he held that such was the union between Adam and his race, that the whole human family stood their probation in him and fell with him in his first transgression, so that all the evils which are the consequences of that transgression, including physical and spiritual death, are the punishment of that sin. (*Systematic Theology,* 2:162)

The formal relation of personal identity to evil is the central issue for theology, not the material explanation of that relation.

16. Schleiermacher surveys a complex array of explanations for the connection between Adam's original transgression and our subsequent state of sin. Within his system, some are more perspicuous than others. Nonetheless, he affirms the necessary imputation of sin from the very outset of personal existence. "We certainly admit," writes Schleiermacher of his modifications of received teaching on the relation between original sin, guilt, and the identity of persons, "a universal imputation of the first sin, an imputation resting upon the belief that to whatever human

that we need to change because of who we are, not because of bad social circumstances or a general condition of disordered desire or inherited defect. Sin is a properly personal problem.

For Christian teaching, then, our need for change is universal, unnatural, and determinative, just as Kant outlined in *Religion within the Limits of Mere Reason*, and that need is imputable. The Christian and humanistic accounts of why and how our need for change is subject to all four conditions vary. Under the constraints of we-matter-most humanism, Kant must preserve a human nature that retains the potency for change, and he explains imputability in terms of free self-determination. In contrast, Christian teaching has theological reasons for denying that sin is natural and provides no single explanation of how sin comes to be imputed to each of us, as individual persons. Nonetheless, in each case formal parallels obtain, and the common problem of anthropodicy emerges. We are all evil, and thus the need for change extends to all persons. Evil is unnatural, and as a consequence, the possibility of change, whatever the source of power, remains a worldly hope. We can affirm that all sin and, at the same time, hope that we, as human beings, might become righteous because none are sinful by nature. This evil is, however, determinative of our identities as persons; therefore, the degree of change is fundamental. Although our natures need not change, our identities as persons must. Finally sin is imputable; it obtains because of who we are. Consequently, the drama of change must account for who we are, as beholden to evil, in order to preserve a basic continuity of personal identity. These four features, for Christianity as for the humanism so rigorously advanced by Kant, define the problem of change. They establish the particular soteriological form of the problem of evil, the problem of showing how becoming righteous is consistent with being evil.

To agree on the problem in no way guarantees a common mind about the solution. Kant embraces the need for change that characterizes the Christian story of the soul, but in no sense does he follow

---

individual had fallen the lot of being the first, he, too, would have committed the sin" (*The Christian Faith*, par. 73.6). Even if we do not all fall in Adam *actually*, we do so *modally*. Whether such a modal participation is, finally, an adequate explanation for the imputable status of sin is of little consequence. For Schleiermacher, as for the Christian tradition generally, the affirmation of imputability follows from his view of redemption. Only if the need for change is personal—that is to say, imputable—will the consequences of change be personal. Kant suggests a similar modal participation in Adam's fall, and for the same reason. See above, chap. 4, n. 26.

the Christian plot as he explains how persons change from evil to righteous. Quite the contrary, Kant adopts an anti-Christian anthropodicy.
For Kant, we possess the power necessary and sufficient to escape the
condition of universal, unnatural, determinative, and imputable sin.
Our identities as persons are supremely consequential for the highest
good. Nothing could be further from the Christian approach. For
Augustine, the story of his own soul in his *Confessions* turns on his
abandonment to the power of God in Jesus Christ. All his advances in
learning and career, moral insight and self-discipline, were of no consequence. They only produced tears born of the torment of wanting to
become different but knowing oneself to lack the power to change.
Only when Augustine heard the command "Take! Read!" out of the
mouths of children and obeyed it, did he change.[17] Augustine enacted
what Paul taught. The gospel of Jesus Christ, not Augustine or you or
me, is the power of God for salvation (Rom 1:16).

What, exactly, is the gospel of Jesus Christ, and how should we
understand its power to effect change? In its most extensive sense, the
gospel of Jesus Christ is the account of his life, teachings and healings,
death and resurrection, as told across the four gospel stories of the
New Testament. The gospel of Jesus Christ is his identity as narrated
in these stories. The good news about Jesus is that he is who he is. For
Paul, this gospel admits of epitome. For example, he tells the believers
in Corinth that they should cling to his preaching, "For I have handed
on to you as of first importance what I in turn had received: that Christ
died for our sins in accordance with the Scriptures, and that he was
buried, and that he was raised on the third day in accordance with the
scriptures, and that he appeared to Cephas, then to the twelve" (1 Cor
15:3–5). The gospel, the power of salvation, the matter of first importance, is Jesus Christ, who died for us, was buried and raised, in accordance with the Scriptures. He is the source of redemptive power, the
engine of change in the Christian cure of the soul.

At the risk of false distinction, I propose to analyze the power of
the gospel that Paul received and wished to pass on to the Corinthians
in two aspects. First, the power of the gospel is the identity of Jesus
of Nazareth. As the one who is raised from the dead, he is the necessary and sufficient source of power for change. His identity, and no
other, provides the potency that saves, and this potency is "for us."
Second, Jesus saves because his identity "for us" has incorporative

---

17. Augustine, *Confessions* 10.9–12.

power, which allows Jesus to stand in our place. "While we were still weak," writes Paul, "at the right time Christ died for the ungodly" (Rom 5:6). Furthermore, Jesus' incorporative power draws us into a continuous form of life. "We have been buried with him by baptism into death," Paul teaches, "so that, just as Christ was raised from the dead by the glory of the Father, so we too might walk in newness of life" (6:4). Jesus alone saves. He is precisely that person who dies on the cross, for us and for our salvation, and does so with the effective power of new life. Nonetheless, if we distinguish the Christian affirmation of salvation through Christ alone from the conviction that Jesus' death "for us" functions to incorporate us into his actions and power of new life, then we can understand more clearly the role of our identities as persons in the Christian view of change. This heuristic distinction allows us to consider the ways in which the Christian cure of the soul handles the Augustinian concerns about the true source of potency for change and the Athanasian concerns about continuity across change. Thus, we can more closely compare Kant's faith to the Christian story of the soul and see how Christian teaching, unlike modern humanism, offers a self-consistent view of the potency for change and the conditions for personal continuity.

Potency for Change

Divine love does not triumph through a radiating and universal potency. Jesus is the power of salvation, and like you and me, Jesus of Nazareth is a person with a distinct and particular identity. A first-century Palestinian Jew, Jesus was born in Bethlehem, lived in Galilee, was tried by Pontius Pilate, was executed on a cross outside of Jerusalem, was buried, and was raised from the dead. Precisely as that person, and no other, Jesus is the gospel, the power of God for salvation. Therefore, his potency is not personal in a general sense. It is not a potency of Jesus' reason or experience, his existential disposition or form of consciousness. Jesus—not what he represents, embodies, or manifests—saves. Jesus' potency is bound to the uniqueness of his identity.[18] So, we should say that Christianity shares with Kant's

---

18. Modern theological projects have foundered on this specification of redemptive power. Again and again, hermeneutical and conceptual gymnastics of the highest order have been employed to translate Jesus' identity into some something else that we can more easily grasp as a form of effective power. He is an "event" that precipitates decision. He is a "praxis" that animates a distinctive form of life. He is an embodied "consciousness" that inspires. He is an

humanism a commitment to specific and particular personal potency as the necessary and sufficient condition for the highest good. Modern humanism and Christianity, then, disagree only in specifying *who* possesses the potency sufficient for the highest good. For Christian teaching, you and I do not—Jesus of Nazareth does.

Here, modern theology has often been blinded by the formal parallel between Christianity and modern humanism. Since both affirm a personal potency, theologians slide toward the conclusion that "personality" is the key to attaining the highest good. This apparent convergence is reinforced by the tendency of an increasingly dominant scientific culture to presuppose a reductive materialism that restricts power to physical forces and natural processes. However, this confuses personhood, or some general category of "the person," with personal identity.[19] Neither Christianity nor modern humanism identifies a general feature of persons as necessary and sufficient for the highest good. For Kant, "personality," "freedom," and "reason" cannot effect personal change; you or I must. For Christianity, Jesus alone is the power of salvation, not his personality or God-consciousness or "praxis." Thus, in order to avoid this tendency to slide toward a false convergence, we must be clear about the formal status of the Christian affirmation that Jesus saves, just as we have been clear about the logic of we-matter-most humanism. Jesus saves because of who he is, just as, for Kant, each of us effects righteousness solely because of our

---

"archetype" that stimulates consciences. He is the "concrete universal," the self-alienation of Spirit that gathers up history into eternity. The list is potentially endless, but the basic form is always the same. Jesus saves because he possesses something of redemptive power. This approach is inconsistent with classical Christian teaching: Jesus saves because he is who he is. For a clear account of the juxtaposition between modern and classical accounts of the power for salvation in the gospel, see Bruce D. Marshall, *Christology in Conflict: The Identity of a Savior in Rahner and Barth* (Oxford: Basil Blackwell, 1987). To a great extent, modern theology consistently seeks to translate the identity of Jesus into something more "real," something more self-evidently potent, because his identity seems so spectral and elusive. For an account of why Jesus' identity can seem so empty and impotent, see Hans W. Frei, *The Eclipse of Biblical Narrative* (New Haven: Yale University Press, 1973); and even more provocatively and profoundly, Ephraim Radner, *The End of the Church*.

19. For a classic example, see William Temple, *Nature, Man, and God* (London: Macmillan, 1951). Temple's work is dominated by an alliance with modern humanism in which traditional Christian concepts such as incarnation and sacrament are shifted away from the person of Jesus Christ and directed toward "personality." We have seen, as well, the way in which Ernst Cassirier's neo-Kantianism uses "personality" to ease the offense of modern humanism's implausible claim that personal identity is sufficient for the highest good. See chap. 2, n. 26. Both are entirely plausible spiritual and moral visions. Neither is fully Christian nor humanistic.

decision to affirm duty for its own sake. Personal identity is the key, not any generic human attribute or power.

The idea that potency for change should come from a person at all—whether you, me, or Jesus—is strange. As Kant recognized, the ubiquity and determinative status of sin makes persons singularly inauspicious candidates for effecting the dramatic, revolutionary changes necessary to bring about the highest good. If we are utterly captive to ignorance and prejudice, then some greater power or principle would seem a more likely candidate. Indeed, one need not specify a doctrine of radical evil, as did Kant, to have doubts about investing mere personal identity with potency for change. We seem so inappropriate, simply by being who we are, for such an important role. Not surprisingly, then, we cast about for surrogates. Perhaps Being or Science or History or Democracy has the power to overcome evil, or at least to restrain its worst excesses. Or maybe Blood and Soil or the Führer Principle or the Dictatorship of the Proletariat will do the trick. Against all such suprapersonal principalities and powers, Kant continued to believe that we can, indeed, change, and change for no other reason than because of who we are as creatures of conscience and freedom. He insisted upon the personal-potency requirement. Only if we are necessary and sufficient conditions for the highest good can we matter most in a full and complete sense.

In order to make sense out of this conviction that persons possess the power to change from evil to righteous, Kant assumed that persons are unlike any other thing that has identity. We can be who we are such that evil is a determinative feature of our identities, and we can, through the exercise of our freedom, become righteous, such that righteousness is a determinative feature of our identities. Unlike the acorn, which always remains that thing determined by its propensity toward becoming an oak tree, we are not always those persons determined by our propensity toward sin. Kant calls this personal potency "freedom." His terminology and formulations, as I have argued above, are not crucial. The important point is the possibility of change in identity. What is innate at present need not be innate in the future. We-matter-most humanism makes no sense without this affirmation. Without it, either evil is not personal, and we are simply victims of external malevolence, or we are captive to our innate evil, unable to change. Neither alternative is consistent with the faith of modern humanism. Therefore, Kant makes his controversial claim: we must believe that personal identity differs from the identity of any other thing insofar as persons possess the power to change their identities.

Christian faith motivates a different and even more controversial metaphysical innovation. In Paul's understanding, Jesus died, was buried, and was raised from the dead, in accordance with the Scriptures. These very Scriptures identify the God of Israel, who created heaven and earth, as the sole power of salvation. The psalmist prays to the LORD for deliverance. The prophets urge the people of Israel to turn to the LORD in repentance and obedience. God and God alone can make all things new. To say that Jesus possesses just this power—not as a messenger or representative but in his identity—creates a dilemma, for if Jesus' identity is the power of salvation, then he is identified by exactly that which identifies God. Jesus has the power to save; the LORD alone has the power to save. The implications of these claims about Jesus' identity encouraged early Christian theologians to argue that Jesus is a person of a very different sort, not only different from acorns but also from other people. He is a person who is God. Only as such can his identity provide the potency necessary for salvation *and* can the God of the Scriptures be the proper object of worship and devotion.[20]

The particular ways in which Christian theology has made the metaphysical distinctions necessary to coordinate the identity of Jesus

---

20. See Robert W. Jenson, *The Triune Identity* (Philadelphia: Fortress, 1982). Because of the connection between an affirmation of the saving power of Jesus' identity and Trinitarian reflection, the array of modern theological projects that seek to specify a saving power that supervenes upon Jesus' identity—that he manifests, possesses, or evokes but never simply *is*—are necessarily a-Trinitarian theologies. Modern theologians may articulate a doctrine of the Trinity, but such doctrines amount to speculative adventures with no necessary logical relationship to the claims about the power of the gospel. Schleiermacher offers a typical illustration. He rightly observes that the doctrine of the Trinity must be a soteriological doctrine; that is to say, it must emerge out of the conviction that Jesus is the power of salvation (*The Christian Faith*, par. 170.1). However, Schleiermacher identifies Jesus' perfect God-consciousness, not his personal identity as such, as the power of salvation. Complex and difficult questions emerge: How might a man's God consciousness be perfect? Why should we regard Jesus' God-consciousness as perfect? What are the means by which perfect God-consciousness exerts power and transformative influence over others? Though Schleiermacher's systematic theology is taken up with these questions, he is not faced with the logical constraint of concluding that Jesus *is* the power of God for salvation. As a consequence, he rightly concludes, on the basis of his own definition of saving power, "that the main pivots of the ecclesiastical doctrine—the being of God in Christ and the Christian Church—are independent of the doctrine of the Trinity" (par. 170.3). That is to say, if Jesus' God-consciousness and sinless perfection save, then one need not worry oneself about the difficulties of saying that Jesus saves. Or again, using Schleiermacher's formulation, if the being of God is in Christ, then one is relieved of the strenuous task of explaining how Christ *is* the being of God.

with the God who created heaven and earth constitute the tradition of Trinitarian reflection that serves as an indispensable bedrock for the intelligibility of Christian beliefs. The details of that reflection are beyond the scope of this inquiry. Nonetheless, two points are necessary. First, once the identity of Jesus is explicated in Trinitarian terms, then the claim that he possesses the power to change our identities becomes analytic. God has the power to make something out of nothing, and the prospect of making a "new man" out of a person determined by sin presents no problem for the Christian imagination. Insofar as Jesus is God incarnate, he possesses such power. Second, the reasons why Christians are motivated to think this way about the identity of Jesus and his relation to divine power are formally parallel to the reasons why Kant affirms a personal potency for change. No general metaphysical principles warrant Kant's distinction between acorns and persons. Kant's doctrine of evil, not his principle of personal potency, garners empirical support. That none are pure of heart seems a plausible generalization, but the contrary affirmation—that we have the power to change nonetheless—is hardly obvious. No empirical observations buttress the belief that people can change their identities all the way down to the root of who they are. Nonetheless, the sheer certainty of a humanistic faith that we matter most for the highest good carries Kant forward. No matter how implausible, we *must* have the power to change.

Christianity proceeds in much the same way. Paul was well aware that both Greek speculation about divine power and the scriptural horizon for messianic expectation are confounded by the proposition that Jesus is the power of salvation. Aristotle's metaphysics do not speak in favor of a triune God. Moreover, in antiquity, common sense associated redemptive power with impassability and freedom from suffering. One need not be captive to ancient ideals of impassability to see the problem. The idea that the crucified Jesus could be the power of God for salvation directly assaults such common sense. How can one whose identity is defined by the problem—suffering and death—be the solution? The gospel stories themselves anticipate the question. If he could not save himself, how could he possibly save others (Matt 27:42; Mark 15:31; Luke 23:35)? In addition to the difficulty of seeing how a dying man can save, for Jews, the sharp distinction between God and creation, which is reinforced again and again in the scriptural polemics against idolatry, militates against the belief in an incarnate God. The LORD might reveal his hindquarters to Moses but He cannot *be* the "new Moses." In each case, only a conviction that Jesus is the power of salvation can overcome the objections. Only such a belief can motivate Trinitarian reflection.[21]

In both cases, then, a presumptive specification of the power necessary to effect change controls. Modern humanism and Christianity agree that this power must be a person, which makes both very different from any number of alternatives. Platonism, for example, surely endorses redemptive change. Yet, the potency for change, the Forms, is not personal; it is a suprapersonal power in which we, as rational beings, participate. Not by accident, then, have many modern theologians endorsed an alliance with modern humanism. In contrast to Platonism, as well as other accounts of transformative power that transcends personal identity, both Christianity and modern humanism advance a *personal*-potency requirement.[22] They differ, however, in the identity of the person who possesses the power for change. As we have seen, modern humanism treats the identity of each person as supremely consequential, and for this reason, each of us must exercise the power for change for ourselves only, and not for others. In contrast, the basic beliefs of Christianity identify Jesus as the sole power for salvation, and for this reason, the classical Christian form of the personal-potency requirement is Augustinian. Christ and Christ alone is the person who exercises the power for change, and he does so, not for himself, but for others.

Because the potency of Christ is "for us," it follows that the Christian view of change endorses a consequential role for personal identity. We, not just Jesus, matter. Who Christ is in suffering and death revolves around our sinfulness; his identity is shaped by our situation as persons determined by an imputable evil. The Son of Man did not come to serve himself; he came to serve others. Our identities, however dependent upon his, could not matter more. Of course, this sense of consequential personal identity is at odds with the assumptions of modern humanism. As the logic of we-matter-most humanism

---

21. See, e.g., Thomas Aquinas, *Summa Theologiae* 3.48.6. The specification of Christ alone as the proper subject for the predicate "redeemer" motivates a discussion of the relationship between Jesus and God, a discussion that requires a Trinitarian framework in order to be intelligible.

22. For this reason, twentieth-century theology has mistakenly attempted to use Martin Heidegger's philosophy to undercut the humanistic pretensions of modernity. Heidegger's account of Being may be anti-Platonic in sentiment and logic, but like Plato, Heidegger treats the fundamental power of Being as suprapersonal. Jesus' identity, therefore, cannot be the power of change, for he is a person.

stipulates, none can be "for another"; we must all be "for ourselves." However, this stipulation merely restates the primitive convictions of modern humanism. It does not provide a basis for assessing the merits of Christianity in comparison to modern humanism.

I have no interest in guiding the reader through the tangled webs of inference, evidence, and aesthetic judgment necessary to form a judgment about which specification of the power for change—Jesus "for us" or each of us "for ourselves"—is more plausible, a prospect all the more daunting because the idea that *any* person would have such potency is so implausible. I wish only to observe that Kant's humanistic conviction that we possess the potency for changing our identities is not prima facie at an advantage. His humanism can seem more plausible because it entails fewer controversial convictions. It involves a distinction between persons and all other things. In contrast, Christianity's commitment to the saving power of Jesus initiates a massive theological project of rethinking an array of fundamental assumptions about divine and created reality, time and eternity, substance and person. A great deal of what Christians claim about God, the world, and persons is controversial. Nonetheless, the parsimony of Kant's we-matter-most humanism may not be an asset.

The natural and social sciences are predicated on the assumption that human phenomena are continuous with other nonhuman phenomena; therefore, a strong metaphysical distinction between persons and things runs contrary to the way that the best available science trains us to think. Furthermore, these sciences scrupulously repudiate any teleological description of natural phenomena, human or otherwise. As a consequence, the entire humanistic project of morally motivated criticism and active efforts to change societies and persons so that some greater good might be achieved also runs counter to the way that the best available science trains us to think. Therefore, the metaphysical parsimony of modern humanism risks being absorbed into the outlook of modern science and its presumption that persons are inconsequential in the larger scheme of things. Evolutionary theory is indifferent to the fate of any species, much less any individual instance of DNA. When biologists turn to analysis of the human species, the modern humanist can do little more than protest that persons are not things. That protest is honorable, but increasingly feeble. The charge of "speciesism" too easily strikes home.

Because Christianity invests Jesus' identity with the power for change, and because Jesus is who he is—the one who died, was buried, and was raised in accordance with the Scriptures—Christian teaching must entertain a wide array of ambitious theological propositions. These propositions, in turn, support a comprehensive account of all that is, both in origin and purpose. This theological ambition, triggered by the connection between Jesus and God, has the advantage of making modern science subordinate, rather than superordinate, in a comprehensive account of everything. The inability of modern science to distinguish between persons and things need not, therefore, be taken as final. A superordinate and comprehensive theological account can justify such a distinction. Therefore, Christian theology does not simply assert that persons differ from things; it offers a rival account of everything based on the Trinitarian consequences of saying that Jesus saves. As a result, the adequacy of scientific patterns of explanation as a whole, not just the scientific conclusions about the relation between persons and things, is challenged by an alternative account that is able to engage both the epistemic practices and material conclusions of modern science at many levels.

Whether or not any particular Christian theologian successfully shows how modern science fits into the larger theological framework, or successfully justifies the distinction between persons and things in light of that larger framework, is a matter for dispute and demonstration. The important point, however, remains. Christian Trinitarian theology, founded on the ambitious claim about Jesus as the potency for change, may have the theoretical resources necessary to provide a satisfactory account of the need for and possibility of morally meaningful change that has its basis in personal identity. Modern humanism, because it does not entail the expansive array of theological claims, does not have such resources. To put the matter more plainly, in a context in which modern science dominates the training of our minds, we most likely need to say a great deal about the world and our role in it, a great deal more than modern humanism does, in order to affirm rationally the unique value of persons. Sometimes saying more makes greater sense than saying less. Christianity does say more, a great deal more; therefore, the difference between Christianity and modern humanism on the question of the personal potency for change is not a collision of two equal and opposite forces. In the face of real contemporary challenges to the conviction that persons matter in any special or unique way, Christian teaching offers greater resources for argument than does modern humanism.[23]

Continuity in Change

Redemptive hope requires more than a proper potency for change. In order to matter at all, we need to be continuous persons across the gap between who we are—determined by evil—and who we wish to become—determined by righteousness. We must be sufficiently self-identical across change to be able to see how that person who *needs to change* is really connected to that person who *has changed*. The old man must be linked to the new man. Change cannot be a matter of self-renunciation, a covert form of forgetfulness, or self-denial. Otherwise, the problem of overreaching emerges. For this reason, Christianity, like modern humanism, acknowledges the personal-continuity requirement. Athanasian concerns are as important as the Augustinian.

For Kant, moral categories of debt and payment, punishment and satisfaction, offer means for expressing the continuity of identity across change. To be a certain kind of person, determined by good or evil, creates a horizon of deserts; righteousness merits reward. In order to secure the conditions for the possibility of the realization of that reward, Kant postulates the existence of God and the immortality of the soul. God

---

23. The following argument may cast helpful light on the margin of argumentative advantage held by Christian teaching over modern humanism. (1) The mind is suited to the world. Our beliefs, on the whole, either are or cannot be thought to be otherwise than suited to the task of navigating through the world. This is the principle of epistemic adequacy. (2) A rationally responsible argument is one that increases our ability to know that which is under discussion; such an argument reinforces the adequacy of our beliefs. (3) An ambitious argument is one that calls into question one or more fundamental beliefs about that which is under discussion; such an argument casts doubt on the adequacy of our beliefs. (4) In view of the principle of epistemic adequacy, ambitious arguments having to do with the world are very likely to be intellectually irresponsible, and responsible arguments are very likely to be unambitious. In other words, responsible arguments tend to confirm or modestly adjust our web of belief. (5) God is the only matter available for discussion that is different from the world. As such, theology is the only discipline for which the principle of epistemic adequacy does not obtain. Therefore, only in theological analysis is it likely or normal for arguments to be both responsible and ambitious.

If this argument is cogent, then we can apply it to the case of modern humanism. To the extent that modern science provides the dominant elements of our web of belief in late-twentieth-century postindustrial society, the distinction between persons and things is ambitious and, therefore, likely to be irresponsible. In contrast, because Christian teaching makes the distinction between persons and things on the basis of arguments about the being and nature of God, this ambitious distinction is likely to be responsible.

so orders the world that we can, across the duration of eternity, hope for the union of righteousness and happiness that, through merit and reward, is based on who we are. The same holds true for evil. An unrighteous person deserves punishment; we remain accountable for our lives. We do not leap into the future blindly. We do not rush forward as if the past were of no consequence. Our identities as persons make a difference, an imputable difference, and insofar as our identities are determined by evil, Kant must speculate about atonement as the condition for the possibility of continuity across change.

As we have seen, Kant's rigorous application of the logic of we-matter-most humanism produces difficulties. Because moral predicates are determinative of persons and the difference between evil and righteousness is disjunctive, the change entailed in moral transformation is a fundamental change in personal identity. Kant simply asserts the possibility of this change, as we have already seen. Establishing continuity across this change, however, is another matter entirely. Constrained by the humanistic, anti-Augustinian form of the personal-potency requirement, Kant must show how we can be "for ourselves" as agents of atonement, much as we are "for ourselves" as the potency for change. Christianity's affirmation of the Augustinian claim that Jesus is the sole source of redemptive change raises exactly the same problem. Christianity must show how Jesus can be "for us," not just as the power for change but also as the agent of atonement. The Athanasian concerns about personal continuity must be addressed. How can we be saved if we are made into something new? How can we matter at all if we simply are broken across the gap between present and future identities?

Jesus' power "for us" establishes personal continuity because Jesus' identity is not simply potent with the power of divine love. Jesus' power supports our continuity as persons—our ability to endure both judgment and change—because his power is *incorporative*.[24] This cru-

---

24. For Barth, the specific form of God power in Jesus Christ is that of "exchange." As he explains, "The conversion of the world to Himself took place in the form of an exchange, a substitution, which God has proposed between the world and Himself present and active in the person of Jesus Christ" (*Church Dogmatics,* vol. 4, pt. 1, p. 75). This exchange has two sides. First, Jesus accepts complete solidarity with the sinner, and as a consequence, he is judged in our place. He endures the "no" of divine judgment that we cannot bear in our bondage to sin. Second, "in Christ we are made the righteous of God as Christ was made sin for us" (75). This takes form as the call to a ministry of reconciliation in which we are brought into God's righteousness as "mouthpieces of reconciliation" in a life of witness to Jesus Christ (77–78). My use of the term

cial premise in the Christian cure of the soul specifies Jesus' saving power as incorporative, thus giving Christianity the ability to provide a consistent account of continuity through change. Jesus is the power of the gospel in this very specific way. His power incorporates us into him, and for this reason, Jesus' power can be imputed to us in such a way that our identities as persons have continuity.

To analyze the Christian view, I will divide the incorporative power of Jesus "for us" into two aspects: the apocalyptic and the pneumatological. The first has to do with classical concerns about atonement: divine justice and satisfaction for human sin. As we have seen in our analysis of Kant, these concerns have an anthropological dimension. Debt and payment express the conditions for continuity across moral change, and a cogent account of the way in which our past is connected to our future is basic to an account of continuity across change. The pneumatological aspect of Jesus' incorporative power "for us" does not yield clear formulations of debt and payment. Here, at-one-ment is enacted and inhabited rather than imputed. Nonetheless, clarity about the way in which Jesus shapes our identities can provide insight into the personal and social continuity that Christianity provides for persons seeking change. Not only is Jesus "for us" as the one who pays our debt and bears our punishment; he is also "for us" in the determining form of apostolic faith and practice. In both ways, apocalyptically and pneumatologically, the power of Jesus for change ensures personal continuity.

The Apocalyptic Aspect

Students of Western theology are familiar with the apocalyptic aspect of Jesus' incorporative role "for us" as it appears in theories

---

"incorporation" seeks to capture both sides of Barth's pattern of exchange and to do so in a way that clarifies more fully the enduring permanence of the exchange of places that Barth details throughout his doctrine of reconciliation.

Patristic thought emphasizes the incorporative power of Jesus. For example, Athanasius vigorously emphasizes the scriptural account of Jesus as the "firstborn" of creation. Under this description, in *Four Discourses against the Arians*, he assimilates the fleshly body of Jesus with the "Word's body," which is the Church, insisting that "henceforth we, becoming incorporate in It, are saved after Its pattern" (*Nicene and Post-Nicene Fathers*, series 2 [ed. Philip Schaff and A. J. B. Wace; Grand Rapids: Eerdmans, 1987], 4:381). This assimilation is often described, by the Fathers and subsequent commentators, with the term "participation." I prefer "incorporation" for two reasons. First, it stands at a remove from the Platonic metaphysics that gives technical meaning to the term "participation." Second, it emphasizes the fleshly, social, and enacted dimension of Jesus' relation to persons.

of substitutionary atonement. These theories range from Anselm's meditation on the satisfaction that Jesus offers in his death, to Scholastic treatments of the effective consequences of Jesus' sacrifice of his sinless humanity, to Reformation efforts to develop an overarching scheme of human debt and divine payment in Jesus' death. The details of these theories diverge; however, each emphasizes the apocalyptic aspect. Divine holiness requires judgment upon the unrighteous, and we are unable to endure such judgment. We cannot traverse the gap between our current condition and the righteousness demanded by God.

The scriptural background for these traditional accounts of judgment emphasizes the theocentric constraints upon change. The divine hatred of transgression serves a standard trope throughout the Old Testament. "Your eyes are too pure to behold evil," we read in a typical passage, "and you cannot look on wrongdoing" (Hab 1:13). Against the background of Israel's faithlessness, the LORD asks, "Shall I not punish them for these things? . . . shall I not bring retribution on a nation such as this?" (Jer 5:9). The righteousness of God cannot tolerate evil; divine perfection will not allow transgression to pass unpunished. Here, the very continuity of God's identity is at stake. It seems unfitting to say that God prohibits transgression of the divine commandments at one time, and then to say that God permits these transgressions at a later point. Punishment seems necessary in order to maintain divine continuity. It was wrong to sin, and God continues to regard it as wrong.

Since Christianity affirms the continuity of the LORD's holiness, attention shifts to the anthropocentric aspect.[25] The specific conceptual terminology used by classical atonement theory to explain our role in divine judgment is inconsequential. Instead, the basic form of the question is important. Given the continuity of divine demand, how can we pay the debt of sin? Since the proper punishment for sin is death and since God will not repent of divine-established justice, how

---

25. As James Denney observes, classical doctrines of substitutionary atonement are necessarily "anthropocentric." Because of us, God's power of love takes effective shape in Jesus' suffering and death. "The Atonement is not the denial that God's love is free," he writes, for in no sense does our sin require or produce God's initiative on our behalf. Instead, the atonement "is that specific manifestation or demonstration of God's free love which is demanded by the situation of men" (*The Atonement and the Modern Mind* [New York: A. C. Armstrong, 1903], 31). Jesus is the power of change "for us" and therefore meets our need. Precisely because atonement is "anthropocentric" in this sense, it marks for Denney the point of the most violent conflict with the anthropocentric assumptions of modernity.

can anyone endure God's judgment? At issue, then, is not the conviction that God exercises redemptive power in Christ. The problem rests in our ability to participate in the change from sinner to sanctified, from old man to new man, for the continuity of divine identity seems to require a discontinuity of our identities: we must be destroyed in judgment in order to be re-created in righteousness.

No matter how the threat of divine judgment is formulated, the solution offered is the same. Insofar as theologians have identified the problem of continuity in divine judgment, they have proposed a variant of a single claim: Jesus stands in our place as the substitute. He is judged righteous and vindicated where we would be judged unrighteous and condemned. He offers satisfaction when we are unable. He pays the debt that is beyond our means. He endures the punishment that we cannot. He dies the death we cannot survive. However formulated, Jesus provides the conditions for the possibility of personal continuity. He meets the Athanasian concern about continuity.

Here, the particular logic of judgment and Jesus' role is not decisive. Many arguments exist for or against penal or pecuniary or cultic analysis of the transactions effected by Jesus' death. Were our object to probe the mysteries of faith, such arguments would be important. However, our focus is on "mere Christianity," and no matter how one analyzes the effective power of Jesus for change, some account of his role in providing the basis for continuous personal identity must be offered. Therefore, the root issue is the way in which Christian theories of atonement establish continuity in change and do so in a self-consistent fashion.

The clarity of Kant's account of the personal-continuity requirement helps illuminate the Christian approach. Kant was aware that who we are, as persons determined by sin, must be connected to who we should become, as persons determined by righteousness. If our lives matter at all for the highest good, then surely something follows from who we are, surely something about you and me constrains the dynamics of change. The judicial constructions of the problem of atonement—the classical Christian accounts, as well as Kant's—seek to acknowledge and account for this constraint.[26] Because of who we

---

26. Dietrich Bonhoeffer seeks to express this aspect: "God does not 'overlook' sin; that would mean not taking human beings seriously as personal beings in their very culpability; and that would mean no re-creation of the person. . . . But God does take human beings seriously in their culpability, and therefore only punishment and the overcoming of sin can remedy the matter"

are, there is some *x* that must be accounted for in the process of change, and if that *x* is not accounted for, then who we become is not connected to who we have been. Whatever we might think of the religious, moral, or legal limitations of concepts such as debt and punishment, they express the logic of this *x* and the way in which it must influence the dynamics of change in order to ensure continuity.

As we have seen, under the constraints of a disciplined use of concepts of debt and punishment, Kant could not establish the conditions under which continuity can be affirmed. His failure stemmed from the rigorous limitations he places upon moral predicates. Because he was constrained by a humanistic account of the personal-potency requirement, a moral predicate can be imputed if and only if that predicate stems from the identity of the individual person. For this reason, no other could stand in our place, no other can perform morally significant acts on our behalf. Only we can atone for our own past. Yet, precisely because moral change is real, we become different persons. Therefore, even though only we can atone for ourselves, we cannot because we have changed. The upshot is a vision of moral change in which the hoped-for future cannot be "at-one" with the past and present.

Because Christianity rejects the humanistic account of the personal-potency requirement and instead affirms that Jesus alone has such potency, no such problems emerge. Since Christianity teaches that Jesus provides the power necessary for change, and that such a change is "for us," in no sense are morally significant actions limited by Kant's account of imputation. The power for change is the power of

---

(*Sanctorum Communio* [vol. 1 of *Dietrich Bonhoeffer Works*; ed. Clifford J. Green; trans. Reinhard Krauss and Nancy Lukens; Minneapolis: Fortress, 1998], 155). This use of forensic language takes place in the context of Bonhoeffer's observation that "time" places a constraint on the efficacy of Christ's saving power. Here, he does not signal worries about how the past event of Jesus' death can effect salvation in the present. Such a concern is properly a matter of the doctrine of the Trinity, for if Jesus is God, then no such problem arises. Instead, for Bonhoeffer, "time" signifies the duration of human life, our existence with a beginning, middle, and end. If salvation overleaps our personal past, rather than atoning for the past, then it is not at all clear how redeemed life is properly "our time." Unless our culpability is "addressed" by redemptive power, then we cannot tell a story of our souls across the chasm of change. The end will not be connected to the beginning.

Anselm identifies a similar constraint. Should God seek to save by mercy alone, without punishment, "one who sins and one who does not sin will be in the same position before God" (*Cur Deus Homo* 1.12). In short, the particular identity of persons does not matter in a salvation effected through mere decree of plenary forgiveness.

another, and therefore, the idea that some other might provide the basis for continuity contradicts no Christian claim about the logic of change. Thus, when Christianity affirms that Jesus is "for us" as the power of incorporation, his actions on our behalf—whether we see those actions under the cultic concept of sacrifice or the legal concept of debt payment and punishment—are imputable. The way is clear for a cogent account of atonement.

Thomas Aquinas provides a straightforward example of how the premise that Jesus is "for us" with incorporative power allows for atonement. As Aquinas observes, "Christ was given grace not only as an individual but in so far as he is head of the Church, so that grace might pour out from him upon his members." Grace, for Aquinas, is the power of God unto beatitude; it is the potency sufficient for redemptive change. As head of the Church, Christ shows himself to possess this potency as an incorporative, not individual, power, which is entirely fitting, for Jesus is the power of God "for us," not "for himself." Because of this incorporative power, Aquinas concludes, "there is the same relation between Christ's deeds for himself and his members, as there is between what another man does in the state of grace and himself."[27] Here, Aquinas addresses Kant's difficulty directly. By defining Christ as head of the Church, that is to say, in terms of incorporative potency, Aquinas makes the relation of Christ's actions to our identities the same as the relation of our identities to our own actions. Therefore, Christ can do "for us" those things that, under any other circumstance, only we can do "for ourselves."

I need to emphasize that the key to Christian accounts of atonement is not to be found in specifications of *what* Jesus does "for us." There are important scriptural, ethical, historical, pastoral, and mystagogical reasons for arguing in favor of any one account of the material content of Jesus' saving work. I do not want to downplay the centrality of such investigations. Nonetheless, each account advances a common claim that Jesus' saving actions are properly imputed to us. Indeed, many putatively antisubstitutionary accounts of atonement should be viewed as rival attempts to explain how Jesus' identity is "for us" in the full sense of providing the basis for a new life in righteousness. For example, Abelard agrees with all proponents of the classical theory of atonement that whatever Christ does on our behalf

---

27. Both quotations are from Aquinas, *Summa Theologiae* 3.48.1.

has real and personal consequences for the believer.[28] He is engaged in a school debate about just what it is that Christ does. Thus, a broad consensus obtains. What Jesus does may be imputed to us, and insofar as Jesus does all that is necessary to pay the debt or endure the punishment or offer a perfect and exemplary sacrifice, he provides the conditions for personal continuity across change.

The ability of Christianity to articulate a consistent doctrine of atonement may seem a hopeless case of special pleading. The idea that Jesus has redemptive potency, and that this potency takes the form of an incorporative power that allows him to be "for us" in such a way that his life and actions are properly yours and mine, might well appear incredible. If only it could be so . . . My goal is not to persuade any reader that the specific claims of Christian teaching are credible, at least not in the sense that they are normal and obvious. An affirmation that Jesus is the potency for redemption, and that his potency is "for us" as the power of incorporation, follows from what Christians believe and do, not from a concept or practice that has widespread cultural plausibility. For good reason we may reject the idea that people or *ethnoi* or social classes have a power of incorporation that is "for us." Fortunately, Christianity advances no such general claims. The Christian cure of the soul affirms only Jesus as the incorporative power that is "for us," and rejects the claims of other powers[29]

Nonetheless, I do hope that the reader can recognize that Christianity is not unbelievable in the way in which Kant's humanism

---

28. However significant the differences between Abelard and Anselm, the latter clearly thought that exemplary sacrifice functioned according to the same logic as substitutionary death. In *Cur Deus Homo* 2.18, Anselm articulates an account of exemplary sacrifice, and he gives no indication that such an account is at odds with the transactional analysis of Jesus' death in chapter 19. In both cases, the "for us" power of Jesus is rightly imputed—first by a psychological dynamic and then according to the logic of gift-giving and proper reciprocity.

29. See Bonhoeffer's insistence that "vicarious representative action" is not a general "ethical possibility or standard." For Bonhoeffer, Christ alone has such a role, and incorporative power is good news because it is "solely the reality of divine love for the church-community; it is not an ethical, but a theological concept" (*Sanctorum Communio*, 156). See, also, R. C. Moberly's clear distinction between the general possibilities of partial incorporation into the actions of another and the incorporative power of Jesus. For Moberly, the parent might be "in" the child, but "these things are a parable, an aspiration, a glimpse: they still always fall short. It is precisely here that the relation of Jesus Christ to humanity is unique" (*Atonement and Personality* [London: John Murray, 1901], 87). We are "in Christ" completely not partially, really and not figuratively; "he alone was not generically, but inclusively man" (88). For this reason, Christianity can endorse Jesus' incorporative power and, at the same time, strenuously resist the incorporative ambitions of various worldly powers.

(and by extension, modern humanism as a whole) is incredible. To believe something that is self-contradictory, on its own terms, requires us to embrace misology. To believe, as Christianity requires, a whole array of convictions about who Jesus is and the incorporative power of his identity, certainly involves a profound risk of cognitive overreaching. However, at least Christianity has the advantage of proposing a way of thinking about personal change in which personal continuity, defined under the same strict constraints as Kant's account, admits of self-consistent formulation.[30] Jesus may not be "for us" with the power of incorporation. Such is the risk of faith. But if he is, then a consistent doctrine of atonement is possible, and we can articulate the conditions for personal continuity across change. Who we are now can be connected ("at-one") with who we hope to become because we are incorporated into the identity of Jesus, and what he does may be imputed to us, ensuring that we are continuous ("at-one") across the wrenching logic of change.

Because Kant cannot provide a self-consistent account of atonement, he cannot describe our roles in the transformative project of we-matter-most humanism. He cannot tell a story of the soul in which who we are matters for who we must become. He cannot explain, as modern humanism in general cannot explain, how filial piety can cohere with the vigorous assaults upon inherited forms of life demanded by the two poles of criticism. He cannot, as modern humanism cannot, show how a grateful acknowledgment of the sustaining gift of traditional belief and practice (Hume's cherished habits of common life) fits with the seemingly bottomless and caustic requirements of critical freedom and rational justification. He cannot, as modern humanism as a whole cannot, establish a connection between (1) our seemingly recalcitrant submission to authority and overreaching piety and (2) the self-directing form of life necessary to

---

30. I have used Kant's clear categories to motivate the problem of personal continuity in this study. However, Christianity's ability to satisfy the conditions for personal continuity across change is not limited to those categories. The Christian claim about the incorporative power of Jesus "for us" admits of reformulation so that it satisfies Derek Parfit's criterion for continuous identity (*Reasons and Persons*, 245–80). For Parfit, relation R is a sufficient basis for continuous identity, and in this exposition of the Christian view, relation R is incorporation into Christ. Christianity requires no other premise, such as that of an indestructible soul, in order to account for continuity through change. Thus, good reasons may exist to affirm the doctrine of the soul, but such a doctrine is not necessary in order to account for continuity in redemptive change. The fact that Jesus is the incarnate Word of God, and that we are incorporated into him, provides the sufficient basis for affirming continuity.

escape crushing authoritarianism. In short, the apocalyptic failure of Kant's account of personal continuity exposes the pneumatological failure of modern humanism. It does not succeed as a cure of the soul. We need to turn, then, and see how the premise of Jesus' incorporative power "for us" allows Christianity to succeed concretely and pneumatologically, just as it succeeds apocalyptically in the rarified regions of divine judgment.

The Pneumatological Aspect

Paul suggests the pneumatological aspect when he teaches that we are "in Christ" not only before God in judgment but before each other and the world in new life. We long for change; "we groan under our burden" (2 Cor 5:4). This labor is fraught with the anxiety about continuity and the desire for incorporation that so preoccupy theories of atonement. We groan, writes Paul, "because we wish not to be unclothed but to be further clothed, so that what is mortal may be swallowed up by life" (5:4). We do not want to "appear before the judgment seat of Christ" in our nakedness, where "each may receive recompense for what has been done in the body, whether good or evil," for we are determined by evil and can do no other (5:10). However, because Christ has the power of incorporation, his power of life can swallow us up and clothe us in righteousness. Paul's confidence comes from this power: "If anyone is in Christ, there is a new creation: everything old has passed away: see, everything has become new!" (5:17). By no means is the new creation forensic or prospective; it is real and present. Not only does Christ's incorporative power clothe us before the judgment seat, allowing God to reconcile the world by "not counting [our] trespasses against [us]," but that same power entrusts "the message of reconciliation to us" (5:19). We are clothed in divine righteousness as "ambassadors for Christ" (5:20). And this role requires us to be shaped and reformed as new creations in Christ, "so that in him we might become the righteousness of God" (5:21). Thus, Jesus is "for us" as the power to make us new persons "in him."

This power of incorporation is effective in baptism and realized in Christian discipline and witness. "Do you not know," Paul asks the Christians in Rome, "that all of us who have been baptized into Christ Jesus were baptized into his death?" (Rom 6:3). As Paul continues, "We have been buried with him by baptism into death, so that, just as Christ was raised from the dead by the glory of the Father, so we too might walk in newness of life" (6:3–4). This newness of life has a specific form and purpose; it involves moral discipline, patterns of mutual submission and communal unity, as well as obedience to the teachings transmitted from the apostles. These concrete forms of Christian practice incorporate believers into Christ. Not without purpose does Paul exhort his readers: "Present your bodies as a living sacrifice, holy and acceptable to God" (Rom 12:1). He details the consequences of this exhortation by describing a pattern of communal life: a harmony of gifts ordered by sober judgment and mutual affection (12:3–13), submission to worldly powers in humility and obedience (12:14–17), communal discipline that shames the dishonor of the world with the honor of God's righteousness in Christ, made manifest in those who "put on the armor of light" (13:12). The pneumatological drama of atonement is, finally, the story of incorporation into the Church. The mission and power of the Spirit is the mission and power of the body of Christ.[31]

Paul's most intensive appeals to Jesus' incorporative power join the apocalyptic and pneumatological at just this point of ecclesial mission. "I have been crucified with Christ," he writes, "and it is no longer I who live, but it is Christ who lives in me" (Gal 2:19–20). Here, the horizon of the law and its apocalyptic demands of righteousness dominate. But Christ, in his righteousness, stands in our place: "Christ redeemed us from the curse of the law by becoming a curse for us" (3:13). Systematic theologians, as we saw above, have turned to various forms of substitutionary atonement in order to explicate the effective grace of God in Christ, "who," says Paul, "loved me and gave himself for me" (2:20). Christ met the demands that no sinner could meet.

As vivid as the condemning judgment of the law is throughout the Letter to the Galatians, on the whole Paul is far more preoccupied with the pneumatological force of Jesus' power to form a community of faith. His most immediate concern is the relation of Jews and

---

31. Here, as elsewhere in his remarkable meditations on the relation between atonement and personal identity, Moberly gives succinct expression to the logic of the Christian vision of change. The incorporative power of Jesus, for Moberly, is precisely what Christians mean when they speak of the power of the Holy Spirit, and this power takes form in the life of the Church. Thus, as Moberly explains, " 'I believe in the Holy Ghost,' and 'I believe in the Holy Catholic Church,' are claims which, if fully enough understood, are in fact almost theologically coterminous" (*Atonement and Personality*, 259).

Gentiles who profess faith in Jesus. Against division according to circumcision and uncircumcision, Paul teaches that "there is no longer Jew or Greek, there is no longer slave or free, there is no longer male or female; for all of you are one in Christ Jesus" (Gal 3:28). For Paul, the emphasis on Jewish and Gentile unity in faith is not simply a case of a larger vision governed by a formal principle of unity. He has a specific end in mind. The prophecies in Isaiah tell of a final and consummating journey of dispersed and faithless Israel back to Jerusalem. The people of Israel are to be received and gathered by the LORD to the very summit of Zion, to come before God in the seat of judgment. Yet this return is not singular. The LORD gathers the nations, with Israel, for the return to Zion. The survivors of Israel do not come alone. All the nations travel with Israel, carrying the sons of Israel on their bosoms and the daughters of Israel on their shoulders (Isa 49:22). Those who were far off, echoes the Letter to the Ephesians, shall be brought near (Eph 2:13). All must be made awake in order to travel, in order to traverse the territory that separates them from God. The mountains shall be turned to roads, and highways shall be raised up so that the lost and forsaken might come from far away (Isa 49:11–12). In this consummating vision, the Gentiles shall be incorporated into the full blessings of the covenant. For Paul, Jesus' power is "for us" in a specific way. He forms the faithful into a community of Jew and Gentile joined in common worship and mutual service. The apocalyptic and pneumatological are hinged.[32]

In this pilgrimage to Zion, the pneumatological aspect of Jesus' incorporative power "for us" gives weight and temporal duration to new life. The ongoing body of Christian faith and practice provides a tissue of continuity. The determinative power of sin is countered by the more powerful incorporative righteousness of Jesus, effective in

---

32. Without doubt, the most prominent manifestation of the link between the apocalyptic and pneumatological in patristic thought is the ubiquitous use of Christ's form "for us" as the basis for figural interpretation of the Old Testament. Through the paschal figure, the spiritual and formative power of Scripture is unveiled, and the full blessing of the covenant is applied to all, Jew and Gentile, in order to bring them into the inner sanctuaries of the LORD. Yet, this unveiling of the spiritual power of the Old Testament does not entail discontinuity. The fundamental claim of figural exegesis is that such a reading is continuous with the literal sense. This is so because Jesus has the power to incorporate the historical, ritual, and prophetic details of the Old Testament witness into himself. For a subtle analysis of the dangers of discontinuity that figural reading evokes, and the specific way in which patristic thought overcomes those dangers (with a focus on Origen), see David Dawson, *Christian Figural Reading and the Fashioning of Identity* (Berkeley: University of California Press, 2002).

word and sacrament, taking form as the gathered community of teaching, prayer, and worship. After all, the Christian form of life is not "spiritual" in an ephemeral sense. Quite the contrary, as modern humanism sees so clearly, Christianity seeks to gain control over every aspect of our lives, from dawn to dusk, from sexual to economic relations, from inner sensibility to outward behavior. Further, the Spirit is apostolic, operating in and through inherited language and practice that have a particular, identity-conferring shape and boundary. The inheritance involves *these* prayers, *this* testimony, *these* rituals, *this* communal structure, and not any other. The incorporative power of Jesus, then, has sufficient specificity to give shape to a new life. One is not simply living differently, in a haze of futurity; one is living in a new way defined by a concrete and particular form of life. Jesus has the power, then, to endure in the world, "for us." He provides the tissue of continuity for dramatic change, and he does so in the incorporative power of his body of apostolic faith and practice.[33]

Here, Christianity provides a description of personal change quite unlike modern humanism's. For Kant, morally meaningful change must emerge out of our identities as persons, and from no other source. The power for change, governed by the logic of we-matter-most humanism, cannot be incorporative. It must be purely personal; therefore, our lives pivot on a vanishing point of individuality. The sheer fact that we are who we are, and are no other, must be the sufficient basis for change. As a result, whether or not one adopts Kant's terminology and rigor, change must be noumenal; it must take place outside of space and time, beyond the constraining influences of anything other than the unique individuality of each person. In this way, the personal-potency requirement produces Gnostic sensibilities. It drives historical and communal realities beyond the boundaries of change, to be admitted only according to the careful calculus of merit

---

33. For a standard patristic formulation, see Augustine's meditation on the incorporative power that unites the sacrifices of compassion, sacrifices of the worldly and carnal self, and "the sacrifice which the Church continually celebrates in the sacrament of the altar." All are given the visible "form of a servant" by the sacrifice of Jesus on the cross: "For it was this form he offered, and in this form he was offered, because it is under this form he is Mediator, in this form he is Priest, in this form he is the Sacrifice." Augustine's ascription of incorporative power to Christ is typical of patristic figural analysis of Christian spiritual discipline, sacramental and ecclesial practice. To dwell in the life of the Church is to dwell in Christ. For Augustine, the "for us" power of Jesus shapes us in our inward and outward lives "so that we might be the body of so great a head" (*City of God* 10.6, quoted from translation by Henry Betterson [New York: Penguin, 1972], 380).

and reward. Not surprisingly, a story of the soul cannot be told. Without time, without a particular location, change can be nothing more than a "moment." The new man is not only discontinuous under the gaze of divine justice, unable to pay the debt of the old man; he is disjoined in time and space, unable to identify the social, linguistic, and enacted engines of change that might provide the basis for a continuous story of a life transformed. Still worse, the world in its potent concreteness and particularity (and other persons as part of the world) becomes a rival to the personal-potency requirement, corrupting the necessity and sufficiency of personal identity for the highest good.[34]

In contrast, for Christianity, the potency of Jesus for change takes the form of incorporative power with duration and location. To be "in Christ" entails baptism into the ongoing disciplines of a common life. To become a "new man" involves becoming a very specific kind of person, located in a very specific place. Thus, the changes that Augustine makes the central theme of the story of his own soul have a narrative coherence. He lived in a certain kind of way, and then, in the power of God in Jesus Christ, he came to live otherwise. In this change, the tissues of connection are many. The man of letters pivots from old man to new man with the scriptural Word in his hands. The ambitious professor, caught up in a social world of intensive formative pressures, turns away from one city and becomes the member of another—the heavenly city with very different but even more intensely formative pressures. His highly personal search for the highest good, for himself, is transformed into a public ministry of proclamation, for others. Augustine's new life of faith has a duration and location, and as a consequence, the greatest possible degree of change and disjunction is initiated and takes form across time and within the world of language, embodiment, and interaction. Yet, Augustine can do far more than simply declare, "I was a certain kind of person, but am now otherwise." He can tell a story about his soul. Driven by the motive force of repentance, his narrative can lean forward toward a future that is fundamentally antithetical to the way he lived, and do so without denying, repudiating, or falsifying the reality of the past.

---

34. See R. R. Reno, "Feminist Theology as Modern Project," *Pro ecclesia* 5, no. 4 (fall 1996): 405–26. For an account of the mirrored "hyperspiritualism" and "hyperphysicalism" of contemporary literary theory, with close attention to the moral sensibilities entailed, see David Dawson, *Literary Theory* (Minneapolis: Augsburg Fortress, 1995).

I have attempted to illuminate the Christian approach to the personal-continuity requirement by dividing Jesus' incorporative power "for us" into apocalyptic and pneumatological aspects. These two aspects are often described wrongly as "objective" and "subjective" elements of atonement, as if one related to God alone, while the other related to the human person.[35] In other contexts, the apocalyptic is described as the work of Christ, while the pneumatological stands as the benefit of that work, applied to the sinner.[36] Or again, the apocalyptic is associated with justification—the imputed righteousness of Christ that covers the sinner before the judgment seat of God—and the pneumatological with sanctification or regeneration—the effective power of Christ to change the person over time.[37] In each case, the potency of Jesus is parsed, and the effective consequences of his death "for us" are divided. One train of analysis treats the demands of divine justice

---

35. See, e.g., Louis Berkhof's straightforward presentation of standard Reformed use of this distinction (*Vicarious Atonement through Christ* [Grand Rapids: Eerdmans, 1936], 95–106). For Berkhof, "God is reconciled to the sinner" in the atoning work of Christ, "and the sinner is also reconciled to God." However, the drama of God, Jesus, and sinner cannot remain integrated theologically: "The reconciliation of God to the sinner is primary, and that of the sinner to God is secondary" (96). This distinction between two acts of reconciliation, and their association with "objective" and "subjective," fatally obscures the role of atonement theory in establishing the conditions for personal continuity in redemptive change.

John McLeod Campbell's striking analysis of the role of Jesus as the one who dies "for us" is a sustained polemic against the tendency of Reformed thought to emphasize the apocalyptic aspects of divine judgment at the expense of the pneumatological dimension of Jesus' saving death. See his *Nature of the Atonement* (Grand Rapids: Eerdmans, 1996). For Campbell, "the atonement is to be regarded as that by which God has bridged over the gulf which separated between what sin has made us, and what it was the desire of the divine love that we should become" (127). Placing atonement in the context of change, Campbell structures his reflection according to the drama of transformation rather than the abstract demands of divine justice. The retrospective aspect of atonement, for Campbell, involves showing how Jesus' death leads to an "accounting for" the old man. The prospective aspect of atonement shows how the same death effects the blessedness of the new man. Both aspects are indispensable elements of the way in which Christ is "for us" as the bridge between past and future. For a useful analysis of Campbell's theory of atonement, see Leanne van Dyk, "Toward a New Typology of Reformed Doctrines of Atonement," in *Toward the Future of Reformed Theology* (ed. David Willis and Michael Welker; Grand Rapids: Eerdmans, 1999).

36. See *The Heidelberg Catechism*, questions 40 and 43. Christ suffers death in order to render adequate satisfaction for our sins (answer to question 40), while we receive the further benefit of release from the power of evil lusts (answer to question 43).

37. See *Formula of Concord*, art. 3, Solid Declaration. The vigor with which the *Formula* insists that justification not be confused with sanctification stems from a desire to block all avenues toward works righteousness: "The righteousness alone of the obedience, the suffering, and death of Christ," and not the "incipient righteousness or renovation in us," "can stand before the just sentence of God."

and Jesus' ability to satisfy the demands of divine justice. The other focuses on the need for change and Jesus' effective power as the source of transformation within the lives of believers.

This division is artificial.[38] Jesus' redemptive power saves in and through his potency to effect change in our identities and to do so while preserving continuity. In no sense does Jesus save by quieting the anger of God and then by turning toward the transformation of persons. As Paul proclaims, "In Christ God was reconciling the world to himself, not counting their trespasses against them" (2 Cor 5:19). The satisfaction of divine justice is not separate from real change in the world. "Not counting their trespasses against them" is, for Paul, constitutive of, not antecedent to, God's divine power to bring the world into fellowship with divine holiness, and that fellowship necessarily involves a change, not in God, but in the world.[39] As Jesus teaches in the Gospel of John, the Counselor will come and "prove the world wrong about sin and righteousness and judgment" (John 16:8), and the clarity and power of the Counselor's effective unveiling of the world's destiny will occur because Jesus himself goes "to the Father" on Golgotha in such a way that we will see that "the ruler of this world has been condemned" (16:11).

---

38. See Moberly, *Atonement and Personality.* For Moberly, the juxtaposition of "objective" and "subjective" aspects of atonement as contrasting theories "is singularly unfortunate" (138). His basic project is to join these two aspects. "Without tearing the New Testament to pieces," he writes, "you cannot separate it from its cardinal belief in the effective reality of a historical and objective atonement" (140). Yet, at the same time, that objective atonement is not effective, for us, unless it becomes "an integral part of the experience and reality of our personal consciousness" (143). The signal importance of Moberly's complex and unwieldy reflections on atonement rests in his recognition that the objective and subjective can be joined only under a theological discussion of personal identity and its relation to the identity of Jesus and the highest good.

39. Pannenberg provides an exposition of the unity of Jesus' work in reconciling the world to God, criticizing theories of atonement that reverse the arrow of reconciliation, as if God must be reconciled to the world. See *Systematic Theology,* 2:403–37. His account identifies the key question of "the role of human recipients" as the shaping question in the dominant theories of atonement (415). The problem does not rest with God (constraints imposed by divine justice) but with our participation in the divine initiative. Pannenberg does not develop his account of reconciliation with the same focus on personal continuity that marks this study. Instead, he views the problem of our ongoing participation in terms of "creaturely independence" and the danger of "replacement" by the agency of another (431). These concerns have to do with the source of potency for change, and they address our preoccupation with the dangers of domination. However, the intelligibility of the Christian view also requires continuity. Is it really *me* who participates in the future for which I hope and pray?

Judgment and transformation go together. The apocalyptic and pneumatological aspects, then, function together, and they do so by virtue of Jesus' role "for us." [40]

Augustine's explanation of the role of the testing fires of judgment in 1 Cor 3:11–15 illustrates the joint function. In this passage, Paul evokes the apocalyptic imagery of final judgment. "The work of each builder," he warns, "will become visible, for the Day will disclose it, because it will be revealed with fire, and the fire will test what sort of

---

40. Although John Calvin regards the dangers of Pelagian backsliding from the *solus Christus* power of the gospel as a sufficient reason for distinguishing between justification (the apocalyptic aspect of Jesus' power) and sanctification (the pneumatological aspect of Jesus' power), he follows Paul closely enough to avoid solidifying them into two separate and divided moments. "Although we may distinguish them," Calvin writes, "Christ contains both of them inseparably in himself." For Calvin, justification and sanctification both stem from Christ's power "for us." "Do you wish, then, to attain righteousness in Christ? You must first possess Christ." For Calvin, we "possess Christ" as we are incorporated into him, both in judgment and in the Spirit: "[For] you cannot possess him without being made partaker in his sanctification, because he cannot be divided into pieces. Since, therefore, it is solely by expending himself that the Lord gives us these benefits to enjoy, he bestows both of them at the same time, the one never without the other" (*Institutes*, 3.16.1). We cannot be "in Christ" without partaking of him.

In a very different way, Jenson suggests the same union of the apocalyptic and pneumatological, emphasizing our dwelling "in him" cognitively. Jenson surveys various attempts to explain how Jesus' death provides effective atonement, and he concludes that no particular theory succeeds. To the extent that explanation involves drawing the shadows of the uncertain (e.g., how exactly does Jesus' death save us?) into the light of the certain, atonement theories amount to efforts to inject present reality into the apocalyptic future of divine judgment. The extent to which classical atonement theory restricts itself to the apocalyptic aspect requires privileging an embracing scheme of eternal justice that provides the supervening and always present context for the divine/human encounter. For example, the necessity of debt payment functions as the certain basis on which to draw inferences about what is uncertain about the way in which Jesus saves on the cross. These embracing schemes of cosmic justice, however, inevitably conflict with the Christian premise that the identity of Jesus is the most certain thing one can say about the divine/human encounter. Therefore, when faced with questions about how Jesus' death saves, Jenson proposes that the gospel narratives offer the greatest explanatory power, and not just the narratives but the narratives as recited across the paschal services of Holy Week. "Only as this is enacted in the church," he writes, "is the Crucifixion understood. One is . . . strongly tempted to say: what must happen as the fundamental explanation of the atonement is that the ancient single service of the Triduum, `the Three Days,' the continuous enactment of the Supper, the Crucifixion, and the Resurrection, covering Holy Thursday, Good Friday, and Easter Night, be celebrated" (*Systematic Theology* [Oxford: Oxford University Press, 1997], 1:190). The efficacy of the cross becomes clear only in and through our incorporation into the witnessing practices of the Church. We can understand— dwell in Christ's truth cognitively—only as we participate liturgically—dwell in his truth as a present, enacted reality. In other words, the pneumatological incorporative power of Christ brings his apocalyptic incorporative power to light.

work each has done" (v. 13). In his exegesis, Augustine combines judgment and personal sanctification. "The furnace proves the potter's vessels," observes Augustine, quoting from Sir 27:5. Yet these fires do not simply test; they also cleanse and purify. "Now wood, hay and stubble may," he says of the building materials to be tested by fire, "without incongruity, be understood to signify such worldly things . . . that cannot be lost without grief of mind. And though this grief burns, if Christ hold the place of foundation in the heart . . . [the believer] is saved by fire."[41] Christ is "for us," then, not only to save us from being consumed by the fires of judgment but also to purify and transform us. We are, for Augustine, not only saved *from* fire but *by* fire. We are not only tested but also purified.[42]

In both cases, under the apocalyptic theme of judgment and the pneumatological theme of purification, the central Christian claim is that Jesus serves as the source of continuity. In him, we can endure the test of judgment. As the Letter to the Hebrews warns, "It is a fearful thing to fall into the hands of the living God" (10:31). Yet, by the blood of Jesus shed for us, we can "have confidence to enter the sanctuary" (10:19) and can approach God without fearing the "prospect of judgment" and the "fury of fire that will consume" (10:27). Because Jesus is "for us," we can come into the dwelling place of the LORD. However, to come into the house of the LORD both requires and effects purifying change. Here, the other side of Augustine's interpretation of the furnace of God's holiness comes

----

41. Augustine, *Enchiridion*, chap. 68.

42. In *The End of the Church,* Radner provides an account of the fundamental unity of the apocalyptic visibility of holiness and its pneumatological power. See chap. 2, "Contesting the Visible: Miracle and Holiness in the Divided Church," 57—133. Radner's analysis focuses on the ways in which post-Reformation theology, both Catholic and Protestant, fosters an artificial disjunction between visible holiness and transformative potency. In this analysis, he discusses the status of miracles, figural interpretation, and the visible form of the Church, not the doctrine of the atonement. Nonetheless, his insights help explain why standard Protestant views tend toward a purely transactional assessment of divine justice as the form in which the debt of sin and the costly price of divine love are made visible to the believer, to the exclusion of transformative potency of the *imitatio Christi* within the believer and the Church as a whole. Conversely, he shows why the intensely pneumatological ambitions of post-Reformation Roman Catholic piety of the Sacred Heart and its emphasis on effecting a recapitulation of the christological pattern of reparative suffering seem to exclude the apocalyptic visibility of divine purpose (277—333). A full discussion of the doctrine of the atonement in Western Christian thought must come to terms with Radner's brilliant analysis, and in so doing show the fundamental relationship between Protestant penal substitution theory and Roman Catholic penitential piety.

into play. Because Jesus is "for us," we can undergo the "grief of mind" entailed in renouncing our way of living, a way of living so intimate that it determines who we are. Because he is "for us," we can adopt another, very different form of life, a different identity as a person. The Letter to the Hebrews strikes the same note. In Jesus, we acquire "a true heart in full assurance of faith," and by him, "our hearts [are] sprinkled clean from an evil conscience and our bodies washed with pure water" (10:22). In both aspects—apocalyptic and pneumatological—Jesus' power takes on a specific form. He can endure where we cannot: the burning judgment of divine holiness and the rending disjunctions of real personal change. His blood takes away sin—both before the judgment seat and within our hearts.

Modern Humanism versus Christian Humanism

Our minds are strange. Fantasy bubbles forth, unbeckoned, uncontrollable. Memories often overwhelm us. Old songs on the radio can turn a routine drive to work into a reverie of youth lost. Inferences carry us forward, sometimes to our dismay, as conclusions unwanted follow from premises sure. The mind can seem so powerful, so independent, so sovereign. Yet, prejudice and habit triumph more often than not. Daily tasks abruptly end journeys of memory. Responsibility trumps fantasy. Syllogisms may throw up dams and levies, but the currents of sentiment and everyday life breach and overflow. The best of arguments are worn down by the erosive force of ordinary life. The cold passions of life, solidified around habitual thoughts and patterns of action, control. The mind can seem impotent, victim rather than victor.

I have no illusions about the consequences of this extended analysis of modern humanism and its logical disadvantages. Perhaps the conclusion of the second section of this chapter is correct. In a modern world dominated by the natural and social sciences, the abundance of metaphysical commitments that emerge from the affirmation that Jesus alone has the potency for change does, indeed, give Christianity a marginal argumentative advantage over modern humanism. Cognitive overreaching could be necessary when one is trying to overcome the moral vacuum created by the inability of the natural sciences to justify a distinction between persons and things. If Peter Singer is the voice of sober reason, then pass me the bottle of credulity and I will take a long drink. Furthermore, perhaps the conclusion of the third section is correct. Unlike modern humanism, the Christian account of change admits of a self-consistent affirmation of personal continuity. Since Jesus is "for us" as incorporative power, he can stand in our place before the Judge, and he can draw us into a form of life that gives change location and duration. Surely this ability self-consistently to affirm continuity in change commends Christianity over modern humanism's contradictions.

Yet the arguments melt away as soon as we turn to the projects of life.[43] Martyr and saint, monk and nun, stand as terrible figures. How can they allow themselves to become so absorbed, so overdetermined by dogma and doctrine? They are testimony to the danger of crushing authoritarianism and vain overreaching—impotent and infertile, submissive and self-denying, credulous to the point of renouncing the very principles of life. Yet, absorbed though they are into Jesus, they do not disappear, and even a hard-boiled modern humanist must wonder. How do mere persons, no different than you and I, acquire such power to become so different? How can they survive the scope of renunciation? How can they endure degrees of suffering, the fire and the sword? And suddenly, with such questions in mind, if one stands with the martyrs in baptism, what seemed like diminishment is now quite otherwise. What seemed like an evaporation into ascetical nothingness now appears to be a commissioning toward a life with weight and substance, purpose and power.[44]

The arguments melt, but they leave watermarks. The fact that modern humanism has so little to say about why personal identity enjoys

---

43. In a brilliant set piece, John Henry Newman unpacks a scholarly argument on behalf of a textual amendment to Shakespeare's *Henry V*. His purpose is, not to settle the question, but to illustrate, with an eye towards modern biblical criticism, the limits of argument. "I have introduced it," Newman concludes, "simply to suggest how many words go to make up a thoroughly valid argument . . . ; how little syllogisms have to do with the formation of opinion; how little depends upon the inferential proofs; and how much upon those already pre-existing beliefs and views, in which men either already agree with each other or hopelessly differ, before they begin to dispute, and which are hidden deep in our nature, or, it may be, in our peculiar personalities" (*An Essay in Aid of a Grammar of Assent* [Notre Dame: University of Notre Dame Press, 1979], 221—22).

44. Nietzsche saw this with great clarity. He ends his self-presentation, *Ecce Homo*, with a summation of his message: "Have I been understood?—-Dionysius vs. the Crucified" (*On the Genealogy of Morals and Ecce Homo*, Kaufmann, trans. [New York: Vintage, 1989], 335). For Nietzsche, the power of Christ does not produce infantile dependence or vaporish otherworldliness. It produces persons with remarkable potency and continuity, worthy adversaries indeed.

a privileged place as the sole potency for the highest good creates more than logical vulnerability. The high priests of "clear thinking" inevitably begin to wonder why only human beings count in the moral calculus. Animals feel pain. The biosphere has moral standing. Patrons of the greatest good for the greatest number recognize that larger forces—markets, world government, scientific progress—hold the key to advancing the highest good. A culture of critique comes to see that a moral belief that we matter most is nothing more than a prejudice, the residue, perhaps, of our Christian past, or an inevitable expression of an anthropocentric impulse to favor ourselves. As the intrinsic poverty and contradiction of modern humanism becomes more and more obvious in our age, it has little to say against cultural pressures that push beyond humanism. Why, exactly, do we matter most? Indeed, why do we matter at all? The devout Christian may seem a victim of authoritarian dogma and overreaching superstition, but at least he or she has something to say.

As I have attempted to show, the failure of modern humanism is clearest in the contradictions that surround atonement. Kant's inability to satisfy the personal-continuity requirement signals cultural failure. His inability to offer a self-consistent version of the apocalyptic dimension of atonement suggests pneumatological difficulties as well. And this is so. The children of modern humanism are remarkable creatures. They seem able to endure suffering forever. However disjointed, however dismembered, however torn by promises that cannot be fulfilled, however animated by moral prejudices that lead to contradiction, they soldier on. They embrace demands for change, even if those demands do not permit them to endure as continuous persons. In order to sustain the project of modern humanism, they seem willing to believe anything, no matter how fantastic, in order to avoid confronting the possibility that all the changes necessary to eliminate authority and overreaching will violate, rather than fulfill, their moral convictions, memories, loyalties, and very identities. They seem willing to give up the connective logic of atonement and, instead, construct flying buttresses of explanation, fabricate myths of progress, believe in slogans that sanctify what they cannot understand. In politics, Democracy serves as a talisman of reassurance. A mystical faith in Majority Rule allows them to believe that the massive power of the modern state brings benevolent change. Confident in the bounty of economic growth, they accept the increasingly disruptive changes wrought by the marketplace. Sure that each and every person deserves affirmation—after all, each of us matters most—they embrace a wholesale assault on traditional cultural practices of praise and blame, honor and shame, reward and punishment. They cannot see how any of these changes allows for personal continuity. However, instead of worrying, as did Kant, about the need to understand atonement and the consequent reconciliation of who we are with who we must become, they simply reconcile themselves to the necessity of change. All the slogans of modernity, from "tolerance" to "the triumph of the proletariat," are so many substitutions for atonement. We just need to put our shoulders to the wheel of change and forget about the particular constraints imposed by our own lives.

The postmodern hope of serial self-creation and its attendant ironic tropes are natural upshots. Modern humanism insists on change. We have to make ourselves anew. But no account of continuity in change is forthcoming. The Rousseauian solution continually reemerges. "Just be true to yourself," we are urged. The watermarks of failed arguments are vivid enough, however, to prevent the postmodern from accepting such a solution: " 'I change myself by becoming true to myself.' Yeah, right. Becoming true to ourselves! If only such pieties could be believed." Friedrich Nietzsche has come and gone, and we know that such statements are either acts of self-deception or self-creation, which really amount to the same thing. The Humean solution also reemerges. "These changes," we are told, "are not as disruptive and fundamental as they might seem." Again, failed arguments cast shadows forward: "If they are not fundamental, then in what sense are they necessary? In what sense will they make us and our world different? I see through your moral exhortations. I've read Marcuse. It's just another sales job to try to get me to take seriously something that is really not that important." Or maybe we have just finished reading Michel Foucault, and the reaction is more suspicious still: "Yeah, right, not fundamental, not disruptive . . . do you expect me to believe *that* line? The executioner always smiles while wielding the ax." In any case, we know only too well the subterfuges and deceptions used by the powerful to get their way: "Why not just tell me that I have to change because I don't have any choice, instead of dressing it up in a nice moralistic outfit?" Here, the postmodern often reiterates, whether in grim or gay voice, the one direction that modern humanism can turn without backsliding toward Rousseau or Hume—toward Hegel and the identification of morality with suprapersonal power. Being is becoming, and what is must be otherwise. We have no choice but to jump on the train—or be left behind by History.

Without a doctrine of atonement, modern humanism is animated by prejudices that cannot produce a cure of the soul. It can only produce therapy, management, and the dominion of fate. Christianity does have a doctrine of atonement, and as a consequence, it can motivate a cure of the soul in which change is something we can undergo as continuous persons. As a result, Christianity can give logical form and existential weight to a humanism in which we do matter. Faith in Jesus as the power of the gospel allows us to desire change—in ourselves, in others, and in the world—and to pursue that desire in such a way that each person matters as a subject of Jesus' incorporative power. In order to effectively articulate this humanism, one of the critical tasks of a genuinely postmodern Christian theology is to address the horror of dependence and fear of difference that animate so much of modernity and drive the logic of we-matter-most humanism, for just such prejudices generate the logical and existential contradictions of we-matter-most humanism.

Against the failed modern cure of the soul, Christian theology must show that there is no problem of dogmatism within the Christian cure of the soul. If Jesus saves in and through his power to draw us into himself, then we can never be too deeply "in him." We can never describe his role in the apocalyptic drama of final judgment as too important, too singular, too unique. We can never cast ourselves upon him with too much dependence. And further, to the extent that his incorporative power has a pneumatological aspect with duration and location in the world, we can never overinvest ourselves in the life of the Church. We can never ascribe too much authority to the scriptural witness to Jesus' identity. We can never submit too much to the objective forms of his power in baptism and Eucharist. At every point, because Jesus is "for us" as the power of incorporation, in the Christian cure of the soul, a distinctive prejudice emerges that is profoundly antagonistic to modern humanism and its worries about crushing authoritarianism. Far from horror, a faith in Jesus as the power of the gospel inculcates a joy in dependence upon him.

The upshot is what I call the principle of maximal salvific dependence. One should ascribe the greatest degree of dependence upon Christ that is consistent with a real role for persons. As I have attempted to show, one can say that sinners are saved by Christ alone, and by no other, and at the same time be very articulate about the way in which our identities as persons are profoundly relevant to the cruciform power of Christ. But for our sin, the dynamics of change would be very different. We have no power to change ourselves from the death of sin to the life of righteousness, but we most definitely have roles in the drama of salvation. The power of God in Christ is exercised "for us," and therefore, we are the very objects of divine purpose. For this reason, the Augustinian insistence upon the sole and sufficient power of Christ has given rise to the very humanism that so marks Western culture. Every century has seen debates about grace and free will; every generation has worried that the *solus Christus* restriction of redemptive potency diminishes human life and leaves us with no roles to play. Yet, the consequences have been otherwise. Augustine's dominance in Western Christianity has generated a pervasive anthropocentrism. This is not surprising, for in affirming the principle of maximal salvific dependence, one draws ever greater attention to the only person who has the incorporative power to ensure that we matter at all in redemptive change: Jesus Christ.

Against the fear of overreaching that animates modern humanism and its worries about the continuity of personal identity, Christian humanism must affirm the atoning work of Christ. The incorporative power of Jesus does not invite Christians to wander aimlessly in a spiritual never-never land but provides a determinate focus for the cure of the soul. For example, the rite of baptism is shaped by two major themes, both of which signal the degree of change made possible by Jesus' incorporative power. The first is intensive renunciation. To be baptized requires denying who one has been, a slave of worldly powers. The second is initiation. One does not renounce for the sake of renunciation; one does so in order to become the citizen of a different city, to be marked as Christ's own. The venture in baptism is extreme: to renounce and leave behind just that current of sentiment and common practice that is so profoundly intimate to who we are that neither our minds nor our wills can escape, and to do so only to become captive to a new form of life, a new current of sentiment and common practice. Only the incorporative power of Christ makes such a venture plausible.

Here, a second Christian commitment emerges, what I call the principle of maximal salvific difference. One should affirm the greatest degree of difference in Christ that is consistent with remaining a continuous person. Again, I hope that my sketch of the typical claims on behalf of the incorporative power of Christ, both in apocalyptic judgment and pneumatological transformation, shows that Christianity endorses dramatic change that is consistent with personal continuity. As Athanasius so fervently proclaims, Christ's assumption of our flesh, and our consequent incorporation into him, engages us in such a profound change that we become divinized. Such radical difference seems ripe with an otherworldliness that can only lead to a neglect of the concrete and particular constraints of human life or, worse, an active and violent antagonism. Yet, the arrow of change points downwards as well as upwards. Eastern Christianity, so influenced by Athanasius's ambition on behalf of radical change, has produced a concrete and particular form of life that is so heavy with the weight of tradition that many complain that it is the Immovable Object of ancient thought. Fervent affirmation of the principle of maximal salvific difference enhances, rather than threatens, visible forms of continuity. Again, this is hardly surprising, for the more one insists upon the principle of maximal salvific difference, the more one draws attention to the one in whom the possibility of any form of continuity across change is ensured: Jesus Christ.

In the end, the possibility of a genuine humanism rests in whom one affirms as the power for change and in whom one relies for the condition for continuity. Thus, the critical task of theology, and its fundamental contribution to the protection of persons against dominion and destruction, is not wringing its hands about dogmatism and tut-tutting about fanaticism. The true dangers of crushing authoritarianism rest in the malevolent powers that are for everything under the sun but are not "for us." The constructive theological project is not to reassure those of us who resist authority and fear submission. The true dangers of vain overreaching are to be found in those ambitions that cannot, or will not, articulate a cogent account of atonement. Instead, Christian theology must show how persons are consequential and continuous in redemptive change by giving even greater attention to the weight and force of Jesus' incorporative power in proclamation and witness. He is the truth that we cannot love too deeply, and he is the one on whom we can rely as the trustworthy and enduring way toward new life, for he has given himself to us, with power and in love.

WORKS CITED

Anselm. *Cur Deus Homo*. In *A Scholastic Miscellany: Anselm to Ockham*. Edited by Eugene R. Fairweather. Philadelpia: The Library of Christian Classics, 1956.

Athanasius. *Four Discourses against the Arians*. In *Nicene and Post-Nicene Fathers*. Series 2, vol. 4. Edited by Philip Schaff and A. J. B. Wace. Grand Rapids: Eerdmans, 1987.

Auerbach, Erich. *Mimesis: The Representation of Reality in Western Literature*. Translated by Willard R. Trask. Princeton: Princeton University Press, 1953.

Augustine. *City of God*. Translated by Henry Bettenson. Harmondsworth: Penguin Books, 1972.

_____. *Confessions*. Translated by Henry Chadwick. Oxford: Oxford University Press, 1991.

_____. *Enchiridion on Faith, Hope and Love*. Edited by Henry Paolucci. Translated by J. F. Shaw. South Bend, Ind.: Regnery/Gateway, 1961.

Barker, Ernest. *Of the Social Contract*. Oxford: Oxford University Press, 1947.

Barth, Karl. *The Church Dogmatics*, Vol. IV, *The Doctrine of Reconciliation*. Edited by G. W. Bromily and T. F. Torrance. Edinburgh: T & T Clark, 1956–62.

_____. *Protestant Theology in the Nineteenth Century: Its Background & History*. Valley Forge, Pa.: Judson Press, 1973.

Beck, Lewis White. *A Commentary on Kant's Critique of Practical Reason*. Chicago: University of Chicago Press, 1960.

Berkhof, Louis. *Vicarious Atonement through Christ*. Grand Rapids: Eerdmans, 1936.

Berlin, Isaiah. *Four Essays on Liberty*. Oxford: Oxford University Press, 1969.

Bonhoeffer, Dietrich. *Sanctorum Communio*. Vol. 1 of *Dietrich Bonhoeffer Works*. Edited by Clifford Green. Translated by Reinhard Krauss and Mary Lukens. Minneapolis: Fortress, 1998.

Calvin, John. *Institutes of the Christian Religion*. Edited by John T. McNeill. Translated by Ford Lewis Battles. Philadelphia: The Library of Christian Classics, 1960.

Cambell, John McLeod. *Nature of the Atonement*. Grand Rapids: Eerdmans, 1996.

Cassier, Ernst. *The Question of Jean-Jacques Rousseau*. Translated by Peter Gay. New York: Columbia University Press, 1954.

_____. *Kant's Life and Thought*. Translated by James Haden. New Haven: Yale University Press, 1981.

Collins, James. *The Emergence of Philosophy of Religion*. New Haven: Yale University Press, 1967.

Dale, R. W. *Christian Doctrine: A Series of Discourses*. London: Hodder & Stoughton, 1894.

Davidovich, Adina. "How to Read Religion within the Limits of Reason Alone." *Kant-Studien* 85 (1995): 1–14.

Dawkins, Richard. "Viruses of the Mind." In *Dennet and His Critics*. Edited by Bo Dahlbom. Oxford: Blackwell Publishers, 1993.

Dawson, David. *Christian Figural Reading and the Fashioning of Identity*. Berkeley: University of California Press, 2002.

_____. *Literary Theory*. Minneapolis: Augsburg Fortress, 1995.

Denney, James. *The Atonement and the Modern Mind*. New York: A. C. Armstrong, 1903.

Dewey, John. *Reconstruction in Philosophy*. Boston: Beacon Press, 1948.

Dyk, Leanne van. "Toward a New Typology of Reformed Doctrines of Atonement." In *Toward the Future of Reformed Theology*. Edited by David Willis and Michael Welker. Grand Rapids: Eerdmans, 1999.

Emerson, Ralph Waldo. *Essays: First and Second Series*. New York: Houghton Mifflin, 1929.

Engstrom, Stephen. "The Concept of the Highest Good in Kant's Moral Theory." *Philosophy and Phenomenological Research* 52, 4 (December 1992): 742–80.

Epictetus. *The Dicourses as Reported by Arrian*. Translated by W. A. Oldfather. Cambridge: The Loeb Classical Library, 1925.

Fackenheim, Emil. *The God Within: Kant, Schelling, and Historicity*. Edited by John Burbidge. Toronto: University of Toronto Press, 1996.

Feuerbach, Ludwig. *The Essence of Christianity*. Translated by George Eliot. New York: Harper Torchbooks, 1957.

Frei, Hans. *The Eclipse of Biblical Narrative*. New Haven: Yale University Press, 1973.

Hare, John E. *The Moral Gap: Kantian Ethics, Human Limits, and God's Assistance*. Oxford: Clarendon Press, 1996.

Herdt, Jennifer A. *Religion and Faction in Hume's Moral Philosophy*. Cambridge: Cambridge University Press, 1997.

Hodge, Charles. *Systematic Theology*. New York: Scribner, Armstrong, 1872.

Hume, David. *Enquiries Concerning Human Understanding and Concerning the Principles of Morals*. Edited by L. A. Selby-Bigge and P. H. Nidditch. Oxford: Clarendon Press, 1975.

_____. *Essays Moral, Political, and Literary*. Edited by Eugene F. Miller. Indianapolis: Liberty Fund, 1985.

_____. *The Natural History of Religion*. Edited by H. E. Root. Stanford: Stanford University Press, 1957.

_____. *The History of England*. Indianapolis: Liberty Fund, 1983.

_____. *A Treatise of Human Nature*. Edited by L. A. Selby-Bigge and P. H. Nidditch. Oxford: Clarendon Press, 1978.

James, William. *Pragmatism and the Meaning of Truth*. With introduction by A. J. Ayer. Cambridge: Harvard University Press, 1975.

Jenson, Robert W. *Systematic Theology*. Oxford: Oxford University Press, 1997–1999.

_____. *The Triune Identity*. Philadelphia: Fortress Press, 1982.

Johnson, Samuel. *The Poems of Samuel Johnson*. Edited by David Nichol Smith and Edward L. McAdam. Oxford: Clarendon Press, 1941.

Kant, Immanuel. *The Conflict of the Faculties*. Translated by Mary J. Gregor. New York: Abaris, 1979.

_____. *Critique of Judgment*. Translated by James Creed Meredith. Oxford: Clarendon Press, 1952.

_____. *Critique of Practical Reason*. Translated by Lewis White Beck. Indianapolis: Bobbs-Merrill, 1956.

_____. *Critique of Pure Reason*. Translated by Norman Kemp Smith. New York: St. Martin's Press, 1965.

_____. *Kant on History*. Edited by Lewis White Beck. New York: Macmillan, 1985.

_____. *Kant's Political Writings*. Edited by Hans Reiss. Cambridge: Cambridge University Press, 1970.

_____. *Religion within the Boundaries of Mere Reason and Other Writings*. Translated and edited by Allen Wood and George di Giovanni. Cambridge: Cambridge University Press, 1998.

Keble, John. "On the Mysticism Attributed to the Early Fathers of the Church." In *Tracts for the Times*. No. 89. New York: AMS Press, 1969.

Kelly, Christopher. *Rousseau's Exemplary Life: The Confessions as Political Philosophy*. Ithaca: Cornell University Press, 1987.

Lindbeck, George. *The Nature of Doctrine*. Philadelphia: Westminster Press, 1984.

Livingston, Donald. *Philosophical Melancholy and Delirium: Hume's Pathology of Philosophy*. Chicago: University of Chicago Press, 1998.

Locke, John. *An Essay Concerning Understanding*. Edited by Peter H. Nidditch. Oxford: Clarendon Press, 1975.

Lucian, *Peregrinus*. In *Selected Satires of Lucian*. Edited and translated by Lionel Casson. New York: Norton, 1968.

MacKinnon, Donald. *Borderlands of Theology*. New York: Lippincott, 1968.

Manent, Pierre. *An Intellectual History of Liberalism*. Translated by Rebecca Balinski. Princeton: Princeton University Press, 1994.

Marcus Aurelius. *Meditations*. Translated by A. S. L. Farquharson. Oxford: Oxford University Press, 1989.

Marshall, Bruce D. *Christology in Conflict: The Identity of a Savior in Rahner and Barth*. Oxford: Basil Blackwell, 1987.

_____. *Trinity and Truth*. Cambridge: Cambridge University Press, 2000.

Menke, Karl-Heinz. *Stellvertretung: Schluesselbegriff christlichen Lebens und theologische Grundkategorie*. Freiburg: Johannes Verlag, 1991.

Michalson, Gordon. *Fallen Freedom: Kant on Radical Evil and Moral Regeneration*. Cambridge: Cambridge University Press, 1990.

Michelet, Jules. *History of the French Revolution*. Translated and edited by Gordon Wright. Chicago: University of Chicago Press, 1969.

Mill, John Stuart. *On Liberty*. New York: Everyman's Library, 1992.

Moberly, R. C. *Atonement and Personality*. London: John Murray, 1901.

Mueller, Julius. *The Christian Doctrine of Sin*. Translated by William Urwick. Edinburgh: T & T Clark, 1885.

Munzel, Felicitas G. *Kant's Conception of Moral Character: The "Critical" Link of Morality, Anthropology, and Reflective Judgment.* Chicago: University of Chicago Press, 1999.

Nellas, Panayiotis. *Deification in Christ: The Nature of the Human Person.* Translated by Norman Russell. Crestwood, N.Y.: St. Vladimir's Seminary Press, 1987.

Newman, John Henry. *An Essay in Aid of a Grammar of Assent.* Notre Dame: University of Notre Dame Press, 1979.

Nietzsche, Friedrich. *On the Genealogy of Morals* and *Ecce Homo.* Translated by Walter Kaufmann. New York: Vintage Books, 1967.

Nussbaum, Martha. *Cultivating Humanity: A Classical Defense of Reform in Liberal Education.* Cambridge: Harvard University Press, 1997.

Pannenberg, Wolfhart. *Systematic Theology.* Translated by Geoffrey W. Bromily. Grand Rapids: Eerdmans, 1991–1998.

Parfit, Derek. *Reasons and Persons.* Oxford: Clarendon Press, 1984.

Plamenatz, John. *Man and Society.* London: Longman, 1963.

Quinn, Philip L. "Christian Atonement and Kantian Justification." *Faith and Philosophy* 3, 4 (October 1986): 440–62.

_____. "Saving Faith from Kant's Remarkable Antinomy." Faith and Philosophy 7, 4 (October 1990): 418–33.

Radner, Ephraim. *The End of the Church: A Pneumatology of Christian Division in the West.* Grand Rapids: Eerdmans, 1998.

Reno, R. R. "Feminist Theology as Modern Project." *Pro ecclesia* 5, 4 (Fall 1996): 405–26.

_____. "Pro Nobis: Words We Do Not Want to Hear." In *The Rule of Faith: Scripture, Canon, and Creed in a Critical Age.* Edited by Ephraim Radner and George Sumner. Harrisburg, Pa.: Morehouse Publishing, 1998.

Ricoeur, Paul. *Oneself as Another.* Chicago: University of Chicago Press, 1992.

Roche, Kennedy F. *Rousseau: Stoic and Romantic.* London: Methuen, 1974.

Rorty, Richard. *Objectivity, Relativism, and Truth.* Vol. 1 of *Philosophical Papers.* Cambridge: Cambridge University Press, 1991.

Rossi, Philip J. "Moral Autonomy, Divine Transcendence, and Human Destiny: Kant's Doctrine of Moral Hope as a Philosophical Foundation for Christian Ethics." *Thomist* 46, 3 (July 1982): 434–56.

Rousseau, Jean-Jacques. *Confessions*. Translated by J. M. Cohen. Harmondsworth: Penguin Books, 1973.

_____. *Emile*. Translated by Barbara Foxley. London: Everyman's Library, 1993.

_____. *The First and Second Discourses*. Edited by Roger D. Masters. Translated by Roger D. and Judith R. Masters. New York: St. Martin's Press, 1964.

_____. *The Rêveries of a Solitary Walker*. Translated by Charles E. Butterworth. Indianapolis: Hackett Publishing, 1992.

_____. *Rousseau, Judge of Jean-Jacques*. Vol. 1 of *The Collected Writings of Rousseau*. Edited by Roger D. Masters and Christopher Kelly. Hanover: University Press of New England, 1990.

_____. *Of the Social Contract*. Translated by Charles M. Sherover. New York: Harper & Row, 1984.

Russell, Bertrand. *The Problems of Philosophy*. Oxford: Oxford University Press, 1959.

Schleiermacher, Friedrich. *The Christian Faith*. Translated by H. R. MacIntosh and J. S. Steward. Edinburgh: T & T Clark, 1928.

Shell, Susan Meld. *The Embodiment of Reason: Kant on Spirit, Generation, and Community*. Chicago: University of Chicago Press, 1996.

Sherman, Nancy. *Making a Necessity of Virtue: Aristotle and Kant on Virtue*. Cambridge: Cambridge University Press, 1997.

Shklar, Judith. *Ordinary Vices*. Cambridge: Harvard University Press, 1984.

_____. *Men and Citizens: A Study of Rousseau's Social Theory*. Cambridge: Cambridge University Press, 1969.

Starobinski, Jean. *Jean-Jacques Rousseau: Transparency and Obstruction*. Translated by Arthur Goldhammer. Chicago: University of Chicago Press, 1988.

Taylor, Charles. *The Ethics of Authenticity*. Cambridge: Harvard University Press, 1992.

Temple, William. *Nature, Man, and God*. London: Macmillan, 1951.

Thomas Aquinas. *Summa Theologiae*. Blackfriars edition. New York: McGraw-Hill, 1964.

Williams, Stephen N. *Revelation and Reconciliation: A Window on Modernity*. Cambridge: Cambridge University Press, 1995.

Wolf, Susan. "Moral Saints." *Journal of Philosophy* 79, 3 (August 1982): 419–439.

Wood, Allen. *Kant's Ethical Thought*. Cambridge: Cambridge University Press, 1999.

INDEX

Abelard, 227–28, 228n.28

Adam, 201, 205, 208, 209, 210nn.15–16

Adams, Robert Merrihew, 175n.19

Alembert, Jean le Rond d', 78n.24

Anselm, 175n.18, 224, 225n.26, 228n.28

apathia, 4, 17, 18, 78n.25, 89

Aquinas, Thomas, 227

Aristotle, 217

asceticism
and fanaticism, 37n.15, 41–42
in modern humanism, 21–23, 22nn.4–5

Athanasian principle regarding continuity, 150–51, 156, 157, 168n.16, 174n.17, 186, 195, 213, 221, 222, 225, 245

Athanasius, 222n.24

atonement, doctrines of
anthropocentric aspect of God's judgment, 224–25, 224n.25
and apocalyptic aspect of Jesus' identity, 195, 222n.24, 223–30, 224n.25, 225n.26, 228nn.28–29, 235–39, 237n.40
Augustine and, 237–39
Christianity and cure of the soul based in, 11, 195–96, 243
and the Church, 231, 231n.31, 237n.40

and continuous identity, 6, 170–82, 174n.17, 177n.21, 221–39, 225n.26, 229n.30, 232n.32, 235n.35, 236n.39
failures of modern humanism regarding, 177–83, 241–43
Kant and, 170–83, 174n.17, 177n.21, 178n.22, 194–95, 241–42
linking of apocalyptic and pneumatological aspects, 235–39, 236nn.38–39, 237n.40, 238n.42
personal continuity and Kant's radical-evil view, 170–83, 174n.17, 177n.21, 178n.22
and pneumatological aspect of Jesus' identity, 230–39, 231n.31, 232n.32, 233n.33, 237n.40
redemptive change affirmed in, 6
substitutionary atonement, 195, 223–25, 224n.25, 228, 228n.28, 231
vicarious substitution, 176–77, 178–79, 180, 181

Auerbach, Erich, 32n.11

Augustine
on atonement, 237–39
and incorporative power of Jesus Christ, 212, 222, 233n.33, 234, 237–39, 244